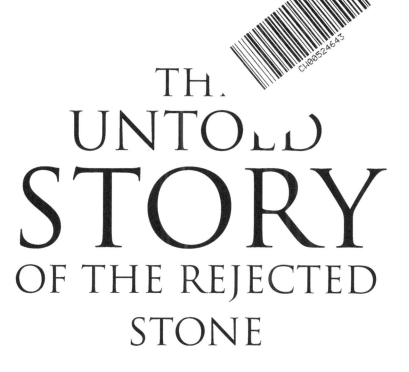

THE
UNTOLD
STORY
OF THE REJECTED
STONE

PART 1

ROSE ADDO

NEWMAN SPRINGS PUBLISHING
320 Broad Street
Red Bank, NJ 07701

First originally published by Newman Springs Publishing 2020

ISBN 978-1-64801-602-8 (Paperback)
ISBN 978-1-63692-308-6 (Hardcover)
ISBN 978-1-64801-603-5 (Digital)

Printed in the United States of America

CONTENTS

ACKNOWLEDGMENTS

To God be the glory for his mercy, grace, and favor on me. Rose, a high school dropout, who was so dumb and nervous out of all sorts of abuses and bullying that she couldn't even express herself in English language in public all her lifetime in Ghana. But she was able to survive death and being able to write about her own life story.

Not in a million years have I dream of becoming an author, and neither do anyone who knows me, including my own family, and giving them higher education, and so, for that reason, I thought that they will write about me after I am dead. My dreams and goals were to see my grandkids born and to babysit them; therefore, I am humbled and blessed by the Lord Jesus the Christ for everything.

I dedicate this book in the memories of my sweet mom, Christina Masike Alihano Dzeagu, who died at the age of forty-five out of depression and anxiety though her wishes were all to live long to babysit my children and to enjoy life; to my kind and loving uncle Francis Odoi Dzeagu, who died in his late teens at his secondary school education by food poisoning from his best friend; to my third born daughter, Diana Adukwei Addo, who died at age of three at other woman's care (only God knows the cause of her death because I was kicked out of the house); and also, to all the saints in heaven who are praying for me.

And my next appreciations goes to all my children and especially my grandkids, who love me most, and they pray every day for me to be blessed exceedingly and abundantly in order to send them to Disney World and to surprise them with expensive gifts, and my granddaughters told me to buy them American girl dolls truly yours and etc.

And am also grateful to God for angels he sent to my life to help me in all aspects whenever I feel lost and I thought that there isn't a way out. Among them is my arch or top angel Oprah Winfrey (since 1987), who helped me a lot through her show with her encouragements and her empowerments, and she also made me believe that I can be whatever I want to be, and she taught me how to fight back no matter what and to never ever lose hope and much more.

And my next angel is Mrs. Cassandra Largea, who was a midwife in Ghana, and she also encouraged me to stay and care for my kids no matter what happens.

Felicia Loebbaka at 1121 West Berwyn Avenue, Chicago, Illinois, 60640 in Crickets Wireless Phone store in 2014, who was sweet and patient with me, and she taught me like a kindergarten on a paper, where she drew signs and arrows pointing how to text, e-mail, and then sent, copy and paste, and many more for months; and because of that, I am able to write my complete story on my phone since I have little knowledge of computer.

My primary doctor Ryan Levenhagen, DO, of Swedish medical group at 5345 North Sheridan Road, Chicago, Illinois, 60640. I met him since February 2018 when I was so depressed and in pain. He didn't treat me only like a patient but like a family. He was so sweet and caring. His positive words were that I will be fine and have my life back in no time on each visit. He referred me to a psychologist, and he also encouraged me toward my story, and he introduced me to Newman Springs to publish.

My psychologist Robin Gilson of Swedish Covenant hospital professional Plaza North California Ave Chicago Illinois 60625, who was so kind and sweet and was emotional whenever she saw me crying. She was used to transform my mind and to see things differently and to love myself and accept the brand-new me.

Also, Rae Phoenix, a navigator at library at 6800 North Western Chicago Illinois 60645, who was used to join my writings together and then to portion them to transcripts for submission through the computer.

My sincere thanks also goes to all dementia and Alzheimer's patients in the world and those I cared for as a caregiver since 2015 in Chicago, Illinois, and those I was associated with, especially at Presbyterian Homes at Evanston, because they made me see how lucky I am to remember my past, since I was little, like everything happened yesterday until now.

Finally, as a good Christian and a woman of faith, my big thank you to some of the best motivational speakers like Pastor John Mensa Otabil of International Central Gospel Church in Ghana. I listened to his messages of hope on the TV each week when I lived there, and it increased my faith whenever it dropped down. If God has never forsaken any of his servants in the past, then he will not forsake you today. God will remain faithful to you to the end. Same thing to Bishop Duncan Williams of Actions Chapel International, who liked to share some of his life experiences in his sermons that gives me hope that it is through prayer that we destroy the kingdom of darkness and enforce the judgment written that the gate of hell shall not prevail. To Pastor Joel Osteen of Lakewood Church in Houston, Texas, since 2017 until date, where he taught me to let go and let God be the vindicator, and he will pay me back with good measure, pressed down and shaken together and running over, will be poured into my lap and many more. Also, I learned, from him, that I will definitely arise because God has bounced back the spirit inside me like a palm tree. To Pastor Victoria Osteen who reminds me of myself when it comes to quotes of Bible verses in Malachi 3:8–11 concerning giving tithes and offerings, and that motivations make me feel happy to continue giving my tithes and offerings and sharing the little I have with the needy too. To Bishop T. D. Jakes of the Potter's House of Dallas I listened to on YouTube, where one of his messages clicks my mind each time since 2018 whenever I feel so depressed. And if quitting the race or suicide thoughts came, then I remember how Paul survived the storms and waves, and he swam for many days, and then just few yards away to make it to the shore, he almost gave up hope that he might drown, but eventually, he made it to the shore because of God and more. To Pastor Joyce Meyer reminds me that I can't live or do anything without God, and much more, I should acknowledge him in all my ways in order for him to direct my paths. Also, to Pastor John Gray, an associate Pastor of Lakewood

Church, where one of the sermons he preached in Lakewood Church in 2019 when I was living with family and going through hell, and I decided to move into a shelter place. Instead then, I changed my mind afterward because I learned from him that I was going through those challenges because God made me so complicated and complex. Like those masterpieces watches that take six years to complete one by the manufacturer, God is taking his time in fixing my problems and keep praying because am coming out big-time.

1
CHAPTER

My name is Rose Aku Addo. I was born in December 20, 1956, at a coastal village called Lolonyah in Damgbe East District in the eastern part of Greater Accra Region in southeast of Ghana. My mom was a Christian, Maseki Alihano Dzeagu, and Mercy Anumokwuor Dzeagu was my fetish grandma. Before I was born, both of them were fishmonger, who owned their own canoes, nets, and all fishing equipment. My mom's middle name, "Alihano," in the Adamgbe language means "you never know what the future holds," and I didn't understand the true meaning of that when I was growing up. But now I do because of a lot of terrible things had happened, and are still happening, in my life that I don't wish for anyone.

Whenever the fishermen arrived with the fish in the very large quantities, Mom, Grandma, and a couple of their helpmates, and other neighbors too, washed them all with seawater and put them in baskets, and then they laid them on palm branches on the ground in the house, and thereafter, they kept awake in smoking them in special clay-built ovens for fish smokers. Mostly, they didn't get chance to sleep at all until they finished, and after they were done, they spent more time in arranging the fish in large baskets inside covered with used cement papers. When each baskets was full, they then wrapped the top with same used cement papers, which was dangerous because cement is a chemical that shouldn't be eaten, but God, being so kind, protected us all from being harmed. And then the baskets were packed in a big track, with passengers also, to Makola Market for sale in Accra, the city of Ghana.

In my village, Lolonyah has two types of work, fishing and farming. And so, part of my family are farmers, mainly in livestock like hen, ducks, and especially black pigs, though they were fed mornings and evenings in their stable with pounded fresh cassava mixed with water—so did other neighbors—and then they were allowed to step outside until late evening before they returned to their stables. They all rushed to the beachside, and because we didn't have toilets in the village, we eased ourselves there, so those aggressive black pigs took advantage of the situation, and they gripped the bowel movements before they land on the sand, and then they eat it. And to be honest with you, it seems scary, especially for men holding their penis whenever they squat down as protections, and we kids as well and the owners did not help the situation, maybe because they keep the beachside clean and smelled good. Only the sick people or really old folks and toddlers eased themselves in the chamber pots, and still, it had to be carried to the beachside to dump. One more thing I observed about the black pigs is that they have skins like thorns, so when they are slaughtered, they are put in a big basin with hot water before they are able to pull out all those thorns, and then they cut it in parts for sale or cooking. And you know why I observed that because there was a time Mom used to buy black pigs and she went through the same procedure, and then she caught them into medium sizes, and she prepared soup with tomatoes, hot peppers, onions, and salt, and she also prepared banku alongside. She carried the soup in a pot covered with a lid, and someone else carried banku rolled in small balls in a large calabash covered with to keep it warm for house-to-house sales at Lolonyah. So the rest of them in farms grow crops like tomatoes, onions, cassava, hot peppers, okras, and many more. And some of the men also go fishing for the canoe owners and are being paid.

And aside from that, four miles from my village is a river called "Songo," which seasonally naturally turns to salt for months. And when that happens, many people all over Adamgbe District go over with their food baskets and sacks to collect them for free, and traders from other regions come around to buy.

And so, some people from my village also took advantage of that to get extra money out of it, but the only side effect of that business is that they hurt on the back, feet, and toes because of walking on the salt river barefoot and without boots on. But years later, it changed because partners got involved, and they used others machines to produce more salt, and iodine was added to it. And people were not allowed over anyone. Though I haven't been over, Mom did one time in the '70s when we lived at Ada Foah and she needed money so badly to care for us.

My mom was one of the most beautiful women at Adamgbe District. She was short, about four feet eight inches tall, with long black bushy hair, round face with a tribal mark on the left side of her cheek, broad eyes, light-colored skin, and well in shape—and workaholic as they became successful because of that. If the Miss Ghana beauty pageant existed in those days, she could have won because in those days, their main concern was outward beauty before anything else. And they also thought that being educated doesn't mean everything, but beauty and wisdom count.

I knew Mom was kind and sweet and with a great sense of humor. Crazy people even felt comfortable with her, and she treated them like family, but she also demanded her right and fought for what belonged to her even if she had to fight physically. So according to Mom, a lot of rich men in the village loved her and would do anything to have her as a wife. But since love is so blind most times, she chose my dad, Osumanu Adjetey Allah—a seventeen-year-old truck driver—instead because she fell in love with him as soon as she set eyes on him.

How they met was that my dad's father, who was born and raised in Labadi in the Greater Accra Region, was a professional driver. And so he drove his truck to Lolonyah—which was a seven-hour drive because of rough roads in those days—and Goi, which is next village, to pick fishmongers and their loads to Accra Makola Market once a week for sales, and then he'd bring them each home in the middle of the night. And these traders also had the opportunity to buy some groceries and other things on their way home.

And since my dad dropped out because, on vacations, his dad took him and a couple of his half brothers with him to work as help mates in loading and unloading stuff. And so they had access to money they collected from passengers, and so he chose money over school. And so after he learned how to drive, his dad who was called Allah Tsuru "Tsuru" means red in Ga Lang because he had light skin you know Ghanaians describes a light skin person as red skin but dad was black just like his mother. And so Grandpa handed over the truck to him as the older son with my grandma because he had other wives and a son who was way older than my dad, and he preferred to go to school until he graduated from college, and he had a great office job, his own home, and his family, which I was aware of that. Grandpa gave Dad a fixed amount of money to pay after work each day on the truck. So Grandpa focused on his farming business rather because both his parents were farmers from a village called Gonsee, where part of his family lives to date, which is part of Greater Accra Region.

And so after Mom and Dad dated for a while and loved each other, nothing could stop Mom from marrying him, not even my grandma, who wasn't happy about her getting married to a simple man, especially because they came from different places. And so they had a traditional marriage. And in those days, church weddings were only for educated people who were Christians, and so only a few people had such a type of marriage, but engagements topped it all and are well-recognized just like church weddings, and the only difference is that the men give their wives rings, and they don't have any. And so, on that day, according to Mom, both families arrived and invited guests, and they all sat under old-fashioned canopies made out of joint bags of flour and with hardwood benches well-arranged under those canopies. And among the requirements of Dad's family, they brought sewing machine for Mom; both nonalcoholic and alcoholic drinks like local and foreign drinks for families and guests; also, traditional weaving cloths called kente, six yards each for my grandma and my grandpa, which is normally called "mother and father peeing clothes," meaning that my mom pee in their clothes when she was a baby; and then a fixed amount of money in three envelopes, one belonged to grandma and the second to grandpa as gifts to them for caring for Mom and then the third envelope money was for the entire Mom's family to share, no matter how little it was, right after the occasion was over to indicate that they all witnessed the marriage.

They made the occasion look like fun that day by letting both families sit across each other and face themselves with enough space in between them. And each family brought a spokesman to speak on behalf of the family, and so, meanwhile, Mom was in her room with a couple of her friends, and she was well-dressed in kente cloths. It was made out with different patterns with a blouse, and she wrapped the two-yard cloths on her waist down like a long tight skirt, and her natural hair was stretched with an old-fashioned stretching comb and styled. And she also wore makeup, gold jewelry, slippers, and then perfume. She was so nervous about the situation, and her friends calmed her down. And so after Dad's family was asked what brought them over after, they said, "Knock, knock, knock." They said that they saw a beautiful flower in the village, and so they came over to pick it. And so Mom's side's spokesmen asked for a few young women to be brought in front of the audience for them to identify the flower they were looking for; and when they searched, they didn't find what they were looking for.

And so they paid more money for the second time, which was given traditionally as transportation, though Mom was in the next room, but they made it more interesting for people to laugh, just like spicing meat up before frying it. And so finally, when Mom was escorted out and was brought in front of the audience, everyone was like, "Wow! We haven't seen such a beautiful woman like her before," and she had a great applause.

And then Dad's family's spokesman said, "Yes, it is the flower we were looking for." And so she sat in the front row on a chair with Dad by her side, and all the items, from cloths to slippers, were arranged in a big brass basin for such occasions, and a medium-size box carrying those different types of jewelries, including her engagement ring tied in white handkerchief. And so all were displayed in public for all the village to witness and give them something to talk about. And they also brought along a large wooden box made of one of Ghana's expensive woods called *odum*.

And so after everything was presented to her, they were given some charges, just like in church. And then Dad put on her the ring, and both parents of Mom were given their cloths and money and what belongs of her family as well.

And thereafter, libations were poured to bless the marriage, and everyone else was served with drinks, and the only thing Mom's family did was cook plenty of Ghanaian dishes for them to eat. And since it was a small village, everyone was around to witness and to enjoy the occasion. And so Dad stayed for a few days, and his family went back to Labadi. Such traditional marriages still exist in Ghana and is called engagements before church weddings, and then they sign papers right after the vows in the church and then get their certificates. Some also prefer to leave right after the engagements to the Register General office to sign papers and receive their certificates. And so my fetish grandma inherited all her family voodoos her late teens way back before Mom was born. And Dad's fetish grandma called Atswei inherited her family voodoos and then his father called Allah Tsuru, and "tsuru" means "red" in Ga language because he had a light skin color, and so after his mother died, he also inherited the family voodoos, and he was also a chief linguist of his neighborhood.

Mom got pregnant with me after her first son was stillborn, and because she was a strong and hardworking woman who endured pains, she worked herself from fish smoking and also for sales each week till her ninth month. And so, on December 20, 1956 that early morning, she traveled to Accra to sell as usual, and she was able to shop for all she needed for Christmas and other things, and then she started having some contractions, and she was in labor pains afterward. And instead of going to a hospital or the nearest midwife health center, she preferred giving birth in the village. And no matter how much she was encouraged to birth me at Accra, she refused. And so she bought an ice cooler and filled it with some ice. And as the truck moved in potholes, she felt even worse pains. According to her, she kept on sprinkling cool water on her belly to calm me down from continuously moving in order for her to get a little relief till they finally made it to the village at nighttime.

And as soon as she was helped to get off the truck, she worked herself slowly to the stinky palm-branch-fenced bathroom—without a door—on sandy ground with small rocks in the middle covered with mold to stand on to shower, and it had a small entrance without a door. And so you have to use your own cloth as cover for privacy and your own bucket of water, soap, sponge, and towel. In fact, it was a bad place to shower because the ground was socked with pee, which was combined with water, since there was no gutter for it to pass through. And for that reason, it smelled worse, and I wonder how they managed to shower in that place twice a day.

She went inside just to pee before she would need help, and then I naturally dropped out right on the ground, but thank God my head didn't hit the rock, or else I don't think that I could have survived. Rather, I could have bled to death because there wasn't any health center in those days.

What blew my mind away was when Mom told me about how I arrived into this world. I grew up to witness types of bathrooms we had just like she told me, and even as a child, I couldn't stand the smell, and so I chose rather to bathe in our chocolate-colored pond with other kids, which wasn't hygienic at all. Just like a swimming pool, someone can pee inside, and no one notices it. But it didn't stink, and the worst thing could have happened to us in that village was that we drunk water from it, and people even washed clothes by the side of the pond and rinsed inside.

And I sometimes ask myself what if my head happened to hit the rock during my birth? And so as soon as I came out from my mom's womb and I fell on that stinky ground, my loud crying voice drew the passengers' attention toward the bathroom because it was just a few minutes of arrival and some of them were still off-loading their things. And then a native midwife was called immediately to cut my cord, and she wrapped me with Mom's two yards extra wrapping clothes she had on, and both me and Mom were sent to her room, and she was cleaned up, and she went to bed to rest, and I was bathed and dressed in my clothes and wrapped with another cloth, and I was laid by Mom's side of the bed. In fact, everyone was so amazed and happy at the same. And my birth turned to be a historic event and also the talk of the village and surrounding villages because it was their first time experiencing a miraculous baby born in such a place. Trust me, as a curious child, I sneaked and I watched few family pregnant women in contractions, and some were birth in the kitchen covered with sand to protect the baby's head because they were standing in pains, and their both hands were tight up against some thick roof sticks. And some also have blanket and sheets were laid on the floor in the room for protection, but unfortunately, a couple of them died together with their babies for some reason like bleeding. But in my case, I could have died in my Mom's womb since she insisted giving birth to me in the village rather than the maternity clinic in Accra, but I was saved by the supreme God because I am one of his chosen ones from pagan parents before I was.

And also, women in those days bought baby clothes before childbirth. But the good news was that all baby's clothes were neutral, and so either of them could wear the same clothes, and they kept it for the next child to save money, and there were also no such thing called crib. And so a day before my naming ceremony, my Dad and some of his family came over to the village to perform as custom demanded, and Mom was given three white African wax prints with different designs and also three African wax prints in different colors, which were six yards each. And she was also presented with scarfs, slippers, jewelries, and a set amount of money for her needs since she won't be working for a while. And I was presented with baby clothes, a medium-size bucket, a bigger basin, a mat, towels, and napkins, and they also brought both local and foreign alcoholic drinks as well.

And so early the next morning, which was a week after I was born, around 4:30 a.m., both side of my family gathered in the compound, and I was stripped naked and laid on the ground by one of elders from Mom's side, and he poured a drink in a small coconut shell at his right hand and a small calabash half filled with water, and he poured libations to their gods and ancestors, and he asked blessing from them and also to protect me from all forces of darkness and for me to be a great person in the future, and then he sprinkled a bit of water on me, and he finally picked me up and dropped some in my mouth with his fingertips.

And then he continued by giving me charges and was like, "You, Atswei Adjetey, drink this water for long life and good health and to be a respectable child too. And when you hear something, let it go out of other ear. When you see something, be quiet about it. And after sunset, before you open your mouth and talk"—and all these while Mom nearly had a panic attack because I was almost out of breath since I cried so much because in December in Ghana, especially close to Christmas, it becomes cold and breezy, and so I was freezing too, and she quickly picked me up as soon as the ritual was over.

Thereafter, everyone who gave money as gifts, names were mentioned, and everyone said loudly, "We sincerely thank you!" And drinks were served along with the traditional drink made out of corn kernel for nonalcoholic drinkers.

And so days later, a rich man in the village with a hunched back drilled a hole in a good amount of coin, and he used a thick white thread as chain and the coin as a locket and placed it around my neck and tied it around my neck like a necklace as a gift, and he told Mom that I was so pretty and he would like me to be his future wife. Those expensive gifts of mine became the talk of the village, and people thought that man was being crazy because though some people did put money on their kids' necks but not such a huge amount of money that Mom could have used for some valuable things for me. And Mom said people were jealous of me for only being an extraordinary child with a precious gift, but to me, though, no one should be born in such an awful place. According to Mom, everywhere she carried me at her back, everyone stared at me and were like, "Wow! This family might be super-rich!"

My parents used to mess with me about Abui the hunchback man when I was five years old after they told me the story that he will be my future husband, and that made me so mad each time because as a child, I thought he was the ugliest man on earth. I recently understood that maybe, like David was anointed by Samuel to be a king at his young age, I was also marked as one of God's chosen ones and untouchable by that hunchbacked man.

It took me two years to walk when I was growing up, though I talked like parrot and was very healthy. But I couldn't walk on my own, though. My Mom bought me a medium-size wooden three-wheel toys that helped kids to walk faster as they continued pushing it on their own.

And so, as pagan parents, I was sent to Labadi to my dad's father, Allah Tsuru, the chief linguist and traditionalist, and he bought me an *Oheneba tokota*, which means "princess slippers," for me to wear because after consulting their voodoos, they said that I was his reincarnated great fetish mother, and she was called Atswei too, and so she wanted her son to notice me, and all she asked of him were those traditional expensive slippers. And to their surprise I started walking on my own as soon my tiny feet fit those little slippers. And so my Mom returned back to Lolonya with me, and she left me with my grandma each time she traveled to Accra to trade or she wanted to be with Dad.

I had an aunt who was just a couple of months older than me, and so Grandma treated us like twins and carried us both on her back if she had to go somewhere. And according to her people, jaws dropped watching her with two kids at her back. Ofliboyo was her name, and she was right at Grandma's back, and I was next to her, and she used *kente* cloths about three yards length to tie us firmly so we don't fall, and she used a large scarf also to tighten us more.

And with that, you know how strong my grandma was. She was the first and last woman because I never saw or heard someone who did such a thing aside from her. I saw her when I was little, as far as I could remember, when she took both me and Ofliboyo to Accra Nugua, a town that wasn't far from Labadi (where her little brother called William lived with his family), for a few days' visit, and she carried both his two kids at her back, though she put the first child on her back, but she was helped by someone to put the second one on her back. And when she tied them so firmly, she walked around the neighborhood, and we followed her around. And then I saw what she was talking about, how people looked at her surprisingly. And the funniest thing also was that she was four feet and eight inches like Mom and was slim but so strong because of her hard work.

I had Guinea-worm disease at age five. It was surprising because I was the only victim out of kids in our home, though we bathed in that dirty pond without soap, or sponge, and we didn't bother to rub our bodies with shea butter when we returned home. But what she did was that we cracked dried palm kernels about a handful each and then we bathed as much as we could, and so after we bathed the dirty pond as much as we wanted and we were about to leave for home, we stepped out from the pond, and then we chewed three cracked palm kernel at a time and then we spit it on our palms and then rubbed our body from hair to toes, and then we returned to the pond to rinse ourselves and stepped out again and wipe ourselves. And then the oil in the cracked palm kernel moisturizes our skin like shea butter. And we drank and washed our clothes with pond water. With the help of chemicals, we sprinkled a little inside to make the water clear, but it tasted salty because we had no tap water, and then we wore our old-fashioned panties that were a special red material with white designs inside, and it was cut in pieces according to ages from babies to elder women, and we all have multiple beads on the waists right after birth, and so we covered our private part with the help of the beads from the vagina with that medium-sized material called in Adamgbe language "subue" in between our legs, our batts, and then through the bead again. And so we're at all times half naked, and some teenagers' breasts were showing, but who cares? And we didn't feel cold because our system was used to it. And when we kids were sent to buy food, money was tight at the back tails, and when the food was sold, the seller untied the money and tied the change back from where she took from. And combing the hair after was optional because some of us don't mind. Aside from pond bathing, we never bathed in the ocean because it was dangerous, and grown-ups were easily drowned.

And me and my friends like playing some amusing games like "ampe." It's a game that two kids have to start by clapping hands and then jump at the same time, and then both of us have to stretch legs at the same time and to the same direction; but if the stretch change to different legs, that make one of us a winner because before we started the game, each of us chose either left or right leg. We also play hide-and-seek at night. With the darkness under the moonlight, we used kerosene lamps and local light made out of milk and Milo cans with a long cotton rope, which also uses kerosene, but we normally use them outside or in the kitchen because black smoke comes out of the flames, and even sitting closer to it, your nostrils turned black and the room too, and much more, it easily burns things. And we used the lamp, including that dangerous thing, to see at night because we didn't have electricity. And so during those days at Lolonya, almost 90 percent of the people from toddlers to elderly folks who were strong enough all slept at the beachside every night in groups from household because those rooms were so hot and mosquitoes dangerously bite also. And the mosquito nets were made from big material sacks of flour sewn together.

And to sleep inside was like sleeping in an oven. But on the beachside, fresh air prevented mosquitoes from biting. And so, one time, we all went to the beachside to a sleepover, but in the middle of the night, I saw myself in a river stream called Bakah that divides the beach and the village, and it led straight to the sea, and it was heavily raining too. And the worse part was that nobody was around and I was soaking wet and terrified too, and so I got out of the stream. I ran, and I knocked on the door before it was opened, and I went inside and changed myself, and I couldn't sleep until morning. And so, according to my family, I went to the beach with them, but they called everyone when it started raining, and they made sure I was walking with them, but they didn't know I was sleepwalking or I was left behind. And my great-grandma said that I was lucky to be alive because ghosts of dead people in the sea hurt people in the middle of the night when nobody was around, and the sea god also released her kids to play around the beach waves and no one supposed to see them and live. And so the incident haunted me for years before I told my mom about that, and she calmed me down. And one more thing, during those days, only a few people like to keep their girl's hair, but the rest of them, including Mom, like our haircut just like boys because of hard work, and so they have no time, and our hair was caught until I had my first child. We didn't normally wear clothes from morning till night, and we felt okay even in the Harmattan season, but we wore our stinky two-yard cloths—which wasn't washed for months—to sleep at the beach. The Guinea worm is a kind of long silky white worm that is very thin, like thread. And not only did it move in different areas of my legs and feet, it also poked me really hard—like contraction labor pains—continuously with no break at all. I also describe it like needles in my blood, moving and poking me so badly. It eventually got swollen at one area day after day, and for that reason, I couldn't eat or sleep, except cry myself out day and night. And when that happened, I couldn't walk on my own. And I was stocked at one place and lay on a mat outside at daytime, and at night, I was carried inside. Can you imagine me as a healthy, smart child, who was just enrolled in a school where I carried my own chair and table back and forth and also missed all the fun I used to have with my friends, especially in the pond, and sleeping over at the beach, and now I was rejected and in pains too?

And so I was so depressed and stressed out because no friend of mine or nieces and nephews wanted to come close to me anymore because it is an infectious disease, and they were warned. And it took weeks for one of the swollen parts to burst or was cut by a herbalist with a sharp razor for the blood and milky liquid to come out, and then after that, the tiny silky worms also popped out of the wound. And it was tied with black thread around my legs, or else it would return back inside, but the thread pulled it out faster, and it was pulled out, then it was cut.

My Mom had my baby sister at Labadi when I was two years old, and she chose to stay with Dad and Adzoa, my little sister, and she found another work because Grandma lost her nets and canoes because there weren't enough fish to catch. So Grandma also focused on her voodoos, and people from the village and surrounding villages came by to know about their future, and they were charged for it, and she also asked them for either goats or chickens along with ingredients to cook and rituals to perform, including foreign drinks.

And after herbal medicine wasn't working for me, Grandma asked a local nurse who went from house to house to heal patients to give me shots a few times, but that couldn't cure the Guinea worm disease. And the rituals Grandma did for those women one at a time in the different day was that she sent them to the dumpster near the beach in the middle of the night and then she slaughtered the live-stock, like a goat, herself with a sharp knife, and if it happened to be a chicken, she twisted the neck to die. Before she cut off the head, she poured the blood in a medium-sized clay pot filled with a bit of cassava, plantain, tomatoes, onions, and peppers. And thereafter, she poured liberations with alcoholic drinks to the Most High God, the Mother Earth, and then the voodoos to get rid of all forces of dark spirits and also problems in that person's life. And then she carried them the pots, and she sang strange songs, and she rang a tiny bell, and surprisingly, both will be shaking themselves for about thirty minutes until grandma asked her to dump the pot at the dumpster, and then they returned home with either the slaughtered goat or the chicken. And then they departed, and Grandma returned to bed, and in day's time, she prepared dinner with some of the meat or chicken for us to eat. I saw all those rituals done because I was curious to know everything, and luckily too, I don't sleep deeply like other kids, and so I sneaked outside each time Grandma woke up in the middle of the night and she stepped outside, and she never saw me since it was dark, and I then give a little space between us. And so for that reason, Grandma had enough money to support me and Afliboyo. And so that same month, my village and all the surrounding were filled with water from the Volta River, which happened for some reason, and all houses were easily destroyed because they were built with clay and palm branches and roofed with dried grass. And so we all moved to the beach because it was the only surviving place, but we couldn't also live without food because there wasn't any way for trucks to come over, except small canoes, and it even came to a point that the small space on the sand also was about to be flooded, and so everyone had to leave without a choice. And so as the news spread all over Ghana, my Mom surprisingly came over to the village with a small hired canoe to evacuate us to a safe place, and so did all families too.

And so Mom hired a canoe, and Mom, Grandma, Ofliboyo, Adzoa, and I in that medium-sized canoe were on our way going to the safe place. And so when we finally made it to dry land, Mom carried me on her back, and auntie Ofliboyo and Grandma walked beside us to the road, which was many miles away, and then Grandma and Auntie Ofliboyo took a lorry to Ada Foah to live with her family and to sell smoked fish at the market because though she lost everything, we all survived, and that matters.

And so Mom took me with her to Labadi, where I continued my treatments with herbs instead of sending me to the clinic because being pagans, their mentality was that Guinea-worm disease was caused by spiritual means. And so she sent me to a few fetish shrines too, and that too didn't work, so she brought me back to Grandma at Ada Foah, one of the largest towns in the Adamgbe District, and lots of rituals were performed for me with other herbs because where she lived, there was a big shrine with many rooms all built with clay and roofed with grass.

And so Grandma took me to the chief fetish priest in the shrine, concerning the same disease, and all sorts of nasty, stinky, fermented herbs mixed with akpeteshie, the local alcoholic drinks, was forced on me to drink as a cure. And secondly, other rituals were made, where the fetish priest fetched a bucket full of the same nasty and stinky herbs mixed with chicken blood from a large pot in the shrine, and I stood close to the dried grass roofs, and then that bucket of herbs water was thrown on the rooftop, and then it poured all over me from hair to toe every morning for a couple of months. And that was even worse because it felt cold, and I started shaking for a while, and the odor became part of me because he didn't allow Grandma to bath me with clean water and soap. He gave Grandma grind herbs to place in the affected areas, but he couldn't cure me because the worms were alive in my blood. And so after a part of my legs got swollen with pains for days, it was cut, and the milky mixed with blood came out, the worms were pulled out from the wound, and then the tip of the worm was tied with black thread, and then Grandma tied it around my leg. And that made the worms pulled out more, and then it was cut off, and the tip was tied with black thread again. But days later, the wound healed on its own. And so then another part of the leg started to swollen over again, so the more I continued suffering. That dangerous disease was so crafty. It gave a few days of relief, then it worsened my situation because it went straight to the back of my left foot, and it hurt so badly that I couldn't even walked at like formerly when I started walking with a long stick at the shrine and in weeks later after suffering and continuously, drinking of bitters, as those herbs mixed with alcohol were called, my foot got swollen and was cut with razor. And so when all the liquid came out and the worms were finally pulled out and the wound was healed, the bad news was that I couldn't walk by myself again unless I used a stick, and even with that, the back of my left foot couldn't land on the floor because the muscles and nerves were stocked.

And in all these months, Mom was there right beside me with my little sister Adzoa. She did care for me and the rest of them. And as for Grandma, she bought smoked fish at Ada Foah on market days, which is Wednesdays and Saturdays. And she sold them for her costumers, and she was able to buy groceries and to support the family financially, and she paid for every treatment too. My Mom was so sweet and patient with me, and I knew that she felt my pains because she cried most times when I was in pain, and she encouraged me to keep fighting that disease and that it would be over soon. And so it came to a point that I felt comfortable limping on my left toes because my heel hurts so badly whenever I tried to land it on the ground. And my mom wasn't happy at all because of that and encouraged me by saying that "Mamkpa Atswei." "Mamkpa" in Ga means "big mama." "You know you are so beautiful, smart, and someday, you will become a great person. And it doesn't suit you to be disabled, and so please try to land your heel on the ground and try to ignore the pains." And till now, I still remember what she said to me whenever I am in a tight situation, and I told myself that was it.

And honestly, those got me like injections, and they motivated me to land my left foot completely on the floor when walking and crying out in pain at same, and Mom still helped me walk—more like exercise—and she repeatedly told me each time, "Great job! You can do. It just keep on walking." And in no time, I started walking well without limping, but I just became used to walking a little slow.

Dad went to police training course at Accra Police Department as a professional driver, but his little brother joined the army because he completed his secondary education. And so my dad and the rest of his other half brothers lived in single rooms at his father's two plots of lands at La Abormli, and he shared them for his firstborn of other women. And so he reserved the rest of the land to those of his children who wanted to build a house on their own. And that was what illiterates did those days because they didn't feel comfortable with lawyers, and so they liked to share their own properties before they died.

And so after months living at that shrine and I felt better, my mom returned to Labadi with my sister and I. But this disease was determined to get rid of me this time, and so weeks later I, felt sharp pains around the left side of my abdomen, and that part started poking me, and it got swollen again the day after, and then my pains got worse, and Mom also was so frustrated because all these bad things were happening to me, and she couldn't focus on trading anymore to provide for us.

She continued with treatments from different herbalists with different herbs, but aside one I had to apply on the swollen areas, I still had some mixed with alcohol to drink as an antibiotic. And so during those unbearable weeks, my dad's brother Kojo came out of nowhere in the middle of the night and told us to leave the room because he was on leave. In fact Mom's jaws dropped hearing him say that, and then she told him that first, the place belonged to her husband, and he had no right to move us out; and second of all, I was in a delicate situation right then, and so we were not going anywhere. And then he started yelling at Mom with insults, and he threw our stuff out of the room, and so all three of us were crying out loud, but none of Dad's family came out to ask what was going on.

And so she had no choice but to carry me on her back, hold my four-year-old baby sister, and she went and knocked on the door of a woman she knew back at Lolonya. She was living with her husband and three kids in her chamber and living room, and luckily enough,

ROSE ADDO

they had a corridor where she cooks and offered us that space to sleep in a mat on the floor. And she, being so kind, allowed our stuff in her bedroom, and I even cried more that night because Mom couldn't stop crying either.

And still, months passed by, and we didn't hear from Dad because after he graduated, he was transferred to Ave Afiadenkpa is an old town in the main Denu-Ho road, to drive the inspector there with a police jeep, and we had no other source of income aside from the money Grandma gave Mom before we left. And so she had no choice but to leave me by myself at home in that compound house with other tenants, who also had jobs to go to every morning. She assisted her friend with her chop bar business, which was shady where she cooked different African dishes like *fufu*, which is either boiled cassava or boiled plantain and pounded in a mortar with a pestle till it's softer, and it's served with soups like light pepper soup prepared with either fish or meat or palm or peanut paste soup with fish or meat and along with tomatoes, hot peppers, onions, garlic, ginger, and salt.

Omotowo also is boiled rice, and after it's cooked and softened, she used wooden a spoon to mix it together till it turned to a small dough, and then she rolled it smaller into football shapes and sold them, and it's served with all of the above soups. But when it comes to boiled rice with measurable salt, she prepared tomato stew, and after it was cooked, she added either fried fish, fried meat, along with boiled eggs.

And so, Mom left home early morning with my sister Adzoa and her friends to work what was about five hundred yards away from home. They cooked all these foods under a big shade roofed with palm branches, and so they didn't cook when it rained. And so the fufu preparation started with fresh plantains and cassava, well-peeled and placed in a large-sized aluminum pot with water added to it and covered with the lid and placed on set firepot full of firewood. And so, in an hour, when it was well-cooked and then it was pounded in mortar and pestle that Mom pounded—and then her friend called Afi—sat, and used her hand inside the mortar to push the fufu in the middle of the mortar until the fufu was soft and ready to sell. When everything was ready, neighbors brought their own bowls to buy, but passerby sat on short benches and tables, and they were being served with Afi's own bowls. And including Malians, whose main work was in Ghana, was filling up people's barrels and pots with free water from the taps by the street, and they charged for that. And something funny about them Mom told me was that they didn't buy meat or fish at all whenever they bought food, not because they were vegetarians, but they said that they had both meat and fish in their mouths, and so they bought only fufu, rice or omotuwo, and the collected soup or stew just to save more money on their return to their country. And so when I was alone, I cried out in pain and fear of being alone, and the only things that I was surrounded with were food, water, a chamber pot, and alcohol bitters in a big bottle with a small glass beside as pain killer. And I couldn't walk again because the muscles and nerves from the left side of my abdomen were hurting so badly through my legs. And what Mom normally said to me before leaving was, "Atswei, take care of yourself. When you are in worse pains, drink some bitters, okay?"

And so I have no means to contact Mom at the chop bar in case of emergency, which worried me, but as a seven-year-old child who didn't know who God is even though I heard his name from fetish priests each time they poured libations. And the way they humbly addressed him first in Twi language that "Almighty Supreme God, have your drink before anything else," so I thought maybe he is one of their voodoos. And so I talked to him to help me get well.

The next thing I saw up there hanging on the well was a box radio, which was provided by the government and was outside all homes. By 9:00 p.m., it was off till 6:00 a.m., and it sometimes distracted me with the music. I got drunk to lessen my pain by drinking more than I should, and that got me a couple of hours' sleep, which happened at daytime but not at night, and I hope those who had been in some kind of worse pains before knows what I was talking about.

My pains got more aggressive, as if I was being stabbed many times at the affected areas, and I felt weaker each day because of lack of sleep, stress, and not eating well too, and that made Mom also cry along with me, and she told me many times that she wished she could switch places with me because I was too young to continue to endure such pains. It took a while for Dad to receive Mom's letter she sent through a trader, who went to buy goods at one of the market days, and so Dad also wrote us an invitation letter to come over and live with him but that he would deal with his brother afterward.

And so Mom packed our things, and then we left Labadi for Ave Afiadenyigpa safe and sound. But unfortunately, after the Guinea worm disease left my legs and thighs and the wounds healed, it tackled the left side of my abdomen. And so that area got swollen, and it always came with a big price, and I was in bitter pains like I was bitten by a living being inside me continuously. And when the swollen area was cut and those liquids came out with the worms, then later, clear water started coming out with tiny pieces of white hard something compared to broken pieces of china plates from my wounds, but it wasn't hurting like before.

And so Ave Afiadenyigpa was an old small town and in a very thick forest in the sixties, and the main crops, I still remember, are palm trees, plantains trees, bananas, trees, huge cotton trees, and also crops like corns, cassava, tomatoes, hot peppers, onions, and many more. And hunters also hunted for animals like grass cutters, rabbits, and many more, and also, they hunt for snails and mushrooms and crabs. So because my parents like snails, mushrooms, and crabs, Mom bought in quantities to them, and she raised them in pots with lids, and she even placed a stone on the lids, else they will pull the lids and get out of the pots. And she fed them with fresh palm nuts and sugarcanes cut into pieces, and whenever she prepares meals, they are not left out in the soup or stew. And the entire town is in gravel ground, so all the houses turned red, and there wasn't tap water or electric, so we drank from wells, and we fetched water by using a medium-sized bucket tied with thick rope, and we add the same chemicals in Lolonyah to clear the dirts that went underneath the bucket or pots. And we drank clean and sweet water during the rainy season. And we sleepover with kerosene lamps, and we used the same local lights made out of milk can and Milo cans like Lolonyah. But we used flashlights whenever both our parents and we stepped outside to visit neighbors during late evenings, or we had to use the toilet that was separated from the bathrooms.

And so not only were we so excited to see Dad, but he was too, and he told us repeatedly how he missed us. And you know Dad wasn't an abusive father at all in any way and not even with Mom, but he was so sweet, caring, and passionate with us. And I still remember that my sister and I used to lay on him in the bed in the daytime when he was available, and we naively suck his breast, and he laughed loudly, and as we continued, he then laughed at the same time including Mom. Mom was rather the tough one and who was so hard on me when it comes to chores aside from her sweetness. But she didn't physically or verbally abuse us. Instead, she yelled at us when she got mad since we refused to listen. And so I never followed Mom to the market before, but she went several times with Adzoa, and when she had measles too, she sent her to hospital treatments, and they returned home with a gallon of oil and also dried powdered milk in a box. And the case of Guinea worm disease, they believe that was a spiritual disease, and so it involved fetish's treatments, and so few weeks after my abdomen wound got healed, and I thought I was freed, it got swollen again close to the healed wound. And so as usual, Dad and Mom sent me to a herbalist at Ave Dakpa, a small town just a couple of miles away from Ave Afiadenyigpa. And so he also told him to bring the same things that the other fetishes demanded and with a fixed amount of money, and he gave me some concoction made from herbs to drink and herbs Mom had to grind and apply to the affected parts. And so at the end of the month, when Dad received his salary, he sent him all he demanded. And so Mom got depressed because as a hardworking woman, she had nothing to sell at the police barracks.

And once a week, Mom slaughtered chicken to prepare soup and fufu for the family aside from the different dishes she prepared every day. But what I had no idea of was that the blood of those chickens was poured on Dad's voodoos he got under the bed until one day when Mom and Adzoa went to the market to buy groceries and Dad was at work. And so I went to the room and looking for my slippers because it's funny that we kids walked around without slippers, except when we were about to go to bath and use the toilet. And so I couldn't find one slipper, so I went on my knees to look for it with a flashlight under the bed, and I saw something else unusual, and so I pulled it out, and I surprisingly found out that it was a medium-sized voodoo placed in a clay pot. And it was molded in a human head, shaped with eyes, nose, and mouth, and dried blood was all over it. And so, in fact, it was an unforgettable day for me because I was traumatized, and I started crying and shaking out of fear that the voodoo would kill me instantly for being curious, like the saying, "Curiosity kills the cat." And so I begged the voodoo not to kill me, but I will keep it a secret, and I wouldn't tell anybody about it.

And now it sounds funny to me whenever I think about it, begging a graven image that has eyes but couldn't see, nose but couldn't smell, and mouth but couldn't eat either to spare my life because I was little and so naive that I didn't know that is only God whom all powers belong to. And I think I negotiated with the voodoo also because I grew up in midst of voodoo worshippers, and I was brainwashed what they were capable of doing. And so thereafter, I couldn't tell any of my parents to get in trouble though Mom saw me acting so weird on her return from the market, and so she asked if everything was okay. And I replied yes! And so after all that Ave Dakpa herbalist did for me to get better, it didn't work, and instead, it got more swollen, and I was in bitter pains, so my parents were directed to see another old couple with their gray hairs in two miles away by a friend of Dad. And so when we reached the gateway to the shrine, we were told to walk backward until we got close to them before we turned and face at them. And so Dad already had two bottles of schnapps, an alcoholic drink like his friend told him, so the male herbalist examined the swollen part of my abdomen, and then he poured liberations for their voodoos with a little bit of the drink in a glass and kept the rest like the other, and then he charged Dad a fixed amount of cash to buy things himself for rituals.

And so he also gave them herbs to mix with the alcoholic drink with tiny glass like that of tequila shots to drink a full glass three times daily to destroy the worms inside me and some herbs also to grind and apply to the affected areas. And so when we were ready to leave the shrine, we did walk backward to the gate before we turned forward toward home and did all that because it was one of the rules of that shrine. And so my parents were sure that it would work this time because they were so old and experienced herbalists, and so as I continued with the treatments, this time, Dad used his razor to cut a little of the swollen area, unaware. And so as usual, those nasty liquids got out, and then afterward, the pain wasn't severe anymore, and those worms were pulled out. And my reasons for describing them as a living being is that not did those worms poked me so hard when moving in my blood, but if the tip of swelling part was caught and those tiny long worms were pulled out with the thread tied to the worms and it was cut off, it moves like earthworms on the floor, but it didn't take a long time to die because it survives in the blood. And so I was addicted to alcohol as a child because the herbs were mixed with it, and my parents also thought it was okay since I got painless from it, and that gave them also relief, and they also thought that the herbs in the alcohol would kill those worms.

And because of my disease, Adzoa went to school ahead of me, located about half-mile away, and before she was enrolled, the teacher told her to lift her right hand and placed on her head and then shift it to the left ears. And so when she was able to do that, she was qualified for school, and that was the interesting thing done those days, and then they asked Mom about her informations, and the teacher wrote everything on the admission forms because they knew that a lot of people are illiterates. And that is still funny to me, and I can imagine kids with short heights, they would be disqualified from school because of their short hands since the school didn't deal with age because only a couple of them have birth certificates, but the rest of us who were born at homes were with no certificates, and some parents didn't even know the day and date of themselves, or neither their own kids.

And so since nobody could notice my wound and with the pains reduced, I asked my parents to enroll me in school, and I went through the same procedure that Adzoa went through, so I sat in the same class with her. But to be honest with you, she was smarter than me. And some of the challenges we faced in class was that all subjects

31

were taught in the Ewe language like math, history, science, and we read Ewe books too, expect English period before the teacher speaks the English language. But that wasn't done in Accra schools; instead, all subjects were taught and well-explained in the English language, expect in Ga lessons before that teacher taught us in Ga language, and we also read Ga reading books and Bibles too. And so it wasn't easy for me because I didn't know the Ewe language, but I tried to cope with that. And because I am a fast learner, I picked some of the languages, and I understood what went on in the class.

And also because Ave Afiadenyigpa is a farming town, so in part, there was a large garden, and corn was the main crops before okra, cassava, plantains, tomatoes, onions, and many more. And something else bad about the school also was that we drank water from the well, and all classes from one to six had medium-sized pots and covered with trays, and on top of the trays were four plastic drinking cups. And so when someone fetched water with a cup and drank, then he or she placed the cup on the tray with leftover water inside. And so when someone else came to drink water, all he did was just dig the cup with leftover water in the pot and fetched some water and drink. And even if when someone finishes drinking, she passed on the leftover, and when somebody else to drink without second thoughts, she would get any disease out of that. And the teachers were okay with that, and in their cases, they had old-fashioned clay cooler in each class for one teacher with one cup to use. And so some-times, I asked myself what if someone got infected with my Guinea worm disease or I was infected with other illnesses like hook cough virus or tuberculosis disease and many more?

And rather, the teacher taught us how important it was to wash our hands after we used the toilet and before we eat, and that was it at hygiene lessons, and so I compared how unsafe the water was to Lolonya, where we had two extra-large pots in the house—one was on the side of the compound, and the other pot was at the hallway in the room—and they were covered with plastic plates as lids and a small calabash on top of each other. And so when someone fetched water and drank, then the leftover water was in the calabash and was left in the plate for someone who felt tasty drink or just the calabash containing water in the pot and fetched water to drink, and those calabashes were there like forever in the plate, and no one cared to clean them with soap and sponge. And those pots were topped with water more each day, and nobody cared to pour out the dirty water from those pots and clean them before filling them with clean water. The bad part was that sometimes when water was fetched from the pot, it sometimes contained tiny little worms in the calabash inside them, but we still drank most times without noticing. And in case we find out, we still drink and just made sure that we didn't swallow any of those worms.

And so when it was few days for the end of the semester, the teachers stopped teaching, and instead, we harvested our crops in the garden, and the dried corn kernels were peeled off in each class into big basins. And so on the last market day before vacation, some of the corn kernels were sold in the market, including some of the tomatoes, cassava, onions, okras, and hot peppers, and the money was added to the little contributions from the parents, and the teachers bought meat and dried fish. And the senior class students collected firewoods from the bush, and some of them also went to grind the leftover corn kernels at the mill into powder. And so on the day of vacation, teachers borrowed bigger sizes of aluminum pots and firepots from neighbors, and then they themselves prepared okra soup with the meat and the dried fish, and it was easy to prepare as soon as the meat and dried fish were tender after cooking for hours with salt water, and then they added grind tomatoes, onions, hot peppers to the soup to boil for about twenty minutes. And they cut the okras into pieces, and then they put them in another aluminum pot, and they added a certain amount of water to it, and then they add a small amount of kawe to make it more slippery and a chemical from a particular rock in Volta region.

And after twenty minutes, the okras turned soft and slippery, and by then, some of the teachers, on the other hand, were also preparing their traditional food called akple, so that too, after plenty water in the aluminum pot, placed on another firepot boiled; then they mixed smaller amount of powder corn with water, and they poured it into the boiled water slowly and stirred it at the same time to thicken like porridge. And then they fetched some of the thickened soup inside a bowl, and then they poured the corn powder into the boiling water, and they continued stirring with a thick long wooden spoon until it became thick, and so they added the reserved boiled water to soften it, and the stirring continued until the akple turned smoother and softened. And thereafter, they fetched all in a big basin, and it was covered with a white plastic bag to keep it warm. And we, the students, brought our own small bowls with lids like we were told to. And so after the meal was ready, we formed a long line, and some of the teachers dished akple inside our bowls, and some also fetched the okra soup and a little bit of meat and fish on the akple. And so the teachers did a great job on that day, and they worked as a team, especially because they were all female teachers.

After we ate, we sang songs we were taught, and then the senior students cleaned all the pots and basins used for cooking, and then we went to the assembly, and we were given our report cards, and then we went home with some leftover food. And so some interesting things about calabash was they used those in different sizes. The smaller ones were used for selling palm wine drinks, which naturally comes out from palm trees, and it was sweet and had alcohol inside, and the medium-sized calabash was used for drinking water, and then the large sizes are like food warmer, and so kenkey, banku, and abolo was sold inside with its same lids, and I describe it like pumpkins.

So Mom sent me back to Grandma because of the same Guinea worm disease in the same part of my abdomen that couldn't heal. The pains also didn't stop, and the water didn't stop coming out of the wound. But she moved this time to Adokope, which is part of the Adamgbe District, and she lived with her last born, Ofliboyo, and she continued her fetish practices there like she used to do at Lolonyah. And Mom, Adzoa, and I traveled with a truck, and then we passengers and trucks got inside the old-fashioned lounge, and so we paid the fare, and we were given tickets, and we passengers sat on seats at different parts of the ship, and the truck also was at the other side, and we crossed the Volta River. And then we got inside the truck, and again, it drove us to our Adokope Road, and we exit, and then we walked for a while before we finally made it to the village.

And so Grandma was happy to see us, but she was worried about me, and she wondered why I was still suffering and also how infectious that disease is, but it didn't infect any of the family, except me. And she lived in a rental house built with clay and roofed with dried grass like Lolonya and other villages, and there lived an experienced elderly herbalist called "Kwuatse," and his dead wife called "Kwuanye" because they had twins. And the funny thing about the Adamgbes is that they believe twins are monkeys since they called monkey "Kwua," and so those names mean "monkey's dad and monkey's mom." And it is the names given to the twins' parents to date, and also, their term of asking how the twins are doing is that "Are the monkeys dead?" And then the parents respond, "Yes, they are all dead." Meaning, that they are all doing well. In case any of the twins died during childhood, the parents made a custom wooden doll, either a girl or a boy, and it was named after the dead child. And they make sure the wooden doll wore the same clothes with the living child out of the leftover materials, and whenever they eat, the wooden doll was around the table. And they slept in the same bed with it, and whenever the twins' mom carried the child at her back on her way out, then she carried the doll on her chest in between her breasts and with his or her face showing for the public to know that her twin dead. And so their mentality of doing all those was to support the live child to continue living when I asked Grandma about the reason why the twins' mom went through all that trouble.

And even when the twin grew up and got married, he or she carried the wooden doll to the marital house as a family. And so at Adokope, Grandma introduced us to Kwuatse, the herbalist, and he took a good look at the wound in my abdomen. And so he told Grandma that he wasn't charging her for anything because of the good friendship they had, but after I am completely healed, he would accept anything given to him. And so to be honest with you, I didn't see any voodoo in his living room, except a small eating table and a couple of stools, and then part of it was like a kitchen where he had his cooking pots, coal pot, a big pot of drinking water that they fetch from the river close the village, and the same river they trapped smaller fish with bottles and they bathed in the water. But I have never been to his bedroom before, and he lived with his young son in his late teens called Doo, and Kwuatse also raised many doves as pets, and he understood them, and they also heard him when he talked to them in birds language, and he had small cages in the same living room hanging on the roof, and they stepped out and flying around the village, and they returned to his room through the open windows.

And the interesting part is, whenever Kwuatse fed them with leftover grind corn powder he got from the mill, those new moms among the doves also fed their little one's mouth to mouth, and when they drank water too, their little ones also had some from mouth to mouth until they were grown and started feeding themselves because they were little to eat like the grown ones. I spent most of the time with Kwuatse and just watching those amazing doves.

And so Kwuatse started treating me with herbs mixed with an alcoholic drink, and he ground some herbs on his own grinding stone in his room, and he personally gave some to drink, and he applied to the affected areas each after I bath in the morning and evening. He poured liberations with water in a calabash rather when he started the treatments continuously day after day. And so Mom and Adzoa left back to Ave Afiadenyikpa in a week's time, and she told Grandma that in case of emergency to send her a message through traders at Adokope who traveled all the way to Akatsi Market days in the Volta Region, which is not too far from Ave Afiadenyigpa with dried fish and other foodstuffs, and in their return to the village, they either exchange with foodstuffs that traders at Volta Region also got, or they collected cash. And so I was left with Grandma, but because Kwuatse was so kind and patient with me and his doves also gave me some excitements, so I was mostly with him since he was our neighbor too. And I wasn't a burden to Grandma at all because she was free and minding her business, and Ofliboyo also preferred to step outside and keep her friends company. And weeks later, same left part of my abdomen really got swollen, and I was in excessive pains like my whole belly was stabbed repeatedly, and Kwuatse kept on encouraging me to stay strong because after those liquids were out of my system, I would be out of danger for good. And as a result of that pains, I lost my appetite, and I couldn't sleep at all, so it came to a point that swollen part was so soft, so Kwuatse decided to cut it with a knife in order for those poisonous liquids to get out of my abdomen before it poisoned my blood and killed me. And so he kept that a secret from everyone else, and that afternoon, he prepared tomatoes soup with tiny tilapias, which has lots of bones inside, but they are so soft, so they are safe to swallow the bones. And he prepared banku alongside, and then he invited all kids in the house to join us eat, and I think he did that because I haven't eaten any heavy food for days and also in order for me to get excited and eat more to gain the strength to stand strong for what I was about to face. And so when we were about to eat, he gave me alcohol herbal bitters more than he should, and so he got me drank and I had much appetite to eat more than anyone else. And so everyone had enough, and they all left for outside to play, and I was left with him and his son. And so he told to fetch a full calabash of water and drink all. I also thought that he wanted me to stay hydrated even after those liquids come out from me. And so, after we finished and the rest of the kids stepped out to play, he asked me to come closer for checkup, but what I didn't know was that he had a sharp knife in his pocket, and so he poked the swollen part while I was unaware. And then I was rolling all over the floor, crying and really thought that was the end of my life at the moment, and my loud noise brought neighbors around, and Grandma was called from the mill when she was grinding corn kernels. In fact, I was just crying on top of my voice out of pain, and I thought that my intestines poked because of milk and blood mixture flowing out of that part like opened tap water, which no one stopped. And so, everyone, including Grandma, thought the same thing too, so they cried as well, and thereafter approximately two gallons of those nasty poisonous liquids fluids came out from the fresh cut wound, and then followed by blood slowly coming out from the same wound for a while and the it stopped instantly. And then I was relieved and the swollen part dropped down to normal. I was lifted from that clay ground, bathed, and changed by Grandma, and the herbalist applied ground herbs on the wound and asked Grandma to clean the wound and apply some on it on a daily basis and continue giving me bitters to drink as well. In fact, the whole Adokope village and the herbalist said that I was a destiny child because only few survived what I went through with the swollen belly because in most cases, it burst inside them, and that liquid poisons the blood completely and kills them.

And even those dangerous worms could have torn my intestines into pieces, or I would be disabled, just like many people I witnessed out of this disease. And so a few days later, Mom and Adzoa returned as soon as she received the message to be with me for weeks. And I was so grateful for all Kwuatse did to heal me. And so he still continued the treatments, but he changed the herbs, and as usual, he continued my treatments himself, and he was glad I healed faster than he thought, and my pains stopped completely. And so when my wound was almost healed, Kwuatse gave Mom herbs to take with us because we left Adokope for Labadi since Dad was there because he was on vacation, and he wanted to deal with his young brother who threw us out of his own room. And one more thing on my own experiences, almost herbalists are voodoo worshippers like I saw them from shrine to shrine, and Grandma also told me that she had been in the thick bushes in different places, and she healed people with malaria, tuberculosis, and many illnesses with herbs, and she also knew the poisonous one. But I wonder if so, why didn't she heal me? And the Guinea worms nearly took my life.

And so, it took months for me to be back to a normal kid again at the age of eight, who walked by herself without any trace of disability, except the scars, which reminds me of what happened to me as a child. And a strange thing also happened when I was a child. I never came across any retarded kids or kids with special needs and also some with superbig heads, etc. because they were forbidden from the society for reasons that they would bring disasters to the villages or towns they were born in, and for that reason, as soon as those babies were born, fetish priests were consulted, and then they demanded money, alcoholic drinks, goats, and food ingredients. And after those items were collected from those naive parents who had no choice than to let them go because wherever those babies will be hidden, someone else will tell the chiefs in their towns or villages, and she will be fine with extra money for disobeying their rules. And so those poor babies will be handed over to the chief's fetish priest and his followers, including all those items to the bushes, and so they poured libations, and then they slaughtered goats, sprinkled the blood on the babies laid on the ground, and then they told the babies that they didn't belong to the society. Then they asked their voodoos to turn them to snake, and then those wicked people turned their backs on the babies, and they walked back home. No one pressed charges against me because the police also believed so. And nobody knows if that was true, and I doubted that because they might be eaten by wild animals in the bushes. In fact, I felt so sad when my Grandma, the fetish priest, told me that story because I thought no one was ever born with special needs, though I saw some people both kids and grownups crawling on the floor in my village and a few places I visited, but I was told that some got crippled because of Guinea worm disease, and some also fell from trees. And so I believed Grandma after she told me that sad story of how some Ghanaian babies lost their lives because of the lack of knowledge since I also could have been dead or crippled out of the Guinea worm disease if it had not God that could have been treated in the hospital just like measles or any disease. And even my Dad's older sister, called Adjeley, went through this terrible experience with her firstborn son called Okpoti. He was born as a child with special needs, and he couldn't sit on his own after he was five months old, and his neck bone was weaker, and water comes out of his opened mouth. And he looked at things so weird because she had never been to school before, and she believed those lies that her son might be a snake. So she never sent her child to the hospital before, but rather, she hid him in the room, and she didn't bring him outside in the compound house. And he started biting her when she breastfed him, and she rather continued to feed him with baby formula and porridge. And aside from everything, she loved her child because he was handsome like his well-educated husband who was so supportive, but they weren't living together, and he was so shy to come over. Rather, Adjeley was the one who visited his place alone in a family house, and so he actually didn't know the real problem with his son.

And so in eight months time, his hair started falling, and his light skin also continued to peel off, and he stank, but she still didn't think of seeking medical treatment for him, and rather, she handed him over to the fetish priests with the requirements, which her dad happened to be one of them, but he wasn't in the group who sent him to the thick bush and left him over. And so she said the most painful part is that they refused to allow her to go with them to say goodbye and to see if he turned to snake for real. And so concerning to the same sad story I was told to in the sixties, I am talking about what I witnessed one in 1979. Jack, my husband's brother, called that Kwabena's wife gave birth to a son who had an extra big head than his entire body. And so after he visited them at Korle Bu Hospital and he returned home, he wasn't happy about that, and he also thought his child didn't belong to the society, and he will turn to a laughingstock in his neighborhood, and so he paid a nurse, according to him, to put him to rest like an old dog or cat. And so he lied to his family members that the baby was stillborn, and he warned that the truth should be told so. He was placed in the coffin and buried in the cemetery. And I was so sad hearing that because I was pregnant with my third child, so I asked myself what if the same thing happened to me, how am I supposed to handle that? This really hurt me emotionally because it's so sad for a child to be born to this world, and for some reason, because of his or her special needs, he has to be killed inappropriately with false accusations.

And so thankfully, after Guinea worm disease, I didn't have malaria out of mosquitoes bites or any other illnesses. And thereafter, Dad was transferred to Elmina Castle, which was a police headquarters in the sixties, for police recruiters and also prisons for smugglers and those who broke the laws.

And for some reason, I still have no idea Mom left me with my grandpa's little sister called Kai at Labadi, who lived at the west side with her daughter and a granddaughter of his son in a family compound house, and she followed my father to Elmina with my sister Adzoa, who was six years old. I was left with money and my personal stuff, but living there was actually like Cinderella and her wicked stepmom and sisters. And so Kai, my stepgrandma, enrolled in a public school at the province of Labadi in the farms, and it was called Africa Unity Primary School, and the classes were halfway built with old aluminum sheets and roofed with aluminum sheets too with holes all over, and so we looked on the sky through the holes, and we had no windows because it wasn't completely different, and we had short gates on each of the classes and cupboards, where we kept our books, and benches and table that three kids sat on each bench, and we write on the same table in front of us. And we had no toilets or bathrooms, so we used the bush near the school as a toilet and bathroom. The teachers had their medium sizes and chairs in front of us. And the floor wasn't even cemented, and to be honest with you, only kids from poor families attended the school, and because of that, Kai's granddaughter, called Koshi, attended a mission school of the Presbyterians. And the whole building was well-built with cement blocks, and they were roofed with slate sheets and with windows and doors and all facilities like libraries, assemble hall, toilets separated from bathrooms, one child had a chair and table to sit comfortably, and many more. And so my school was two miles away from home, and she didn't give me any breakfast but a little coin that affords only snacks like both roasted corn kernels and peanuts or "agblekaklo" prepared from fresh cassava that tasted good with a dried piece of coconut. And because we ran shifts, morning classes started from 8:00 a.m. to 12:00 p.m., and afternoon classes started from 1:00 p.m. to 4:00 p.m. And so until I returned home, she gives me a little coin to step out and buy foods sold at each corner of Labadi, like both roasted plantain and peanut, rice, and tomatoes with meat, fish or boiled eggs or fufu, banku, kenkey, or konkonte with different kinds of soup or hot pepper and fried fish. But unfortunately, the money given to me could afford boiled rice only with nothing else except stew in it, and so I mostly buy toasted plantain and peanut instead just to keep on surviving, and then evening time too with the same little amount of money. But when it comes to Koshie, she had more money than me to buy whatever she craved for and to be satisfied.

I turned to a beggar at school and begging every break time from classmates, and I didn't care about all sorts of fun made of me as long as I had enough in my tummy—that mattered. And step-grandma Kai had a full-grown son and a daughter, and she is a fetish priest, and because of that, she is called "Aawon." It means in Ga language a "female fetish priest," and so half of Aawon consultation room was filled with voodoos in different images. Some are wooden dolls, human heads molded with clay, wooden masks hanging on the walls, small sizes of pots painted black, and all filled with beach stones and water and a tiny coconut shell she filled in an alcoholic drink whenever she poured libations, including the wooden stool she sat on, and they were all sprayed with blood exactly like Mom's mother consultation room, and she also had few different kinds of schnapps alcoholic drinks, and at the end of the day, Aawon covers them with white large material.

You know why I was able to see all these? And so my reasons for observing all these because I slept with them every day alone until I left. And she rather slept over her husband's house and returned in the mornings, and her job was somewhere like a psychic, and she pretended to be in motion and then asked her costumers, "Why you came?" But she didn't read cards; instead, she poured libations in one of the pots, and she also started by asking the supreme God to have a drink, the Mother Earth too, and her voodoo comes last. And then the funny thing was, she said all the time that her voodoos have traveled, and they need a certain amount of money before they return and solve their problems. And then she told them a bunch of lies they wanted to hear about witches, witchcrafts in their families, trying to harm them, and so out of fear, her costumers provided her with everything she asked from them, even if they had to borrow money. And then Aawon got enough money out of that, and there is a saying in Ga language, "A fool doesn't turn fetish priest" since wisdom is common sense. And I witnessed all these because whenever I had after shifts at school, in morning hours, she called me by her side whenever she had consultations. And Aawon was kind me, and she didn't abuse me in any way. Rather, once in a while when she cooked, she gave me some leftovers and a roof over my head. Because they have ways of putting fear in people—mostly women—since we are so easily convinced. And to be honest with you, I never witnessed a man going for consultations from them, but some said twenty per-cent out of one hundred percent.

Stepgrandma's granddaughter Koshi was a clever thief, and rather, Kai thought that I was the thief, and she instead was treated like a princess, and she did nothing in the house to help in the house chores. You know, she had a small kiosk where she sold local drinks that was akpeteshie, cigarettes, matches, sardines, sugar, etc., and so after school, I filled all pots and barrels of water in the house with water I carried in a big bucket from the roadside about a fif-teen-minute walk away on a rocky ground because we have no tap water in the house except those tap water around all roads sides built by the British.

And aside from that, they also built us superlarge bathrooms, which contained about forty people at once with showers and tap water inside, and all we did was bring our own sponges, towels, and soaps but some grownups brought buckets because they were scared of using shower, and even some of us washed dirty laundry over there. But some who were disabled or had something in their body, which they didn't feel comfortable for others to see and to gossip about, bathed at home with buckets of water by standing in a big basin. They stood in the big basins to bath the houses because 90 per-cent of those houses in those days had no bathrooms or toilets. And so mostly during mornings and evenings, long lines were formed in the public toilets, built by same British, and those toilets contained about twelve people at a time, and they were like small space with twelve round small holes, and sewage tanks were built underground to contain the feces. And some weren't divided, and so when some-one squats and easing and passing gas, then somebody else would be watching. And sometimes when the sewage tanks got full and the upper tankers delayed to flush the toilet, then because there weren't doors on them to lock them, people continued to ease themselves all over the floor. And so all those toilets turned nastier, and they stank and also full of worms. And so we, the kids, placed empty milk cans from the dumpster on the feces before we eased ourselves and also some used newspapers and used cement papers to wipe themselves because I didn't see toilet paper with my own eyes until 1980 when my husband and I had a trip to Daphne, Alabama, here in States. Because toilets papers were like a treasure and imported from Britain, only the rich could afford it. And one terrible thing was some of us kids, who had no access to newspaper or cement papers, did without thinking twice was that whenever we used those toilets, we were about to step outside without panties halfway down and then to the sharp edge walls of the toilet facing outside, we bunt, and then we wipe ourselves on that sharp edges. And though we saw dried feces that was never cleaned, we continued doing that and not thinking that we might be infected with some diseases. And also at school in the bush, where we eased ourselves too, after we were done, we just picked up any used paper for wiping. And when I think about now, I knew that we were all under God's mercy, else I wouldn't be alive.

And so, Kai, my stepgrandma, told me to sell each evening till late night in her kiosk after water fetching, and she gave me a coin, which afforded food just to survive on, and she told me to leave sales money in a small drawer inside the kiosk each time I was about to sleep. And so in the middle of the night, Koshi sneaked out from the room where both she and her grandma sleep, and she unlocked the kiosk with a key, and then she opened the drawer where I put money out from things I sold. And she took some out of it, and then she returned to the room, and she spent the money at school. And so each time I accounted for my sales, the rest of the items left in the store didn't march. And Grandma Kai didn't believe me that I had nothing to do with those missing money, and then filthy insults followed every day. And she abused me verbally in that big family house every day, which really hurts if being accused with something you didn't do, especially being disgraced in public, and so I cried myself out every day. And as a child, I asked myself, "Why didn't Mom take me along like my sister?" I didn't have enough for dinner to eat, and I was afraid to complain too because to her, I was the thief, and she didn't stop me from selling or to collect even to money from me after sales since she sleeps early with her granddaughter Kiosk at same room, but my place was to sleep among the voodoos. And my point is that when I talked about being verbally abused by Grandma Kai or the Ga people, in general, especially the elderly women, is it's the filthy insults that I wouldn't like to write in my story and not even compared to some of African Americans terms over here like, I respectfully say, "Eat my ass," "Fuck you," "Motherfucker," "You stink," and much more. And she yelled my name in anger tones, and that really hurt because I did nothing wrong, and by nature, I am humble and respectful, and I didn't deserve such treatment. And to honest with you, those people born and some raised in Ga-Mashie, Chorkor, Labadi, Teshie, Nugua, Tema, and all those Ga coastal areas knew what I am talking about. And so I was totally rejected in the house, and even the kids over there were warned to stop playing with me because I was not a good example to them, and so my only place of comfort was school. And so I was excited about being around my classmates, but I was sad about returning home. And so I slept in a room with the voodoos, not because I wanted to, but it was where I was offered to sleep. And so, at first, it seemed scary to me because though I was born and raised around them, I haven't been sleeping with a bunch of them like that before. And so I had a sleepless night for days, and I got worried why I was the only child sleeping with them. But after I thought about it that, from my own experiences, all voodoo worshippers have the same things in common when it comes to pouring libations. And that is the way they addressed God, lifted his name on high, and he always came first, and their drinks pointed up there before Mother Earth and their voodoos. And so, for that reason, I asked myself, if so, then why didn't I talk to that Most High God instead for protections? And so then, instantly, I started talking to God by lifting my face toward the ceiling, and I imagined him right by my side and taking good care of me. And so, I started talking to God. I imagined someone by my side to protect me in all ways and help me to have some sleep. And since that night, I wasn't afraid of them anymore, and I slept well till someone knocked on the door because it was daybreak. I continued to talk to God like he was my invisible friend. Because I hadn't been to church before, so I didn't know how to close my eyes and pray, than to talk to him like the fetish priests talks to their voodoos. And I am so obsessed with God that whenever I was alone or I step outside, I talk to God like he walks beside me, and so it's part of me since I accepted God as my

Lord and my savior Jesus Christ at the age of eight until sixty-three years now. I still talked to him with the same feelings when I was at home or outside, and he listened to me.

And it came to a point that my sandals got ruined. Because I didn't have any spare one, so I walked barefooted to school in such hot conditions or if I was sent outside or it comes to chores. It was another toughest situations for me. But because I was encouraged by mom way back that I will succeed in the future someday, so I tried to endure any terrible things that were done to me. We had a new teacher who introduced Wednesday for one-hour worship, and we even had Ga Bibles in our cupboards because the British introduced Christianity to schools, and we had period for that, but pagan teachers didn't care about teaching. And so, that lady Christian teacher taught us how to read and also how to give offerings to God in order to bless us, and she even taught us a song I never forgot, which was, "Hear the pennies falling. Listen how they fall. Everyone for Jesus. He will have them all dropping! Hear the pennies fall everyone for Jesus. He will have them all!" And as a nine-year-old child, something inside told me to save the little pennies every Wednesday for Jesus the Son of the living God, and I should rather continue to beg for food instead because his name has been mentioned each time before their voodoos; that makes him more powerful.

And so I fell in love with the God, and I listened and learned how to read the Ga Bible to know more of his words, and I gave offerings willingly, expecting to be blessed. I saw ninety-nine percent of kids walked out of worship class with excuses to use the bathroom, and some even didn't show up till it was over because almost every home at Labadi had voodoos from the entrance to the compound and especially their rooms and all covered with blood and even at each junction or in the middle of some streets.

And so few months passed by, and I still hadn't heard from Mom, Dad, and Adzoa. I really missed them, and I wondered why they dumped me in a place like a lion's den and if they had totally forgotten about me. And so I felt rejected, and I asked God multiple times if I was born to suffer. And since he didn't answer me, I stopped asking, but that hurt so much, and I cried myself out, especially on bedtime in the midst of those voodoos. And so it was just me and my friend, God, I chose instead of those voodoos, and I asked him to keep on protecting me, to give me the strength to keep on surviving because I didn't have any nutritious food, and God amazingly turned those small carbohydrates I ate, without any protein, to energize me and kept me stronger and beautiful. And I never recorded having any symptoms in my body aside from emotional pains. And at school, in history lessons, I learned that the Gas immigrate from Israel, and after the tough war for years, they finally won over their enemies and settled in Accra. And some of them started fishing right away since it's a coastal town, and some of them also started farming, and they were all pagans who carried their voodoos alongside with them. And so after they have more than enough to eat and then they decided to celebrate and to shame hunger because after they settled, there was starvation, and people died out of that. And so they called that festival "Homowo," which means "to tease hunger" And Labadi festival is in the month of August, and a month before, there is a banned in drumming, music, and hand clapping and so we kids became sad to those periods because of "ampe" and hide-and-seek games.

And so thankfully, they had massive harvests of corn, yams, millets, including veggies, and fresh fruits. And the fishermen also had more than enough fish like herrings, salmons, octopus, snappers, etc. I mean, some canoes began to sink because of more than enough fish, and so they called for help to unload some into other canoes to the shore. And so, they had a set day in August, and kpekple was prepared, which is the main tradition food for the occasion, and after its been prepared, all chiefs and fetish priests representing every neighborhood had people follow them around to sprinkle kpekple on their voodoos and at junctions, even at cemetery, and libations are also poured after each sprinkle as thanksgiving to God and Mother Earth and much more to their voodoos and to their ancestors as well.

You know, I describe the meaning of Homowo also as "hunger has been defeated," and we always rejoice over our enemies when we defeat them, and so that was exactly what our ancestors did, and the traditions continues every year so that there shouldn't be a room for hunger anymore. You know, my Grandma, who was my dad's mom at Labadi told me some sad story when I was eleven years old that during those periods of hunger, some parents had absolutely nothing at all to feed their kids, and as they kept on crying, the only thing they did to calm them down was for them to step out and play with other kids, and they packed stones in big cooking pots and filled them with water halfway on firepots with lots of firewood, and then they lit them up.

And so whenever the stones on the cooking pots boiled for a while and then their kids would come around and complain to their parents that they were hungry, they would ask them that "Can't you see that food is boiling? And so just go ahead and play, and soon, food will be ready to be served, so just relax, okay?" And then they returned to play with the neighbors' kids, and because they knew that food was still on the fire, boiling, and so surprisingly, they didn't feel sad or any weakness for days. And until hunters among them luckily hunted animals like deers, monkeys, grass cutters, rats, rabbits, and buffalos, then they shared with neighbors in order to get something to eat and kept on surviving.

You know, I turned up to be a good cook because I liked food, and so I was around any food preparations and paid good attention when it comes to food preparations since I was a child. Kpekple meals were prepared with food ingredients like corn kernels, smoked herrings, and snapper fish, etc., and both palm oil and palm nut, hot pepper, okra, tomatoes, onions, etc. And so, in the kpekple preparations, measured amounts of corn kernels are soaked for two days and then sent to the mill for grinding, and then it's mixed with a small amount of water to make the dough hard and let it settle till the next day for the preparation because it should not be too fermented, or else it won't taste good.

And so kpekple, as part of the Homowo festivities, preparation has special pots with tiny round holes underneath, and it is placed on top of the cooking pots, already filled with water halfway on the firepots. And that special pot is sealed with corn dough attached to the cooking pots in order for the vapor to go through the top pot. And then a small of local sponge made out a particular tree was placed underneath the potholes to prevent the shred corn dough, which was poured inside from going straight into the cooking pot filled with water, boiling. And then it was covered with a small white cloth and with a lid too for about thirty minutes. By then, it was cooked out of the vapors, and then it was poured in a large basin, and they continued with the same procedure until they were done with the first part. And then it was pounded in a mortar and pestle with a measured amount of palm oil added to it until it was well mixed up, and thereafter, it was separated in powder form with a locally made sieve, and a good amount was dished in another large basin. The rest was dished in big plates.

And so, the second part is to be pounded in a mortar with a pestle after a measured amount of palm oil is poured into it, and when all is mixed together and separated from each other in powdered form them is sieved again with a local sieve to get rid of stubborn ones which is stick to each other. Trust me when I tell you kpekple preparation is a tough job.

And preparation of palm nut soup also is not easy because the palm nut also had to boil on the fire for thirty to forty minutes before it had to be pounded in a mortar and pestle for a while to soften and to have the palm kernels separated after mixing with water and then sieving into a cooking pot. And then smoked fish of choice is added into it, along with salt, tomatoes, pepper and onions, and a small amount of salted fish, and it is left on the fire to boil for thirty to forty-five minutes to cook. And then a good amount is placed in a big basin and mixed with some amount of palm nut soup and fish before a volunteer carries it and walks side by side with the fetish priests, and their duties are to fetch and sprinkle some also on bare grounds.

Thereafter, when kpekple sprinklings are over, the real parties begin in homes with families and drinks (all sorts alcohol and sodas), and then kpekple with palm nut soup is served as dinner, along with yams, fufu with light tomatoes and pepper soup, with fish of choice in it. And so, in a couple of days before the festival, some Gas all over the world and around Ghana come over. And as the celebrations continue to the next day, they change clothes continuously—about two to three times daily—to show everyone how hardworking they are and to throw parties too.

And so, the inheritance of Labadi also get themselves and their kids also well prepared with nice clothes and outfits in their own ways to prove to the travelers also that they are not sitting and doing nothing because you know how some people gossip. And so Grandma Kai l was living with bought nice different materials and had it sewn to Koshi with fancy jewelries and slippers to wear during the day Homowo festival. And then the rest of the kids in the house also had all they needed for the festival, and I was the only one left out with nothing but my old dresses. And so I was emotional about those situations because I was just being used like a slave who wasn't even appreciated. And I overheard how those happy kids talked about things bought for them for the occasion, and that made me so sad, and I cried myself out many times on my way to school or out to fetch water, and I started asking my best friend, God, some questions why Mom decided to leave me with this wicked, total stranger called my family, who insulted me like she was chewing a gum, and she treated me like trash? And they ate and lived comfortably at Elmina without thinking about me? But God said nothing back to me, and it's not fair asking a friend questions, and then he refused to answer back, and that made me cry even more.

And sometimes, I thought that my mom didn't like me, and that was why she dumped me there, and so I talks to God at bedtime, lying on a mat on the floor around the voodoos in that room to help me also dress well in new clothes to witness the occasion, though I had no idea where it was going to come from, which was a night before, and then I slept without noticing it. I was so emotional when all kids and grown-ups were all dressed up at afternoon, and I was even teased by them till I was left alone at home to continue with chores.

But the supreme God proved himself that he hasn't forgotten about me at all, though all hope was gone, and I was crying like someone just died, and then a woman walked in and asked me, "Are you Atswei?" And I said yes. Then she said she knew that because of my description, but she was a friend of mom, and she gave her things I would be interested in for the festival on her way down for Homowo Festival. And so Mom's friends brought a big scarf tied with things, which was an old-fashioned way of wrapping a parcel or gifts for someone. And so when she sat down and she untied the scarf, then I was like, "Wow! This is unbelievable!" because what I saw that belonged to me was breathtaking to wear to the festival. And those were multicolored wrapped cloth and a matching blouse and two different styles of dresses sewn with different beautiful materials and then three different sets of jewelries made out of pure gold, alongside with two different kinds of slippers. In fact, I was covered with goose bumps all over my body because though I was expecting a miracle from God, but not something awesome like that. And also, I was his only follower in the neighborhood, and I had no idea of his capabilities, so I was shocked, and I had tears of joy. And then Mom's friend helped me to dress up quickly, and I chose to wear one of those dresses. I never forget the designs in it because it was so magical to me. And so that particular dress was color blue with white designs of waving hands and hearts in it. And so I said thank you to her before she left, and that was the last time I ever saw her, and Mom didn't tell me anything about her since. And my feelings are unimaginable but maybe like Cinderella. Though I didn't get a chance to see myself in a mirror, I looked like her through my imagination. And also, that miracle confirmed that my teacher Dora said about God that he is alive, and he heard us unlike those graven images that fooled us.

And so I rushed to the roadside, where the festival was going on, with lots of well-dressed people and also some dressed in matching clothes and singing traditional songs and dancing and drumming at the same time in groups, and each group sang its own songs.

And so another funny part of the Homowo festival that I don't like is called, "Shakamo," which means "hugging," and that is done traditionally from generations, and if you don't feel comfortable with that, then you better stay in your room because even when you are in a compound house, anyone can just walk in and hugged you. And so according to the Lakpaa Wulomo, who is like the supreme fetish priest of Labadi, which is now shortened, "La," he explained that "Shakamo is not is like committing a sin, but it's like you haven't seen a friend or family member for a whole year until the Homowo festival, so you hug each other to show some love and unity." And so, from 6:00 a.m. to 6:00 p.m. on that day, you have the right to hug anyone you set eyes on anywhere in Labadi—on the streets, sidewalk, restaurant and bars. You can hug him or her according to the tradition with permission and walk away with big smiles. And I was even told by Grandpa that in the early '60s, President Kwame Nkrumah and his wife Fathia were hugged one time at the Homowo festival by ordinary people and smiled at them, and the bodyguards did nothing because they knew the tradition.

You know, I don't like that part much because some people would take advantage of the occasion, and so they would drink, and they would hug you so tight for seconds and would never want to let you go, and so I hid myself behind the crowd and watched everything that was going on and took notes in my mind.

And so "ooooh goodness," both Grandma Kai and Koshi looked at me with shock and evil eyes. When I returned home later with my transformation, instead of Kai smiling at me and asked my amicably where I got those beautiful outfits from, she rather asked my in an angry tone. And so I told her those were gifts from Mom, delivered by her friend from Elmina. And so I went to the room and showed her the rest of the things, and then in a frown face, she asked if I told her about what was going on with me before she like. And I her, I said nothing to the woman, and then since that day, she hated me more. And so at the least chance she got me, and then those filthy insults continued. And also, because Koshi had me to be blamed for stealing from her own Grandma, so she continuously steals at the least chance she gets. And aside those mistreatments, I still looked beautiful than Koshi, and I think that also hurt Kai. And so my life became more miserable there because those little pennies she gave me for food was also decreased, and so I went to bed still hungry, and I felt sometimes like a total orphan without any relatives, and it didn't even occur to me once to visit my grandma and grandpa, who lived just a mile away, to let him know what was going on because he recommended his sister as a good person and would take good care of me.

And aside from insults I had from that wicked Kai, she also told me to feed myself with stolen money I kept on stealing, and that made me cry myself out every day with lots of questions I still had no clue to that and worse of all was that no one in that house ever fed me with reason I had no idea maybe, she warned them or they also believed all those lies.

Mom told me not to take something which wasn't mine because it's stealing. And also at school, we were taught that God said we shouldn't steal. And so as a good listener. And since then, I repeatedly asked God to feed me through my schoolmates because of the saying, "When both fronts are back doors and closed their windows opens," and truthfully, they felt sorry for me. They cheered me up, and they shared food with me to keep on surviving. So for those reasons, it made me fall in love with God more, and he turned out to be my protector, provider, a good listener, and much more, he gave me peace and calmness whenever I felt so overwhelmed. And so this emotional pains got me I couldn't focus in class anymore, but that didn't stop me from being at school. And so it's amazing how I was protected in that house full of mosquitoes, and I had no bumps out of mosquitoes bites, and some of the kids heard hookworm diseases, but I wasn't affected. And because I feared for my life as results of bad things that Kai was doing to me, I started asking God to bring Mom over and to take me with her though I continued doing my best with house chores, and I also took her instructions. And so one day, Kai was aggressive with me like a lioness concerning the same stealing issues because though she hadn't been to school before, she took notes of all the groceries she placed in her little kiosk, so she would notice when something was missing, and I couldn't provide her money for it. And so that day, I just came back from school, so as those filthy insults went on, I couldn't take it anymore, and out of stress and frustrations for. And so, in fact, I was shocked, and out of frustration, for the first time, I yelled back at her with all the strength inside me, which came out with tears, and I told her that I wasn't like her granddaughter Koshi, who was the real thief.

Then aside from the insults, she rained on me for being a bad girl, and she dragged me on the rocky ground and pulled me to the bedroom full of voodoos and different African wooden masks covered with blood hanging on the walls. And then she said to me,

"Atswei, you see all these masks. They are all part of tigalic voo-doos—very powerful and dangerous. And so if you lie to them, you will die instantly. So if you are really sure that you aren't the thief all the while, then swear to them now."

And so, I said, "I, Atswei, if I'm responsible for all these missing money, then kill me instantly!"

And so, with all aggression, I repeated the same words after her and crying out loud as well. And then my worst nightmare just started after I swore to the voodoos and I was still alive, and she pulled her underwear she wore from in between her legs, which is called *bue*, old-fashioned panties for women and children. Those days in Africa and currently some elderly women still wear them. And also, according to some traditions of Ghana, elderly corpses in funeral homes are not dressed yet without "bue," as its called in Ga language, before burial. It's of red material with white designs and cut in all sizes, according to all ages. As far as I could remember, in my village, I had beads around my waist with this tiny piece of material wrapped from front of my vagina through my legs to the waist beads on my back, and so surprisingly, Grandma Kai pulled out her three-foot-long "bue" from her private part, and she repeatedly hit my face with it mercilessly, followed with filthy insults to me and Mom too. And so I sat on the floor and crying myself out loud, and nobody came to my rescue, and she furiously told that I was disrespectful to her voodoos, and I challenged them because of that. And sadly, nobody came around to help me no matter how loud I cried.

Actually, I wished I was dead already, and I became so weak, and I ran out of breath, and I couldn't shout anymore, and I was still sit-ting on the floor, in sitting postion with my back leaned towards the wall, and I hugged myself and trears naturally flowing on my cheeks. She left me when she got tired and walked away because she also ran out of breath because of all she did to me as an elderly woman. That moment, my thought was that all those voodoos should take my life, though I was innocent, but I wanted to stop suffering on earth.

In fact, it was okay for me to swear to those voodoos to proof my innocence, but it wasn't okay for me to be hitting with that "bue" because they stink, and also, those days, women used them as pads, but the bad thing about that is they washed them whenever they bathed and dried them and changed into another one because throwing them out would be waste of money they couldn't afford. And so I stopped wearing "bue" when I was ten years old until I turned fourteen, and I had my first monthly cycle, and then Mom gave me about four pieces half yards of her old clothes to use as pads because that was what everyone used at Ada Foah in the early seventies. And she also gave me Pine-Sol disinfectant to rinse after I washed it and dried and changed another one. I folded it nicely and kept it month after month when needed. And so, it is forbidden for someone to be beaten with that local underwear, and so I sat at same spot for hours, and then I heard my mom's voice calling my name, and at first I thought that maybe I was imagining things, but as the voice came closer, I saw her for real, and in fact I felt like I was dreaming because it was too soon for her to find out what just happened to me, and so she grabbed me from the floor and held me like a baby in her arms and took me outside.

Mom was so emotional, and she also regrets entrusting me with the heartless Kai, and we both cried because of the awful situations she saw me in. And she got hurt for me being called a thief because she knew I wasn't, but what freaked her out more was my face being hit repeatedly with her "bue" and wished that Kai was right there for her to also pull out her "bue" to hit her too and know how it felt. And thereafter, Mom came out of the room. Those women gave Mom excuses for not rescuing me from her because she was hard to deal with, and unfortunately, people in the family house were all women with kids, and they slept overnights in their husband's houses.

And she also told them about the bad dreams she had about me, and she thought something was wrong with me, and so she put her busy schedule aside and came over, and honestly, she did the right thing by coming. And what even surprised me most was that it seemed like Kai and her daughter and granddaughter had disappeared from the house because Mom waited for hours, and none of them showed up, and so she asked me to ready my stuff for us to leave because it was getting late, and we might miss the last bus to Edina, which was the original name of Elmina before the Portuguese arrived to take charge. All the pure gold jewelries were stolen from my things, but Mom asked me not to worry, but my life matters, and so it seemed like she, her daughter, and granddaughter had disappeared for good by means of witchcraft—as if they knew what was waiting for them.

And so we took one of Toyota's big buses, and we waited for a while until it was full before the driver moved because it was one of the rules since it would be a waste of gas if it was half full. And so in the middle of the night, we were still on the road to Elmina, and on the journey, passengers dropped off and in at each stop by the roadside of the surrounding villages, so some people also sold foodstuffs like sugar bread, kenkey with fried fish, octopus, oranges, bananas, and water sold in plastic buckets with lids on and same cups that were used in fetching water from the buckets that were used for drinking by the passengers. And that was unhealthy, but we had no choice than to buy and drink since we were thirsty. And so Mom bought bread and octopus, and we shared with lively conversations with much joy inside me. And I was thankful to God for saving me after the long-suffering, and both of us kept our belief a secret since she didn't discuss anything concerning voodoos.

And so we finally arrived at dawn because of the rough road and the few stops we made. And so we walked about half a mile from the station to the castle, and after Mom prepared Milo tea with milk and sugar alongside with bread and blue band margarine spread on it to eat and gain energy, she made me sleep by my sister Adzoa's side on a mat on the floor, and she said she was going to work. And I was so glad seeing Adzoa, my little uncle Odoi, and small auntie Ofliboyo too, and they were also super happy to see me.

The Elmina Castle is a big township, and it is about three stories, and it had basements and sub-basement, and it had steps all over and is fenced with thick walls, and it has a couple of main gates. The top floor had many rooms turned to offices, and part of the second floor and many small rooms were given to new police recruits with tiny wooden beds with mattress and blankets on each, about four in a room.

And in the third story was a spacious place without roof and reserved for entertainments like concerts, acting, and jokes, which were well-rehearsed and played by some the police as their professions in the service. And so, sometimes, they were invited to play on occasions, and they charged them, and also, they played right in the castle, and outsiders were invited by posting some posters, and they paid and given tickets before they entered the gate to entertain themselves. And my favorite part was acting because of how the men dressed as women, and they acted funny, and they played women roles well because I never saw a single policewoman in the sixties. And so I found that exciting interesting because I enjoy laughing at them. And as for Dad's driving was of the same profession. He drove some prisoners to court in the town in a police Jeep, and they also made some arrest, but he just sat in the Jeep for others to do the job.

And one more heartless thing Dad didn't do at Elmina Castle was that each morning, outside the main gate of the Castle, all prisoners in the dungeons were put in chains like they did to the slaves during slavery, and they lined them up, and some were weaker and tiny because they were not fed well. And then their names were called in a record book, and they responded, "Yes, sir," until they finished calling them. And then next terrible thing was that the inspector in charge of the prisoners ordered all police officers around to slap each of them as much as he wanted, and so those officers did what they were told with smiled faces, except my dad who refused to do so, and nothing was done to him, but his friends called him a coward. And his reasons were that they did nothing wrong to deserve those punishments since most of them were caught as smugglers who bought clothes and drinks from Togo, and some also were arrested with crimes like stealing goats, pigs, or foodstuffs from someone's farm, and he or she was paying to the society. And so I witnessed that scene once, and I felt sad and emotional because if Africans were treated so horribly and shipped and treated like sorts of wild animals, why do we have to do similar things to ourselves?

And so one Saturday afternoon, I decided to explore the Castle on my own. I saw something horrible in the basements and the subbasements, called the dungeons, and that was carved rocks turned to small rooms turned to cells with no beds, lights, or toilets inside them. And they drilled holes on the walls and put in thicker chains like four and five feet tall, and some also lower parts all over the walls, and those cells had iron gates with iron locks, and prisoners were chained up with both hands up on the walls, and their legs were also chained against the walls. And so they couldn't sit down but just standing up and crying. And also, there was the smaller passage called "gate of no return" because slaves passed through the passage straight to the ships. And the worse part of it was seawater passed through that narrow passage and filled all the cells, so they were standing in chains and also halfway drowned with the sea cold water, and that gave some them pneumonia and fever aside from hunger and thirst, and most of them died just like that. And so as a curious ten-year-old child, after watching those dungeons, which most of them were empty and some were occupied by native prisoners, it made my heart jumped, and I was emotional, and my memory took me way back to history lessons we had in school at Labadi about the "slave trade," and we read in books too, and it made me so sad and scared of where I was, all by myself, and then I quickly squeezed myself, and I stepped out through that narrow passage outside, and I walked on the slippery rocks of the beach next to the passage filled with sea waves, then I ran faster back home. And those moments I imagined how our ancestors suffered in those dungeons in their own country, which was just the beginning before they were shipped horribly to overseas to face realities of their lives. And so I didn't get the nerves to visit there again, and maybe God sent me over to see things for myself and to write about it now. And so I kept it a secret, which haunted me for a long time.

And my family and I lived in of the medium size wooden single rooms built in the ground floor in the castle, and it was shared to the police officers and their families. And there were other wooden rooms a few yards away built for army officers, who come around for a while in some special trainings and without families, and so the cooks among them cooked delicious meals for them from break-fast and dinner, and they had their own silver containers for food and cups and water bottles. And so, after they were all served with lunch or dinner, we kids would rush to collect some leftovers with our own bowls to eat, or else it would be thrown out in the sea anyway, and my favorite food was peanut butter soup cooked with meat and boiled yams.

We had public toilets and bathrooms for men and women; those toilets had latrine pans under each hole and were carried early morning to dump in the sea and cleaned with short bloom before they were returned so they don't stink, like those at Labadi. But everyone was exposed to each other in terms of showering and bowel movements. The small compound kitchen also had two police wives in it, so they stored food, cooking pots, plates, glasses, etc. in it, but they cooked outside the kitchen on coal pots because the space was too small.

Mom had about forty recruits she fed more than the rest of police wives because she really cooked good, and they were being paid each month in cash by the paymaster of the recruits out of their monthly allowances. And so those days, police officers were paid in an interesting and funny way, unlike nowadays, through the bank. And so the thing is that at the end of each month, they formed long lines, and including the recruits, standing at ease positions, and they were paid in cash in sealed envelopes with their names written on it on a big table in front of them yards away. And so their paymaster stood near the table, and he called names, and when someone hears his name, then he marched forward to salute him, and after he collected his envelope, then he saluted him again before he marched back to his post. And so after everyone collected his pay before he shouts, "Dismiss!" and then they all responded, "Yes, sir," and then they leave with smiling faces. And so since I amused myself with that, I didn't miss it.

And so though Mom was illiterate, God blessed her with wisdom, and that is common sense, and so she had a weekly menu in her mind. And so each day, she prepared them with different breakfasts like fermented corn porridge, watery cooked rice, alongside butter spread bread with sugar and milk. And the porridge or the watery boiled rice were all dished in medium-sized metal-designed bowls covered with lids and placed in silver trays alongside with sugar cubes and a small amount of milk all in separate little cups because some of them didn't like too much sugar or milk, and the bread was also placed in a small plate. She made sure everything tasted good and looked nice and decent like well-educated women born and raised overseas. And so because all those took much time, she woke us up as early as 4:00 a.m. to help her prepare the breakfast, and then we carried them one after another with care to the rooms of the recruiters, and then we placed them on top of their small drawers. Thereafter, we bathed, dressed up in haste, and we had breakfast, and Mom gave us pockets money to buy food during break time in school. And then we set off to school, which was a mile away, and I was in class 2 with Adzoa, and because Elmina people speak Fante language, the teachers thought us in Fante. We read books in the same language, except in English lessons before they switched to English, and we read books in English. And so it was different for me to understand at first, but because I am a fast learner, so I eventually learned Fanti language like the Ewe language. And so we attended the same school with Odoi, but he was ahead of us in school, and though he was the only boy among us, he was more serviceable to Mom, and he didn't complain about anything.

After school, on our way home, we passed through a building built on top of the mountain by the Portuguese as their living place before they built the Castle, which was about half a mile away. And inside that mansion was an architecture of the complete Castle on a table, and it looked great and a surprise to me because it was my first time seeing something like that, and someone was there to walked us through the building, and he told us the history too. And in their living rooms had some portraits of those who lived in with their family and old-fashioned couches, rugs, library, and in their bedroom too, they had beautiful iron beds with mattresses, dressers, drawers, and they left some of their clothes in the closets. And outside the mansion was an old-fashioned telescope they used to spy the Castle because of where the mansion is located, and there also had old-fashioned machine guns all fully loaded, in case of an attack, they could defend themselves.

During evenings too, we helped Mom in the preparations for dinners like banku and konkonte. And because konkonte preparation is difficult if it is prepared in large quantities, so after it becomes thicker in the big aluminum pot on the firepots, Mom continuously stirred in with a strong thick wooden ladle. And then we helped her to pound them in portions in mortar and pestle to make it softer and smooth like fufu. And then she dished them all in those recruits' medium-sized plates, but when it comes to banku preparation, she was able to handle it until well-cooked, soft, and smooth in the big aluminum pot, and then she rolled them in medium sizes like balls, and she dished it in their plates. And then those foods were served alongside soups like okra, palm nut, and peanut butter deliciously, cooked with either fresh or dried fish, and she dished it in those medium-sized bowls and covered them with lids. And so we placed them in trays and carefully carried them to distribute to the recruits. Mom faced some challenges with some police wives because she was a good cook, and they were jealous of her because of that. And since she served the recruiter with nice metal bowls and well-designed plates instead of plastic ones, they started stealing them, and so she had all marked with paints to catch those thieves.

And one more thing about the Castle beach is that there were lots of crabs moving around, and they returned to the sea waves. And because Mom and some of the officers' wives liked craps, they trapped them in medium-sized barrels. And so they dig deep holes in the beachside, and then they placed the barrels inside, and then they put fresh-pounded palm nuts around the surface of the barrel, so the good smell drew them closer to the barrels to eat, and they all fell in the barrel. And so early mornings, those barrels were full of live crabs. And so Mom raised them in pots, and she didn't cook without adding some in the soups alongside fish, and that tasted so good.

In fact, life at Elmina was breathtaking to me, though it involved hard work because Mom was a workaholic, and so she was trying all ways and means to become rich. And so there is a huge rock in dividing the Castle border of the sea in order for fishermen not to fish there. And Mom stepped out from the Castle to the other side of the beach to buy fresh small fish from the fishermen, and she returned back to the Castle beachside and spread them on the sand to dry. And so on Elmina market days, she sent those dried fish to the market and exchanged all food items like corn kernels, both fresh and dried cassava, yams, tomatoes, hot peppers, palm nut, fresh peanuts okras, onions, and many, and she saved enough money because of that. And so we were in school one day, and two health providers came to give us shots against measles, tuberculosis, and hooked cough on the left shoulders on with old-fashioned metal instruments like a gun. And so they placed it on each side of our left shoulders, and then they shoot the medicine into our hands with little sound. And then we were told not to put anything there, but it will heal on its own. And so a few days later, everyone's shoulder was completely healed with no more pains except me who had a swollen shoulder. And that really hurts. And then, here we go again, instead of Mom to send me to the clinic right in the Castle, her kitchen mate told her to put liquids that come out from a part of some firewood when it is in flames, and the liquid is thick like honey to rub on the swollen part. And so she listened and applied for a while before finally I was healed. And to date, my big scar reminds me of what happened since 1966, and also, whenever I am about to have a shot in the hospitals or clinics, health providers asked me what happened, and I continued telling the same story over and over again. Just like the three different scars I have still at the left parts of my abdomen, which reminds me of my Guinea-worm disease, which nearly destroyed all my intestines and sent me to an early grave, though I don't feel comfortable talking about it but I have no choice because it will be so rude on my part to tell someone that I don't want to talk about it.

You know Elmina, which was at central region of Ghana, also has a festival called Bakatue which is quite different celebrate from Ga Homowo Festivals their celebration is on Tuesdays in July each year, and they chose that day because fishermen in Ghana never fish on Tuesdays in honor of the sea god. And a few weeks to the festival, Mom bought material color white with red rose designs inside, and we were measured by the seamstress, and she sewed us a nice short dress to look like twins. And so that Tuesday in July 1966, Mom dressed up in her beautiful, expensive clothes that were a lace blouse with long sleeves, and she wrapped from her waist part with about three-yard cloths, and she wore makeup and her gold jewelries and her slippers and a purse.

And Adzoa and I wore our matched dresses, gold jewelries, and slippers. And then Dad also wore his matched top shirt with long sleeves, tight long pant, a hat on, and sandals, and then Odoi too was in his black-and-white design shirt with his pant and shoes. And so I was so excited when I saw myself in those beautiful new outfits just like my family. And so we all walked together and stepped outside the Castle to the town at the festival grounds, and we weren't the only people that were well-dressed, but because it was a great festival and many travelers were there to watch, everyone else dressed in their best clothes like the Homowo festival. And so the paramount chief and his subchiefs from the surrounding town and villages were also well-dressed in their Ashanti kente cloths and the local "oheneba" sandals, and they decorated it with gold jewelries. And some were carried on palanquins, and some of their elders also carried their stools that they would be sitting on the festival ground. And among them were fetish priests too, and so just like kpekple is sprinkled at Ga Homowo festival, rather, they sprinkled cooked Ghana mashed yams mixed with palm oil alongside boiled, peeled eggs around to their voodoos and ancestors and especially the River Brenya.

And after that, they poured libations with schnapps drinks and asking their voodoos for protections and peace among them. And some of them were playing traditional drums and musics, but the most exciting part to me was those grown-up women who were dressed in Ashanti cloths half naked without blouses, but they covered from their breast part with two yards of cloths, and they wrapped from their waist down with another two yards, and they were wearing gold jewelries. And then they sat in one big canoe on the River Brenya, and they paddled around with singing and smiling faces. And so before we returned home, we went to the photo studio, and we took a group family picture, and Mom took one on her own, though Mom had different kinds of pictures with some of her golden jewelries, they got lost after her death as I moved around from family to family house with her big basket, which was the only thing I kept my belongings inside. And so those pictures were the only ones I have on my walls right now that reminds me of my childhood when I was ten years old and of Mom and my little uncle Odoi.

And a little after the festival, we sadly moved out from Elmina because Dad was transferred to Abosseyokai at Accra in a small township in just one-story building as a police barracks in the sixties with about ten police officers. Their wives and kids lived in medium-sized single rooms. And that was an uncomfortable place to stay with only two flushing toilets, separated from two bathrooms, and especially in morning hours, we formed a line to ease ourselves and bathed to go to work or school. And the barracks had no real kitchens to cook, but in the small compound was a shade roofed with aluminum sheets, and the floor was cemented, and it was divided into parts with wooden boards, and so two officers' wives shared the same kitchen. And because space wasn't enough for two people, all their cooking pots and food were in big wooden cardboards provided by themselves, and they cooked in the compound close to their kitchens like Elmina. And I was told by Dad that house wasn't actually built for police officers to live, but it was rented. And because of the inconvenience, Mom being a smart woman as usual. She called Dad, Adzoa, and me at 4:00 a.m. We had bowel movements and bathed before they all got out up from bed, but during evening times, it wasn't everyone that wanted to bath, and they also didn't arrive home at the same time, so there weren't rushing.

And so a few days later, Adzoa, who was the lucky one, never suffered like I do. She was enrolled about couple of blocks away in a public school building, well-built with cement blocks, roofed with slate sheets, and they had a big space and clean classrooms with big widows, cardboards, and toilets separated from the bathrooms and a big space compound. And for some reasons, I was enrolled way far, a couple of miles away at Kaneshie number "two" primary school, and to be honest with you, those rooms shouldn't be space for humans or animals because those small spaces, called classes, were built with real thick aluminum sheets from the rooftops to bottoms, and they were shaped like cages for birds. And they had smaller thick glass widows, and because Ghana being a tropical and so hot country, then you can imagine the situations of students in those classes. And when we sat in those classes, then we started sweating, and I felt like we were grilled in an oven. And the teachers even couldn't stand the heat, so they would, most times, absent themselves to be at school for days, and they got away from it, and they received their pay all right. And even if they arrived in classes, they didn't take their time to teach us to understand more, and as soon as they set classes to work, they stepped out for a while. Before they returned to mark the exercises, as a result of the heat, we had rashes all over our body, and that itches. And one more thing was that there were few schools around us, and those were well-built with cement blocks, and they had the same facilities like Adzoa's school, and we all wore the same uniforms like us, but the badges on the chests parts of their our uniforms differentiate us.

So those lucky ones in better classes made jokes of us that we study in "doves cages," and so all those tough situations really depressed me, and I asked myself several times, "Why do I have to continuously have bad luck, suffer, even being with my own family?" And so I couldn't focus in the class, and because that, I had zero out of ten in all classworks. Our teacher was also being so mean to me, so she drew a big circle with ugly ears, nose, and mouth with a red pen in my exercise books at end of each lesson, and then she showed them to my classmates. And then they laughed at us, the students of that school, and they made jokes about us. And so all those bullying made me so inferior and would have dropped out of school if I had a friend who willingly wanted to drop out because both of us could pretend like we were going to school and all dressed up in uniforms, but rather, we would be roaming around, and then after school hours, we returned home.

And so weeks after we arrived at Abosseyokai, Mom, known as a workaholic, found a place at Odorkor at Akukophoto Poultry Farm, which wasn't far from Kaneshie Market. And in that farm life, frozen chickens were sold, including chicks, eggs in there too, and so customers from surrounding towns came over with their trucks to buy in large quantities for sales. And so she started her chop bar business under a medium-sized shade roofed with palm beaches, and she had few benches and matched tables for the customer to eat on them. And so she had one young woman who helped her, and she paid her at the end of the day, and she so had her daily menu with soups she prepared each day, and those were palm nut, peanut butter, and tomatoes soup, known as "light soup."

And she prepared those soups with few whole frozen chickens she bought the first thing as soon as she arrives on the farm, and then she defrosted and cut them into medium sizes. And since Odorkor was a developing town in the sixties, there weren't passenger trucks to the farm, and so Mom and the helpmate joined the workers in their truck at Accra Liberation Circle for a free ride every day with all her food ingredients packed in a big basin. And because Odorkor inhabitants are mainly Ashantes and Fantes, Mom prepares fufu every day but different soups because it is their favorite food like Ga's favorite food, which is kenkey and fried fish with hot peppers grind with a little bit of onions, salt, and tomatoes to make it spicier. And so each morning after she placed the frozen chickens in water to defrost, they peeled the cassavas and plantains and cut them into medium sizes, and they rinsed them in water, and they placed them in a big aluminum pot, which was half filled with water on the set firepot full of dried firewoods, and covered with a lid to cook until it becomes soft. And then they focused on the defrosted chickens, and those too were cut into medium sizes and then washed and also placed in another big aluminum pot and seasoned well with salt, onions, and basil and placed on another aluminum pot that was on top of the firepot to boil. And so, they would start pounding the fufu as soon as the cassava and plantains were cooked so they didn't get cold because if that happened, it made it difficult to pound, and Mom took breaks to add the rest of the ingredients in the soup. And within six days in a week, she prepared three different soups, which were light tomato soup or either peanut or palm nut soup, which her customers liked.

And so because she was a great cook, workers at farms and in the surrounding areas also bought from her, especially customers who came around to buy stuff, and she also, being so kind, sold on credit basis to workers who ran out of money, and she got paid at the end of the month. And on Saturdays, we followed her to the farms, and while in there, Mom let her help mate relax a bit, and she pushed me so hard as an eleven-year-old to work and to pound fufu for a while, and she refused to let me rest even if I told her that I was tired, and all I heard her say repeatedly to me that she was training my heart, which I found so hard to believe. And rather I felt like I was being punished instead because why not my sister too, who was nine years old? And I completely lost my appetite before eating. And, yes, I did get jealous of my sister Adzoa sometimes because of all these.

She also bought chicken feeds in sacks and eggs for sale as an additional source of income, and she was successful and the only provider for the family and didn't care about Dad's little monthly salary. And she also furnished our room with bed, Vono mattress, radio, DVDs, TV, etc. She also bought a carpet for the floor, and we kids still slept on a mat because that single room was too little for an extra bed. We gladly stopped watching TV from neighbors through their windows.

2
CHAPTER

And so when it came to house chores, I cooked, and Mom gave me orders. I cleaned the dishes, the kitchen, and I pounded fufu with the mortar and pestle, and Mom directed it to the middle position with her fingers because one thing about fufu pounding was to focus in the center of the mortar, else, at least a mistake was that someone's fingers would cut off as soon as the pestle landed on it. And so I continued to pound as she sometimes sprinkled a small amount of water on it until it turned smooth and soft. She portioned the fufu and then dished in plates. And so all Adzoa did was to play with her friends after she finished with her home. In my case, Mom really taught me the hard way as a child, which also hurts me emotionally because I didn't understand her that—she had two girls who were just two years apart, and rather, I have to do everything like a young adult. In fact, pounding is one of the hardest ways for cooking using your whole body, especially your heart, which beats so fast, as if you are working out on an treadmill for hours, and that made me wonder more what Mom meant by she was training my heart.

But in those days, we were not supposed to ask certain questions or to talk back, especially when you have a tough mother like Mom, though she shared some of her past with me when she was little (like my age) and was sweet, caring, and patient with me but not if it comes to house chores. And as an eleven-year-old, I thought I deserve a little break from those chores to do my homework and play like Adzoa does, but Sundays rather were my busiest day of all. Mom woke me up early morning, and she already had all the laundry clothes piled up for me to send them outside in the compound near the tap water to wash and dry everything before the other officers' wives woke up. And one more thing also with Mom was that she was like "the early bird who gets the worms." And because it was hand-washed, I lined up two big sizes of basins, halfway filled with water, and then water in a big bucket and another empty bucket. So I poured some amount of Omo or Surf detergent soap we used for white clothes in those days in the second basin of water. And then I started to rinse the white clothes in the first basin of water, and then I squeezed them into the soapy water, and then I began to wash the armpits parts and the shirt collars before I continue washing every part of the clothes, and then I rinsed them in the bucket filled with water. And finally, I squeezed them into the empty bucket for Mom to check if they were well-washed before I dried them on the drying lines, and then I hold them with pecks to prevent them from falling on the ground.

And so after I finished with the white clothes and then I threw those water away, I then filled those basins and buckets with fresh water, and I started washing the colored clothes with Sunlight sold soap in order for them not to fade. And so I used the same procedure to wash them until Mom said it was okay to dry before I dried them, but as for Mom's clothes, she liked them stiff and well-ironed, so she bought raw cassava starch from the market. So I precooked it like porridge, and so after I washed her clothes, I then poured the starch in another basin, and I added a little bit of water and stirred with my hands to make it smoother before I placed the clothes inside, and I continuously flipped those cloths until they were soaked with starch before I hanged them the dried line.

After I am done with washing, and I had my lunch with just a little break, then I had to help Mom in the kitchen around 2:00 p.m. to cook dinner. And because we didn't have a real dining table and chairs, Adzoa and I sat on the carpet floor, and we ate together, and Mom and Dad too sat on the old-fashioned couch with a medium-sized table in front. They ate as a routine. And so during evening time, my worse nightmare was ironing clothes with charcoal box iron, which had a small space for charcoal fire. And so I started with Mom's clothes, and I sprinkled a little water on them, and I folded them to turn a little softer before I started to iron them, and after I was done, I folded them nicely, and they turned stiff again like she wanted. But it wasn't an easy task at all because I took more breaks than I should since when I ironed a few of clothes then the fire die, the iron turned cold instead of turning hot. And so I had to set fire on the charcoal pot over and over again, and it took me a while because I completely finished ironing including Dad's, Adzoa's school uniforms, and mine came last. And then before my sleep time too, I had to polish Dad's police boots and his silver bottoms on his uniforms with a special chemical to make it shine. And by the time I finished my chores, my family was already snoring, and that made me felt sad and unwanted. Because it hurts a lot when I stayed with Grandma Kai with some of the situations, I supposed be doing house chores by myself, and Koshi, her granddaughter, did nothing to help me. And I told myself many times that "If only I were to be with Mom, I wouldn't have been doing all that by myself but Adzoa would help me."

On Mondays early morning, I felt so tired I was reluctant to get up from bed to bath and ready for school, and so after Mom called me a couple of times, then she sprinkled cool water on me before I got so stressed about it too. And something else was that we didn't have a refrigerator, so we boiled leftover soups late evenings on fire coal pot for about twenty minutes, and then the next day mornings too, we did the same thing before leaving home to keep it fresh for dinner, served with either fufu, banku, or konkonte around 4:00 p.m. And also, when we opened a can of evaporated milk for breakfast, we placed the leftovers in the containers in a small bowl with little water to keep it fresh and also to avoid ants from getting inside, and we used it the next morning for breakfast. And so for safety sake, since we didn't have a real kitchen, we kept our soups and provisions in the room. And so we also bought ice outside across the street in a kiosk, and Mom put it in a flash, and she added water to it whenever we were thirsty, and we bought ice cream and cake, a little bit of pineapple, sugarcanes as desserts from the same kiosk after dinner, and Mom called that "sweet after meals."

And because Mom was gifted with wisdom, we always had healthy breakfasts like either Milo, Horlicks malt, and oatmeal with sugar and milk inside, along with fried or boiled eggs in the buttered bread. That nutritious food kept us all day long, so when I had some snacks at school, I didn't feel hungry until dinner was served. And so because Mom pushed me too hard than she should, I turned out to be a great cook, neat and clean person, well-civilized more than Adzoa, and at first, I wondered how Mom, born and raised at a small village of Lolonya and hadn't been to school before, learned how to cook deliciously without a cookbook and with a weekly menu, and much more, she was so neat and clean, and she dressed well and smelled good with designer perfumes like someone who came from a civilized world? And now I know that it was a gift from the Almighty God regardless of whose parent womb she came out from.

One time, Mom decided we should make a trip to Lolonya to spend Christmas and New Year, and I was happy to go because it had been years since we left, and so we went for shopping at Accra Makola. She needed much money for different materials to sew dresses for us and slippers. She also bought herself new clothes to be sewn, slippers, jewelries, watches, purses, and she also shopped for things to her large family members. She also bought treats like different sorts of cookies, candies, sodas, and alcoholic drinks for her elderly men in the family. And so on December 23, she bought chickens from the farm, and she also bought ingredients for stew and rice on Christmas and New Year's Day, and we packed all our stuffs.

On the next day, Mom, Adzoa, and I left home in the afternoon to Accra Lorry Station without Dad because he refused to take a leave to be with us. So we waited in the truck for a while because the traders who came with the truck had to finish selling their smoked fish and also shopped before we left in the evening time. And since it was rough roads with potholes, the truck moved slowly, and also at each village junction, the truck had to stop for those trades to exit the truck, so we finally arrived at Lolonya late in the night. Mom wasn't happy because one of her chickens was stolen by a trader who claimed ownership of it on the way, and though the driver told Mom he would ask all the traders, it wasn't returned to us. So she let it go, and we had a warm welcome the next day by family members, and also, traditionally, we went from home to home to greet almost every in the village before we returned home, and then they also came one after another and welcomed us for returning home. Though those traditions seemed very tiring, it was interesting because of how happy they were seeing us and sincerely complimenting us about how fully grown we were, how beautiful we looked, also, we looked like we came from abroad, and much more. It made me so excited.

And then on Christmas Day, I helped Mom to prepare stew with half of those few live chickens we brought with us, and it was served with boiled rice. Our family members and some other families came to join us in the house, and we all sat on benches with short medium-sized tables in the compound, and we ate with lovely conversations only without any music because there wasn't electricity. But it was fun to see my childhood friends, asking me many things about Accra, which, unfortunately, they haven't been there before. And after we finished eating, Mom opened bottles of chilled sodas like Fanta, Coca-Cola, and Sprites for everyone, except the old folks who preferred alcoholic drinks. And they made funny jokes about drinking sodas, which has a lot of sugar and will produce more worms in their belly. And those drinks were chilled because, during the Harmattan season in Ghana, the weather becomes cold, especially December and January. And then later, she gave them their gifts. They liked that more than the food because one more thing is, when someone visits villages, especially Accra in those days, they expect gifts, just like someone from the United States or Europe to the third-world countries. And because the villagers drank from well or pond water unless it was rainy seasons before they had rainwater, Mom bought rainwater preserved tanks and for sales, and that wasn't safe because it still contained tiny worms moving in the water. And we sieve it before we drank and bathed in order for us to be safe somehow from illnesses and diseases.

On New Year's Day, Mom prepared soup with the rest of the chickens, and it was served with fufu, and we also had cookies and candies. And then in the early evening, we went to their mini-market, where they played cultural musics and drumming called kpacha.

Mom was a group leader in singing and dancing when she was a teenager until she got married and left Lolonyah. She joined them, and she sang beautifully, and she danced like the rest of them, and the crowd clapped for her. And that day was the first time I saw Mom sang and danced, and they all composed kpacha song to honor her with her name inside as a beautiful Lolonyah Maseki. One more thing, Mom's hand, at the right side, had a tattoo of her name Maseki of Lolonyah as her identification, and not her alone but to almost everyone in Adamgbe District and those of Volta Regions. And Mom told me that they had those tattoos because they traveled a lot, and they never knew what might happen to them, and so with that identity, they would be easily noticed. So I saw those local tattoo artists walked from house to house and worked on people with combined needles, and they put some black powder on the writings, and they charged a small amount of money when I was fourteen years old and staying with Mom at Ada Foah. And so the next day after New Year's Day at Lolonyah, we returned to Abosseyokai, and that was our last trip with Mom and returned to her normal business.

And so I missed my village because I was a normal child who played games just like my age group, but then, my tough chores started again. And one time, after long day chores, Mom asked me to pound fufu. I couldn't focus to place the pestle in the center of the mortar, so I pounded her hand unintentionally, and I injured her thumb, and the fufu was mixed with blood. I saw Mom carried her hand and crying for the first time, and I felt so sorry for her, and I was emotional too. Dad was at home because it was Sunday, so he placed her hand in salt water to stop the bleeding, and the blood stopped. Thank God, it wasn't a deep cut, so she refused to go to the hospital. And Dad treated the wound by applying penicillin ointment, and he badged it with a pain pill to stop her pain. A few days later, she went home to work.

Mom turned so rich, and she kept her money at home under the mattress, and she could have bought a double-story building way bigger than the police barracks or bought a bigger land and build a home and then a chop bar in her own alongside like a restaurant just like few people did those days with musics too. And this could have happened if only she had a loving, caring, and selfless man by her side; rather, Dad convinced her to buy a car for taxis instead to bring her more income and not knowing he has selfish motives for that. And so Mom thought that was a good idea, so she told him to go check for a good car and let her know because she trusted him completely. And days later, Mom gave Dad exactly the amount he told her of the car without second thoughts, and she didn't even demand a receipt. And thereafter, when Mom asked him to find a driver to drive the car as a taxi and to account for it at the end of the day, then "here we go again," Dad lied to Mom that he shouldn't trust any taxi driver because he might end up with excuses in order to avoid the money he supposed to bring. And so for that reason, he will rather work with the car during nighttimes, and then he would be back home to sleep a little bit before he returned to work as a police officer during morning hours, and that was the only way she could make more money and save her car as well. And so Mom agreed, and he started working as a taxi driver at night, and so instead of Dad bringing money home like he said, he started demanding more money from Mom with excuses that he had problems with the car that needed to be fixed.

And so since love believed in all things, she continuously gave Dad money he wants and not knowing that he started cheating on Mom with other women and teenagers. If he moved the car from the house, and he worked a little bit, and he added what he collected also from Mom, he took his lovers to restaurants to eat, drink, and dance, alongside live band musics and sometimes to the cinema too to watch movies. And they ended up in motels, and this was something he never did with Mom who didn't ask him money for anything in the house, and rather, she provided for everything without complaining. And so Mom knew something was wrong because of his behaviors of demanding constantly and not bringing money home and also how he dressed in clean clothes and he wore designer perfumes. A fight broke between them, and he refused to give Mom her car keys when she asked him to, and he kept on denying that he was cheating on Mom until one day, a girl in her late teens, called Ayorkor, went to the family house at Labadi by herself and announced her pregnancy to the family, which was never done, because if you get pregnant, first thing was to tell your parents, and they would send delegates to the man's family house to announce her pregnancy.

As gossip easily spread out, a family of Dad came to tell me about it, and Mom was so brokenhearted, and after she fought Dad, she then hired a van and packed all her stuff, and she stripped the room naked with everything she bought, and she and Adzoa left, except me, again, to stay in Logos Town, now called Accra New Town. And so she rented a one-bedroom, aluminum sheets building in a large compound house with separate latrine toilet and bathroom. And so though Mom continued to work in the farms, people also discovered that eggs and chickens feed business, so she lost her costumers and sold them. Because she needed distractions at home, she brought his nephew Korletey from Lolonyah, and she put him in an apprenticeship to learn fitter. And so she brought Odoi, who passed in West Africa Common Entrance Exams in class 6, to continue his secondary education in Lagos Town and his other brother, who was born before Odoi called Fulani, and she enrolled him in teacher's training college at Kokomlemle next town to Lagos Town. And so Fulani was young, handsome, light skin, and about four feet few inches tall with Afro hair, and he liked it more than anything, so he kept a comb in his pocket always, and he combed it continuously, and he didn't care about where he was. He was also kind of a private person, who barely talks, but he was a nice person, and so he rented a very small room across the street out of his teaching allowance, and he was also still supported by Mom with other needs till he completed in three years' time, and he taught as a trained teacher at a nearby school.

Mom's nephew Korletey also saved his allowance because Mom fed him and supported him financially, and so he rented a single room in that same house, and then he invited his wife and a son from the village to live with him, and Mom still supported them.

My favorite uncle, Francis Odoi Dzeagu, was tall, unlike Mom and Fulani, he was about six feet tall, and he had brown skin and a round face; he was handsome, funny, and a respectable guy. Though Mom provided him with everything, he still sold handkerchiefs and brown paper bags at Aflawu Lorry station on weekends and on vacations too, and he also helped Mom out with every needs. He opened my eyes for the first time about coming to America at the age of twelve. It was Odoi who showed me where American was located in the earth global map of the world, and he also showed me the Statue of Liberty in his book. And then he promised to send me to the United States to live with him and his white wife as soon as he completed his college degree. And so instantly, I totally believed in him with great joy and hope that I will become an American citizen someday and to grow old and be buried, so in my reincarnation, I will rather be a white person because of all the bad things I was going through as a black since I thought that only blacks are born to suffer and also from my perspective of the slavery. And so because of that promise, on weekends and vacations, I spent at Lagos Town. Whenever Odoi ordered me to buy him something from outside, I ran instead of walking, and I almost ran out of breath. And I didn't haste to wash his handkerchiefs or socks, but he washed his own clothes because he said that I washed with energy, and his clothes were so delicate.

Because Mom's nephew Korletey was illiterate and he anxiously wanted to learn the English language and to read and write, he bought a slate and chalks, and I started teaching him the alphabet. He was so patient and humble to me, so he learned fast, and then he also bought kindergarten reading books, and I thought him little by little, and he picked up very fast, and he tipped me for that. Months later, he started speaking broken English, and he signed his signature, and then after he completed the fitting, he rented a space close to the house, and he fixed Toyota and Nissan trucks there, and he gave his costumers receipts after they paid him.

In fact, after Mom left Dad, I wasn't okay at first for the fact that she took Adzoa with her again, but after a while, I got used to it. I had a break from those tough chores I used to do, and also because Dad wasn't abusive at all. He was like one of those dads who spoiled kids and didn't yell at them when they do something wrong but talked with patience. And my reason was that Mom left us enough provisions in the particular drawer made with glass as a showcase those days in the living rooms, and I had breakfast every day as usual since Mom left, except Dad. When the provisions got finished, instead of me throwing those cans of Milo, Horlicks, and dozens of milk away, I rather packed them nicely the way they were. And I couldn't tell Dad about that until one morning, he was about to have breakfast before living for work, and then he realized that they were all empty cans. So he started laughing and asked me that there were more than enough cans of milk, which shouldn't be finished, and what happened. And then I told him that I drank one can also each night before going to bed because of my belly pains. And then instead of him being mad at me, he couldn't help himself laughing. And he was like, "Wow, you, Atswei, and your craftiness." I also laughed and laughed, and he said, "Why didn't throw those cans out? You just wanted to trick me."

He also allowed me on weekends and vacations to be with Mom at Lagos Town, and I think that gave him a chance to spend time with his lovers. And one more thing was that I barely cooked, and rather, we buy food from the roadside like kenkey, banku, and fried fish with hot peppers. Dad did something unusual after Mom left us. Once a week, he brought chicken home, and he gave me money to buy ingredients at Kaneshie Market on my way back home from school. And so I prepared soup with that, and I pounded fufu for the two of us. During dinnertime, when I dished my soup and I was about to eat, he told me not to break the bones and suck the marrow like we normally do, but I should add it to his bones. And when I asked him why, he then said that he was seeing a Muslim Malam, and she told him to bring that for rituals in to get protections and promotion in the police service. And so I pitied him that day for being so naive and still believe those things rather than believing in God, but I couldn't tell him that.

I tricked Dad, and I went to the cinema with him and her girlfriend without knowing until we arrived at the cinema car parking lot because he left me by myself at night to sleep until he arrived in the middle of the night. And it wasn't because he was driving the taxi since it was out of order and he couldn't fix it, so he brought the police jeep after work from Cantonment Police Headquarters. After duties, he used it as his private jeep, so he told me about a new

Ghanaian funny movie in the sixties titled *I Told You So*, and it was acted in one of the Ghanaian languages. That night, I asked him if he could take me to watch the movie, and he said, "Nope!" I dressed up and got in the back seat of the jeep, and I lay down on the seat. He wasn't aware of that, and he drove away and picked his girlfriend to the cinema parking lot, and then I came out of the car like a ghost. Dad was shocked, and he laughed at me, and we all formed a line until we had our tickets, and we went inside to watch the movie.

He dropped off that woman, and he didn't introduce me to her. We returned home late at night, and he didn't complain about that, and it was my last time to watch a movie with him. And so, for some reason, Dad was transferred to Cantonment Police Station in part of Accra, close to a town called Osu. And so there are several one-story buildings purposely built for police officers and their families, and each building had about ten single medium-sized rooms and separate few latrine toilets and bathrooms. And they also had smaller kitchens for each officer's wife, and so for confusion safe, the buildings are boldly marked with alphabet letters from block A and on and on. We lived in block E on the second floor of a single room. So I cooked, cleaned dishes, and washed clothes just for me and Dad. And since Mom left, he didn't stop begging her to come back, but Mom was hurting badly for what he did. And thankfully, she and Adzoa returned to stay with us at Cantonment Police Station, and she still maintained her chop bar business as her only source of income, and she provided for us and my uncle Fulani and Odoi at Lagos Town too. And so though there are schools at Osu, where the officers' kids attended, Mom said since my previous Africa Unity Primary School at La Abormli was a mile away from us, Dad should enroll us in the school. And also because I was familiar with it, we started going to school where I already had friends. And also, walking long distances were part of me, so I was happy about that, but Adzoa complained about the distance and how awful those school structures were.

And though I was glad Mom came back to live with us and I started eating well, my only concern was the tough chores started all over again, and that also depressed me more than I had Mom who loved me, but I couldn't express my feelings for her to understand me when I said I was tired of doing something and I needed help. And I also thought she wasn't treating me fairly because she supposed to share chores, but she listened to Adzoa's complain, and so because she said the school distance was too far for her, Mom talked to one of Dad's stepbrothers in their family house at La Abormli, not far from our school. Adzoa and I went to live with that woman, called Odoley, and Mom provided us with provisions, and she gave her enough money to care for us just for us to be able to go to school. Odoley didn't feed us well, and she loaded us with chores to do, and she yelled and abused us verbally at the least chance she had, which I was used to, but Adzoa cried like a toddler each time, and I had to comfort her.

Instead of preparing us at least fermented corn porridge and sugar for breakfast, she rather prepared flour porridge with sugar for us, which we never had or saw someone had that before, and it tasted nasty, so we couldn't eat it, and she forced us to take it before leaving for school. A week later, Mom came to visit us. She brought food items, and she also brought a big baby doll, and she gave it to Adzoa. She told her that it was hers, but she should share it with me. And so that gave me more reasons to think that Mom didn't love me because she could afford two dolls, but I let it go, and Adzoa shared her doll with me once in a while. And so because of Odoley's bad behaviors toward us, we weren't able to tell Mom because when she came to visit, she pretended to be nice to us, and she accompanied us to see Mom off until Mom's third visit, and luckily, she wasn't at home, so her neighbors told her everything she did to us.

And so Mom got angry, and we packed all our stuff and then left back to Cantonment during her absence. Since then, Adzoa stopped complaining about the distance, and we focused on walking a mile away to school. They still ran shifts, but I stopped begging for food because we had a good breakfast during morning shifts, and Mom gave us money to buy food during break periods. Since then, I started buying real food, and my favorite was konkonte with peanut butter soup prepared with fish, meat, and crabs by an Ada woman. And one amazing thing happened to me after I returned to my old school when I took God seriously again. I listened to my teacher on Wednesdays at religious education, and I even borrowed a Bible to take it at home, and I started reading and prayed. And then, suddenly, I started focusing in class, so I gained good grades in all subjects like a blind person is seeing things miraculously.

And Adzoa's, who rather had good grades all along and my parents surprised her with gifts, grades started dropping down. And though I wasn't surprised by any gifts, I was so grateful for that. Aside from Mom's chop bar business, she decided to prepare kenkey and fried fish with hot peppers for block-to-block sales on Sundays, where she was supposed to rest because she didn't go to work. She talked to someone who wanted to help with her with preparing and also to carry it in a basin from door-to-door sales at the police blocks. And so Mom bought a big sack of corn kernels, and she soaked portion of it in water for three days, and then she removed the corn from the water and rinsed it with fresh water, and then she poured some in a medium-sized bucket and the rest in a big basin. I carried the one in the bucket, and her helper carried that one in the basin. And because there wasn't cornmill at Cantonment, we walked a mile away to Osu Market to grind it. Mom's helper mixed the corn with a measured amount of water, and she made it thick before we carried it again back home, and that made it a little heavier than it should. That was so heavy load for me, and I couldn't even turn my neck because it hurts. Mom rubbed it with pain relief ointment for a while, and she gave me a pain relief pill. Days later, the pain went away. And because it happens every week, sometimes I wondered why she didn't give us taxi fare since she knew how far the mill was. But I couldn't ask her personally, and neither her helper. She got paid at the end of each time she worked for her. After the dough fermented on the third day, Mom then started to mix a certain amount of dough with measured water in an aluminum pot, and she added salt, and then she placed it on firepot filled with firewood and in flames.

And so after she stirred with a thick long wooden ladle until it cooked like banku, the second part was that she dished it in a big basin, and she added shred corn dough to it, and she mixed it together with the ladle, and she allowed it to sit until it cools enough for her to mix with her right hand in portions. And then she started to roll them in smaller balls, and then her helper and I helped by wrapping those balls with corn husks in such a stylish way to protect the dough from messing up in the boiling water until they are cooked, and then the husk is peeled off when it's ready to be served. And so after we finished with the wrapping, which wasn't an easy task on Saturdays evenings, before Mom and her helper fried fish enough to sell the kenkey and thereafter, Mom placed a small amount of corn husk underneath in another big aluminum pot that was on top of the firepot but not set yet, and then she packed all the wrapped uncooked kenkey inside that aluminum pot before going to bed.

And so early Sunday morning, she got up, and then she poured more water on the kenkey, covered them with empty corn kernels sack, and covered the aluminum pot with a lid too. Then she filled the firepot with firewoods, poured some kerosene on it, and she lit the matches, and then it burst into flames. And then she called me to clean the kitchen and the compound, and then I had to grind the hot peppers, a small amount of onion, tomatoes, and a little salt on a grinding stone, and then I dished it in a bowl. Then I had to shower and get myself ready. After a long while and the kenkey turned soft, Mom then covered the base of the basin with a thick large white plastic bag, and then she packed all the kenkey inside, and so she counted at the same time until the basin was full. And then she wrapped the plastic bag well in order for the kenkey to keep warm. She then packed the fried fish inside the tray, and she knew how much that cost, and then she placed the bowl in peppers near the fried fish in the tray. And so her helper carried the basin with the kenkey, and I carried the fried fish with hot peppers in the tray. And so she gave us kenkey and fried fish to eat when we felt hungry as breakfast. And so Mom's helper and I stepped out for hawking on all the blocks from door to door to sell, and when there was still leftover kenkey, we continued to go to the police inspectors bungalows to sell, and we sometimes went to the police headquarters, which wasn't too far, until everything was sold before we returned home and so very tired. And so she paid her helper, and she left for home. And I felt so exhausted, and I wished I could take a nap before anything else, but after I finished my lunch, I had to help Mom with dinner.

Sometimes I found it difficult to do my homework, and I ended up doing it in class before my teacher showed up, but as for Adzoa, she did not help; rather, she played with her friends.

Aside from all sorts of work Mom did to earn more money, she also made a big shade, roofed with aluminum sheets, and covered partially with boards on the other side of the compound, and she raised chicks that turned out to be fat chickens, and she sold them in cheaper prices for the officers' wives to prepare dishes with them for the Christmas celebration with their families. And so, for months, things worked good between Mom and Dad till Mom found out that Dad had married Ayorkor, that teenager he impregnated, as his second wife without telling her, so she got so hurt because Dad complained when it comes to responsibilities, that his monthly pay wasn't enough and yet was able to perform traditional marriage. And much more, he lied to her that she had nothing to do with her, but he will take responsibility for the child.

Those reasons caused another fight to break between them. When Mom demanded her taxi to fix it, she did not know Dad sold the car without telling her about it. And so things really turned awkward between them, and Mom was so disappointed in Dad for blowing the second chance she gave him to make things right and also to be honest with her. And so Mom was depressed and overwhelmed with Dad's bad behaviors, so she moved back to Lagos Town to be with Odoi, Fulani, and Korletey and his family. And so Adzoa and I were sad about these whole situations because Dad couldn't provide us with good meals and other needs the way Mom did. But, on the other hand, I was relieved from those tough chores again for real. A few weeks later after Dad, Adzoa, and I went to visit Mom on weekends, Mom refused to return when Dad begged her.

Thereafter, Ayorkor, Dad's second wife, moved in with us with her one-year-old boy at Cantonment Police Station. And so from the look of things, Ayorkor had no manners, and she was disrespectful and rude to Dad, and she didn't care if we were around. And not only didn't she know how to cook, but she was so messy, lazy, and she didn't keep herself and her own child, called Adjei, clean. And so "here we go again," I resumed my tough chores again, and I cooked, cleaned, washed clothes, and worse part of it was, I washed Adjei's washable diapers and the feces inside. And I cried myself out mostly because I was just twelve years old and too young to be washing those diapers full of feces a few times every day, and some of her panties with menstrual cycle blood inside, and I had to wash them too. And one more thing about me is how Mom raised me the hard way and not to complain about anything, so I learned how to endure pains no matter what. And so though we visited Mom, I didn't tell her much about that woman and how she treated me because I knew she would freak out, and she would beat Ayorkor mercilessly and hurt her she might end in jail. And so Ayorkor argued with Dad always about spending money for cooking, which wasn't enough. She didn't believe Dad whenever he told her he wasn't earning enough money monthly, and she refused to work to help provide for the family. And so we didn't have nutritious food like when Mom lived with us. And now I could see some sadness and regrets on Dad's face each time, and he lost his sense of humor, and I think he realized that "the devil you already know is better than the angel you never knew." And also, you don't know what you have till you lose it." But it was too late for him now.

One time, Mom came to Cantonment Police Station to collect the part payments of the car Dad sold, and he promised to pay something at the end of each month. To be honest, things really got ugly when Mom saw her rival Ayorkor. She aggressively was about to attack her, but Dad didn't allow her to fight Ayorkor. So Mom threw more pouches on Dad. He had more scratches on his face. The neighbors stepped in to stop Mom because Dad didn't lay a hand on her, but all he did was he tried to shield himself, and he repeatedly said, "Ouch! Christie, stop it!" And so Dad next-door neighbor reported what was going on the in-charge officer of the police station, and Mom and Dad were sermoned right away over there. And so the inspector in charge referred the case to the Cantonment Police Headquarters. It was settled, and Dad was told to pay the installment, and Mom was also asked not to come over and attack anyone, but if Dad refuses to pay, she should directly report him at the police headquarter.

And so, one time, we went for a visit to Lagos Town, and Adzoa refused to return with me, but I came back to Cantonment Police Station to continue to face reality. And so because Ayorkor wasn't getting enough money from Dad, she turned out to be a prostitute, and then she used me as her accomplice. Out of her smartness, she started having affairs with prison officers just across the street from the police station at prison officers' barracks. But first, she started by leaving Adjei, her son, for me to watch over him and stepped out for hours, depending on what shifts I had to be at school. And then, later on, she decided to cook for those guys, and because she knew that Dad left home around 8:00 a.m. and he returned so late in the night or once in while he arrived at early nights, she figured everything out so she shouldn't be caught. When I returned from school, around 1:00 p.m., to the house, she already bought food ingredients from the mini-market at the police station, and then I helped her cook boiled rice and tomatoes stew with can fish, like sardines or tuna and boiled eggs, which is easy to cook. And thereafter, she dished the stew in a bowl with lid and rice a plate, covered the other plate, and then she placed the food in a nice basket, and she covered it with a beautiful embroidery material. And then she wore her best clothes, jewelries, slippers, and a purse, and she also wore makeup to cover her big bumps on her face to make her look a bit prettier because for real, she was about six feet, and she looked ugly.

And so when she was busy dressing up, she told me to be in my best clothes too, and then I wore slippers, and I dressed up Adjei. She made me carry him on my back with two-yard cloths, and then we set off to the prison barracks. She knocked on the door of the room where her lover was. A guy opened the door, and he invited us inside to his living room with a bedroom attached to it. Ayorkor took Adjei off my back, and she placed him on my lap after I sat on the couch, and the guy served me with Fanta and cookies on a smaller plate right away. He and Ayorkor went to the bedroom with alcoholic drinks, water, and the basket of the food, and they closed the door behind them. Though I didn't see anyone having sex before, we were taught at biology lessons, so I knew that they actually did have sex also in there.

After Adjei and I spent several hours in the living room, I felt irritated and waiting for us to get back home in order for me to complete my chores even though I liked the Fanta and cookies I had. When it comes to those snacks those days in most families like mine, it was served occasionally like Christmas and New Year's Day. We returned home at night, and Dad wasn't home yet, so after I had my dinner, I cleaned and finished my homework, and I went back to sleep on a mat on the floor as usual. As far as I can remember, I slept on mats on the floor until I was in my midtwenties. Ayorkor continued seeing other men at the prisons barracks and also some at one of the Osu hotels, and it surprised me how she handled her schedule well with her lovers since we didn't have a phone in the room and there weren't cell phones those days. That showed how smart she was because she knew I liked Fanta and cookies, so each time before she and her lover left the sight of Adjei and me, she made sure I was served with that. Though I knew what she was doing was wrong, I told myself that I wouldn't be like her. My mouth was zipped by nature, so I fulfilled my promise to her by not sharing her secrets to anyone. Dad knows nothing about that, but he was glad she wasn't demanding anymore, and they stopped arguing. Dad also told me that he was dating a flight attendant, and I kept his secrets too. Sometimes it was funny when I thought about how they were cheating on each other, and nobody was caught. One more thing about that, life without Mom wasn't easy for me at all because I wasn't given enough money like before to spend for school. My teacher sent me the nearest chop bar to buy her fufu and soup with goat meat inside each break time and, being so kind, gave little fufu leftovers and soup without meat for me to eat and clean her bowl and put back in the cardboard. I was thankful for that because it was better than nothing.

So one time, when I bought fufu, and I should have been served with the boneless part like she wanted, rather, I was given bones part with muscles attached to it and soup. I had no idea about that, so when she gave me the leftovers, I was surprised she couldn't chew her meat. I ate the fufu so fast and took a bite of the meat before I realized that, so I threw it out on the ground in the bush path, and I cleaned the bowl with soap and sponge I had in the cardboard, and

I rushed to the class because she was teaching English subject. But the interesting part was that I regret throwing the muscles part of the meat away because I couldn't remember the last time I had meat since Mom left us. Though she didn't often cook meat, she liked the fresh oxtail and cow tongue in preparing soup and fufu. I was badly craving for that, and I couldn't focus on the lessons, so I asked permission to pee, then I went straight to pick it up from where I threw that contaminated meat in the dirty ground in between the bush where we pee and we ease ourselves. I washed it with a cup of water I had purposely for that meat, and then I put it in the pocket of my PE, or physical education, shorts that I wore under the school uniform, and I calmly returned to the class. After school was over and I was on my way home, I pulled it out, and I used my strong teeth to bite the muscles little by little. I couldn't chew it, but I swallowed them, and though I was nearly choked with the last part, I was content that I didn't throw it out like I did for the first time at school.

And another thing I also survived on was collected leftovers from trash cans in newly built bungalows for whites, and since they knew of some kids' situations in Ghana, their leftovers were well wrapped in aluminum foil for safety before they dumped it in the trash cans. And so I tried to be the early bird to leave home on time before others to dig my hands inside trash cans one after another, and I found leftover food like grilled chicken, beef, pork, bread with butter spread and cheese, baked potatoes, boiled eggs, rice, etc., along with plastic forks and spoons, and I quickly sat myself down on the ground and dug my dirty hands inside food and enjoyed myself. And then I imagined myself in America, eating the same food. And out of that joy, nothing else mattered.

I had more than enough food on afternoon shifts than mornings because when school was over at twelve noon by the time I passed by the white neighborhood, all those trash cans were left with only trash and little leftovers that someone probably hasn't seen. But on afternoon shifts, I left home early before anyone else. One more sad and unbelievable thing about me was that though those days "oto"—which is prepared with Ghana cooked yam with slight salt and then mashed together with steamed palm oil with onions, and it's served with boiled peeled eggs, was for all kinds of traditional cel-ebrations, like birthdays, weddings anniversaries, and many more—unfortunately, neither Mom, Dad, Adzoa, and I haven't celebrated our birthdays before, so I didn't actually know my parents' birthdays, and they also only had guesses for when they were born. If it hadn't been for our education, I wouldn't have known my birthday, and also, I never saw balloons before but in reading books when I was in primary school. That was the reason why I picked a used condom with sperms inside in the trash can, and I thought it was a balloon filled with milk or something. I got so excited that day, and I emptied it, and then I blew air inside, and I tied the knot.

And so I held in my hands up and with big smiles on my face on my way to school until I entered the class and then Ms. Dora looked at me in a shocking face, and she was like, "Atswei Grace, why are you holding that thing in your hand?"

And then I smiled and said, "Balloon, madam."

Then she said, "This is a condom!"

And I was like, "Corn what? what is that?"

And then she said, "Men use it during sex to prevent pregnancy and diseases. And so where did you get that?"

And so I told her the truth, and the whole class started laughing and teasing me. I was ashamed and scared to death because HIV was a common disease I was aware of in those days, and it had no cure, and I turned from a happy kid to a sad kid with lots of negative thoughts. *What if that user had HIV or other infectious diseases? Which means that I'm already affected.* And so I was emotional and asked myself, "Why do bad things continue happening to me?"

And so I couldn't focus a little in class that afternoon, and I went home so sad and I kept quiet about it.

Ayorkor, my stepmom, eventually left us to her family house on the south side of Labadi because her few lovers' money wasn't enough for her since she wanted to live a luxurious life that she didn't want to work hard to get it. Dad also couldn't provide more than he gave her because she had her own room in her family house, so life as a prostitute was easier for her over there. Dad continued to see her with an excuse to visit his son and to give child support, and he had another son with her. Though her own sister continued to tell Dad about Ayorkor's affairs with other men, he kept on having sex sometimes with her until Ayorkor got pregnant again with someone else's child. Her own family put their feet down and told Dad point-blank that it was another man's child. Her baby girl and Dad had nothing in common like her second son. Those days, many Ghanaian young women returned from Abidjan in the city of Cote d'Ivoire richer as a result of prostitution. Ayorkor left for Abidjan for a couple of years, and she turned to international prostitution. Unfortunately, she was tested HIV positive, and she fell sick over there. So she returned home to Ghana for treatments, but she died a couple of years later. Dad also continued having an affair with other women, so he didn't spend time with me anymore like before. One time, I was so sick, but instead of him sending me to the police health center, he sent me to Mom's place. Mom took me to a private health center, and the doctor said I had severe malaria. He referred me to the Kolebu Hospital. After I was examined, the doctor gave Mom some prescriptions to get me medications from the pharmacy right there. He also recommended that I should be admitted for a few days because my temperature was so high, and I was shivering, and I couldn't eat, and most of all, I vomited what I ate. The doctor gave the prescriptions to get my medicines to the admission ward because that was how the system worked those days, and prescribed medications had to be by the patient's side in the small drawer in the hospital rooms, and then nurses gave patients what they needed.

But for some reason, I got scared to be in the hospital for days, and also, my instinct told me that I would die if I was left alone in the hospital without Mom, so I started crying out loud. I begged Mom not to leave me but to take me with her, or else, I would die before her next visit. Mom got emotional, and after she received the prescription drugs from the pharmacy, and she was supposed to take me to the admission ward where she was directed to, rather, she sent me to the roadside, and she picked a taxi back to Lagos Town. I was calmed, and I prayed to God to heal me. Mom continued giving me the medicines, and she encouraged me to eat. One thing she did to stop me when vomiting was she squeezed lemon juice in a cup, and she gave me a spoonful each time I felt nauseous from eating. That worked for me, and I spent about two weeks with Mom. Dad came to visit me a couple of times, and he tried to win Mom back, but he couldn't. Mom didn't trust him anymore, and she was so depressed as a result of after all she did for Dad, and he was unfaithful to her, and he behaved like someone fed with good meals, and yet he still went to the dumpster and picked leftovers from there.

I returned to Cantonment Police Station to be with Dad and continue my education. And so Dad thought I was a burden to him because the little money he made mostly went to other women spending, so he couldn't feed me well or spend time with me and to sleepover. So he lied to Mom and me that because of my school distance, I should rather be with her mother called, Atswei, and her nickname was Aaaaatswei at Labadi in the family house where Grandpa was. If you asked why she was also called Atswei, it is because it's the most common name in towns like Labadi and Teshie. And so Dad sent me over to his mother, Aaaaatswei, even though she lived in same family house at Dzrasee, which means "behind the market" because it is next after Labadi Market, and it has a nickname Abrewankorwe, which means "old folks refused to die" because it came to a point that, for some reasons, younger people died constantly and, rather, the old ones buried them. According to Grandpa, some of the members of the family became Christians, and as a result of that, they refused to contribute money to celebrate those voodoos in the house for years, and they got mad and started destroying the younger generations. And those voodoos I am talking about in the family house are placed in the center of half plot of land with rooms built and facing each other with just a narrow space, and that huge woman-shaped cement blocks voodoo with her big breast without her head, and she is carrying a medium-sized cement pot attached to her. She was halfway covered with a white cloth that looked dirty, and her breasts are showing on that center part. And another male-shaped medium-sized voodoo with a mouth, nose, and eyes. He was wearing a cement hat, and he was right in front of that female voodoo. They were fenced halfway with the same cement blocks walls with a couple of schnapps alcoholic drinks, and they had slate sheets roofed over them. Though they looked kind of scary, but not to me because I saw scary voodoos more than them.

Grandpa was in charge of them and also to the other ones he had in his room, and he poured libations often for them, and some family members from far and near, who had problems too, brought Grandpa money and schnapps alcoholic drinks to pour libations for them for things to work out for them. The female voodoo is called Ayorkoaye, and the history behind those voodoos is that they were bought by our ancestors at Big Ada, which is a small town but the downtown of the towns and villages of the Ga Adamgbe District. So before those voodoos, they dig a deep hole in the center of the compound, a lot of gold and cash was added and buried underground, then those statues were mounted on top because they believed that would make them richer through their businesses if they continued to perform yearly rituals for them like slaughtering of fat goats and preparing dishes and also inviting other fetish priests to celebrate them and to pour libations. Also, the female voodoo Ayorkoraye cloths, weren't changed with new cloths. And so shortly after I moved in there, I saw young people dying, and one more thing also was that whenever someone died in the family, and not necessarily because he or she lived in the house, the corpse would be laid in state in one of the single rooms that someone lives after the person moved out temporarily. And so after the corpse was buried and funeral rights were done, that person returned to live inside, and that happened those days in Ghana.

So according to Grandma Allah Tsuru, when the voodoos were consulted why the future generations of the family were dying one after another, they said because they weren't celebrated for years, and that was the reason they had tragic losses. And so the whole family members from Labadi and other towns and villages came over and donated money, and some farmers among them also brought fresh farm products like a sack of corn kernels, tomatoes, onions, hot peppers, and fruits—like watermelons, oranges, grapes, mangoes—cashews, and many more. And then some of the money was used to buy a fat cow instead of goats, and they bought different kinds of drinks, both foreign and local alcoholic, and they also prepared special local drinks made out of fermented corn called "asaana." And then they invited all fetish priests in Labadi and surrounding town and also from Big Ada and all family members over to celebrate them for seven days straight.

I took sick forms from school, and I faked malaria symptoms to the doctor, like dizziness, nausea, and I actually sat on the sun for a while before I get to his office so my body temperature was hot when he examined me. He gave me prescription drugs, and he wrote a week of rest for me at home, and then he signed the forms. And so I gladly returned it to my teacher, and I came back home to see everything for myself as a curious child. And because there wasn't enough space in the house, but it has about a plot of empty space right in front of the house, local canopies were mounted on the whole space. Many benches were hired and well-arranged under those canopies, so they started the celebration from Wednesday, and since they claimed that Ayorkoaye's favorite day, all the fetish's invited guests came with their few clothes and helpers. They poured libations as usual, and the cow was slaughtered in front of the voodoos. And some of the blood was poured in a calabash, and they sprinkled it all over the voodoos, and Ayorkoaye dirty clothes were changed to white new clothes, and then they prepared fetish's meal called "fotoli" with some of the meat, and it was simply prepared like soup. So when the meat turned tender, tomatoes, onions, hot peppers, palm oil, and a small amount of powder corn mixed with water were added to thicken it. And thereafter, it was dished in big basins and placed in front of the voodoos, and after they poured libations, one basin was for all kids around, and the other basin was for grown-ups.

And so we all dug our hands inside the "fotoli" without washing, and we ate to our satisfaction, and I was so smart to save some meat on my left hand, and I took my time later and chewed them. They also hired traditional cultural drummers like Obonu, Atopani, and fetish songs singing groups, and a couple of more. So they played and sang well, and some of the fetish priests claimed that they were in motions when they danced. That went on continuously for a week. Some people volunteered and prepared different dishes for the guests to eat, and because there wasn't any room for them, they slept on those benches under those canopies, and luckily for them, it didn't rain, and they used the same public toilets and bathrooms just across the street.

And so after the seventh day, all things came to an end, and they all returned to where they came from. And so to be honest with you, since then, those tragic deaths stopped in the family; rather, once in a while, an old folk die, and they never stopped celebrating the voodoos each, but the nickname of the house, Aberewankowe, still remained. And to those days of celebration was so exciting me, for witnessing something I never saw before, and also, I really enjoyed all meals prepared out of the cow meat even though I still believed in the Lord Jesus Christ as my Lord and Savior.

And so my grandpa Allah Tsuru didn't only have light skin, but he was over six tall, huge over three hundred pounds, handsome, kind, loving, caring, and so I describe him as a man with heart of gold. And because traditionally, in Ghana, a man has the right to marry as many wives as he can as far as he can provide for them, he married five wives with a lot of children. And though Grandpa and his siblings weren't able to go to school and they helped their parents the farms, he encouraged his children to go to school and get their degrees. And so he sponsored his first wife's two boys and a girl up to college, and they graduated from the University of Legon in Ghana because they went willingly. And because he was a spoiled dad, he never forced his children against their will, and so Dad's brother Largea and his other son he had with his other wife also went up to the secondary school, and they joined the Army. But the rest of the dropouts boys he thought them how to drive, and the girls became traders in small businesses with money he gave them. And so Grandpa's youngest wife came from Ada Goi, a village next to Lolonyah, and he married her when he used to drive fishmongers and their fish to the Makola Market to sell.

The most interesting thing I saw about Grandma was that at his age of seventy, he was still sexually active, and he got Auntie Dora, his wife, pregnant, and they had a child aside from the nine children she already had, and it turned to a funny gossip in the neighborhood that Auntie Dora refused to let the old man rest at night. Auntie

Dora was a great cook, and she was his only cook who prepared him with breakfast, lunch, and dinner around 4:00 p.m., and his favorite food, that was either goat meat or fish light soup with yam fufu. And so whenever I was around and had his dinner, he called me for leftovers because I was his favorite grandchild who was respectful, and I also reminded him of his mother. One time, I accompanied him, Auntie Dora, and a few of his young sons to his farms, which was miles away from home. And so before we left home, he bought enough kenkey and fried fish with hot peppers, and we had a couple of gallons of water in his truck. We went to his large plots of land on the farm to harvest mainly watermelons, dried corns, cassavas, plantains, tomatoes, hot peppers, and many more. And so I felt like burning in the afternoon on the extremely hot weather because it was my first to have been in such large farms and harvesting those large amounts of crops to that big truck. And the worse part was that he didn't have trees to sit down on the shade and rest, but Grandpa and his family were used to it, so they continued with the harvest inside many big baskets in the truck, and I also joined in somehow. And so after we ate the kenkey with the fried fish, we continued to drink water, and then we ran out of water, so they cut small sides of water watermelons, and then we dug our hands inside, and we ate them to quench our thirst. When the truck was full, Grandpa then drove us back home.

In fact, it was interesting and fun to me because there was much to eat, but it involved hard work on that hot weather. And no one took breaks till Grandpa sat to rest, though he didn't ask us not to, but seeing him so hardworking motivated us to work as well. And at the end of the day, we filled that big truck with watermelons and some cassava, plantains, etc., and we sat on top of those food items in the open-top truck, and only Grandpa and his wife and the little child had space in front.

As soon as we arrived, he already had customers waiting with locally made large wooden pushing carts, and they bought everything, except a few of them left to be eaten and for cooking. Grandpa had diabetes, and aside from medications he took and farmwork, like once in a week, he actually didn't exercise, and he sat at one place for hours from his room to sit in front of his room outside, or maybe he used the bathroom and then back to his room. And so in those days, the Gas called diabetes "sugar disease," so they didn't add sugar to breakfasts or eat anything sugary, but they ate a lot of carbohydrates without knowing that it turns to sugar. And so I heard that he wasn't feeling well for days in his room, and he wasn't sent to the hospital until he had hypoglycemic coma, and he died a few hours in the hospital.

I think in those days, even health providers had little knowledge of diabetes treatments. And so I wasn't the only one who is brokenhearted by Grandpa's death but the whole community because he was known as "Ataa Adjo," which means "Grandpa, it's okay" or "let go." He normally used those words whenever injustices were done to someone and that one refused to let it go and wanted to fight back until he gets the justice he deserves, and then he said, "Let go and let God justify," though he was a pagan. And so he also as chief linguistic, and he solved family disputes most times and relationships, and he did a great job with his wisdom.

You know, in my own experience when I was living there, one time, my friends and I were on our way from school in the afternoon, and then I found a ten-British-pound note on the floor. In those days, we still used British pound sterling, so I quickly picked it from the ground by the roadside. And I was so excited for having such a big note, so I was waving it like my handkerchief, and at the same time, I was yelling and telling my friends ahead of me that I had found ten pounds sterling note in my hand for the first time in my life. And so my friends stopped walking, and when I approached them, they didn't believe until they touched it and made sure that was ten pounds sterling for real, and I took it back from them, and I continued to wave it, and I promised to share it with them. And then out of the blue, the money was snatched from me by a middle-aged woman, and she claimed ownership, that she lost it from her handkerchief. But I said that I didn't believe her, and so she should return to me the money. But she insisted and didn't take no for an answer, though a few people around asked her to return the money to me, but she refused and went to the nearest house.

I went home, still in shock, and I was crying out loud because that woman took advantage of me, and then she stole the money from me. I went straight to Grandpa in his room, and I told him what happened. Right away, he let someone accompanied me to the woman's house, and she was sermoned to meet with him. And so on the set date, the woman came with a couple of people, and Grandpa also invited a few of his elders to settle the case. So after they listened to the woman and me, they concluded that the woman actually stole the money from me and it didn't belong to her, but she insisted because a ten-pound note was a good enough money. And so his elders tried to demand the money from her, but Grandpa said the same thing, "It's okay, Atswei. Let go and let God justify." In fact, I was so depressed and disappointed. As a result of that, I cried myself out for a long while because my Dad left me with nothing, and he told Grandma Aaatswei he would return at the end of the month, and that was it. And so out of that money, even if I shared it with my friends, I couldn't buy new school uniforms, shoes, and books. Grandpa had a great funeral, and he was placed in a custom-made truck-shaped coffin because he was a truck driver and a farmer. It was common in Ghana that most people were buried with custom-made shaped coffins according to their professions like if fish for fishermen or fishmongers, an airplane for pilots, gardening products for farmers and food sellers, etc. to show how wealthy they were because those coffins were expensive. And so he was carried by six strong men around the town before he was sent to the cemetery for burial. I still missed Grandpa and all his kindness toward me, but unfortunately, he was the only person I miss with good memories after living in Dzrasee Aberewankowe in my family house for about a year and a half.

Grandma Aaaaatswei, who was Grandpa's second wife, had her own medium-sized room in the family house next to Grandpa's, but she lived in with her elderly daughter called Adjeley, with her four kids, and also her last born daughter, called Adjokor, and her one-year-old son and all slept in same under the same roof. I also joined them, and so in total, we were nine people living in the same room. And so there were two twin beds facing each in the room, and Aaaatswei, Adjokor, and her son slept in the same bed, and they fit in because both of them were about four feet and a couple of inches tall and tiny. But Adjeley was about five feet, seven inches tall, and she weighed about 150 pounds, and she slept with his few months old boy, and she had a drawer with mirror on top and then also had a table behind the door, and they packed their wooden boxes with clothes and baskets and bags also with kids' clothes with my basket too.

And also, next to Adjeley's drawer, she had a medium-sized can barrel filled with Akpeteshie local alcoholic drink for sales, and then the small space in between those beds was where Adjeley's two boys and her eleven-year-old daughter slept on mats on the floor, so I slept beside them. And though Adjeley had a small standing fan on top of her drawer, the room was still hot because it was also too little for nine people, and it felt very uncomfortable, and I had heat rashes all over my body just like the rest of the kids. And we also had another severe rash that was widespread in Labadi and other parts of Ghana in the late sixties, and the Gas named it "otsokobila" because it had no name English, and they had no cure for that since we visited health centers, and we were given calamine lotions to apply the affected parts. But it didn't work, and those rashes increased and turned to bumps rather, and it affected sensitive parts of the body, like armpits, vagina, in between legs, elbows, etc., and it was so itchy that you didn't care to scratch it wherever you were, and it was contagious too.

The bad thing about it was it felt good when scratching, but blood came out from the bumps afterward, and it hurts, so nobody could focus well, even at work or at school. So we applied local black soaps mixed with a little water on it for about fifteen minutes, which you had to endure the pains, before we bathed with a hard sponge to scratch it well, and then we applied dirty engine oil on it as a cure. And so people made money from the engine's dirty oil by pouring them in smaller bottles for sales, and the black soaps as natural remedies everywhere. And thankfully, a few months later, those notorious rashes disappeared. And so during those periods, I felt like "I was thrown in a lion's den" because of the uncomfortable situation I was in, and then also dealing with those rashes and neither Mom nor Dad came to visit me to see how I was doing.

And so Aaatswei prepared kenkey in small quantity for sales to support herself, so I was like a burden to her, and as a result of that, she couldn't feed me well. She gave me a little money to my old school without breakfast and until I returned home before she gave me little money to buy food, so I bought roasted ripped plantain and peanut. And so Aaatswei was also verbally abusive to me, but not compared to Grandma Kai, so I did my best with house chores like fetching of water from the roadside and filled all the barrels and bigger pots in the house. I cleaned dishes, the room, and the narrow compound. And after school in the morning shifts, I also helped Aaatswei with wrapping the kenkey with corn husks before she started cooking, and then I went to hawk around the town to sell Adjeley's sardines and matches, packed full in a medium-sized tray. And then when I returned home in the late evenings, I sat by the roadside close to the house, and I sold Aaatswei the kenkey she packed in a big basin and well-wrapped in order to keep it warm on a big table, alongside a tray of fried fish and hot peppers. And so the neighbors and pass buyers also bought from me. So I did my homework over there by myself, and I also found that place to be my sanctuary, and I imagined God, and I talked to him about protections and blessings for me someday and to be happy. Because though I was twelve years old, I was smart enough to know that I was even depressed before I was born since I should have been born at Accra when Mom was in labor pains; rather, I went through suffering in the womb to be born in Lolonyah and also all the pains and depressions I went through as a little child. And finally, my parents dumped me in the family house to another Grandma again. It made me felt denied and rejected. And so I felt like the only one that love and care about me is God else I wouldn't be alive, and that makes me love him more.

After I cried myself out in talking to God by the roadside, selling the kenkey and fried fish, I found some instant peace in my heart to continue selling. I had my dinner over there, and sometimes it was just a small ball of kenkey and a little fish, and though it wasn't enough for me, because I needed about two of kenkey and either two or more fried fish, I was limited to just one kenkey and a little fried fish. I will be in trouble if I have more than what I was given because those kenkey and fried fish were all counted. So after each sale, I had to account for that, and sometimes too, I was given just a little coin equivalent to the amount of kenkey and fried fish given to me. And because I liked boiled rice and stew, I bought some by the roadside not far from me, but the sad part was that because I didn't have enough money, I asked the seller to give me the half-burn rice underneath the aluminum pot. And so she gave me more, and she added stew on it in specific large leaves (it was used to sell food in those days instead of takeaway containers). And the interesting thing with those boiled rice sellers was that after they finished selling the first pot of rice and then replaced it with another pot of boiled rice, they then placed the half-burnt rice in another bowl next to them on the table to make it easier for them if someone asked for half-burnt rice.

I couldn't afford meat, fish, boiled eggs, or cooked cow skin called "wele" in the stew, and I had no right to touch any of the counted fried fish, so I had to break those stiff half-burned rice with my unwashed hands into tiny parts before I could take my time to chew. And so I prayed over the half-burned rice, and I imagined myself each in US and eating boiled rice with stew and all kinds of meats and fish to my satisfaction, and that gives me hope to hang in there no matter what. And so I ended up with my sales each night, after the cinema closed around 11:00 p.m., when some people like to buy kenkey and fried fish to eat before bedtime. Also, one more nasty thing: what Aaatswei, Adjeley, and Adjokor did was that, instead of them buying chamber pots and using them every night in the room like Mom did, they rather placed the same big bucket and used it in fetching water into the barrels and pots, and they all peed inside, and so that was not okay to me the first night sleeping with them, and so I opened the door, and then Adjeley asked me, "Why?" And so I told her that I was going to pee outside, and then she said, "I can't do that." They all peed in the bucket placed behind the door. I reluctantly started peeing inside the bucket, because it was their room, and so I had to obey them. Though Aaatswei was responsible for me, Adjeley and Adjokor and her daughters took advantage of me, and they used me anyhow, especially Adjeley when it comes to chores and selling, and also, they sent me outside more than necessary to buy them food or whatever they wanted, just like those Gas, when they didn't like to cook, and so they also sent food like fufu and soup or konkonte and peanut butter soup, and they actually cooked like once in two months. And so Adjeley's behaviors toward me when it comes to yelling and insults in filthy words were like "Grandma Kai," and she reminded me of how good-for-nothing my father was, and he came to dump me on Aaatswei. He was supposed to be support-ing, at least by chance. I followed their orders, and I tried my best not to frown. I smiled even if I was tired or insulted. And you know, Adjokor was the calm one who didn't insult me. She was patient with me, and she even gave me couple of her used dresses to wear, and a couple of times, whenever Grandma ran out of corn kernels and she didn't prepare kenkey, she sent me to the cinema just to care for her child in order for her to sit a little farther from us and to have good times with her boyfriend by kissing and talking. And coincidentally, she also bought me my favorite soda, Fanta, and cookies to eat with his year-old child, and so I enjoyed myself and then watched movies at the same time.

Aside from the stuff that I sold for Adjeley, who didn't support me, Adjeley turned me into a bartender, who sold akpeteshie, a local alcoholic drink, to her costumers, which was filled in bottles with caps on, and they were placed on a table along with a glass in a tray. And so some of her customers preferred to buy a full bottle to share with the friends they came with, and some also like to buy one-half or one-quarter bottles for themselves. And so they sat on benches and tables packed at the corner of the house, and I served them with the drinks. And also, one bad thing that Adjeley told me to do: she had a small plastic bucket which was halfway filled with water, and when-ever a costumer finished drinking in a glass, I should just rinse it and serve another person with that. She did, and I know it wasn't the right thing to do, because someone might be infected with any disease, but I followed her instructions, since sometimes, if I felt like saying the right thing, she said that I had been too nosy. And I also handwashed the clothes of her three boys, and also I sent her child, who was only a few months old, to the health center for weighing every two weeks, and for some reason, I didn't know till date that Adjeley told me to keep all the money from the sales of akpeteshie and even those sold in my absence. She gave it to me later for safekeeping, until the woman who provided her with the akpeteshie returned to collect her money, and she brought another full barrel of the alcoholic drinks. Before she called me into the room to give her the money, she didn't know how much I had. And then after she counted all for a while, she stepped out of the room with a big smile on her face and gave the actual amount of the akpeteshie to the dealer, and then she kept the profits, and she did give me nothing, and she didn't appreciate me too, and truthfully, it never occurred to me to steal from her no matter what, whether I was hungry or needed something. And then I asked myself what her daughter Bole was doing. And so because Boley is Adjeley's only daughter, who was eleven years old, she turned her into a spoiled brat, and she did nothing to help when it comes to household chores or caring for her three young brothers, especially since I moved in with them. And so Boley went to a private school built with cement blocks, roofed with slate sheets, and they had all facilities in the school like a table and chair per child. The teacher had comfortable stuffed chairs and table libraries, entertainment halls, toilets, and bathrooms, which were built in the center of the town, and only the rich kids went to that school. They charged a fortune in paying school fees, and her dad paid for it, since he went to college and he worked as a sales manager in a Philips company in Accra. And Adjeley's two young boys were in day care, and so every morning before they leave for school, she prepared them with either oatmeal, custard, Milo, or Horlicks tea with evaporated sugar, and they were served with buttered bread, and those provisions were bought by her husband. She also gave them money to buy food. And to honest with you, Adjeley didn't serve me with any of those, and she also had some as her breakfast, and she looked heartlessly at me going to school with an empty stomach, and so when Boley and her brothers returned back home, she gave them money to buy food from outside, and when they were done eating, she served them also with snacks like either Fanta or Coca-Cola and cookies. And I tried to become Boley's friend in order for her to share those things with me, but she refused to be my cousin or friend, because to her, I was nobody but a slave. And also at dinnertime, Adjeley gave me money to buy food outside for her younger kids, but she gave Boley enough money to buy her favorite part of the boiled rice, which was the middle soft part, and she bought fish, eggs, and wele with enough stew inside a bowl, and then she bought oven-grilled pork, alongside with sauce, and she mixed everything together, and she ate with a spoon at home. And that was mouthwatering, and so sometimes I pretended to drink water in the house and returned back to my post to sell, and I asked her a little bit of grilled pork that smelled delicious, but she refused to share with me. And when I was about to go to school, Aaatswei gave those little coins that afforded snacks I had in school when I lived with Grandma Kai. And so that gave flashbacks of my bitter past, and that was pain and suffering for me, and I cried myself out on my way to school, and I asked God many times what I did wrong to continue suffering from an okay life to a worse life. And so once again, I started begging for food at school, and I turned out to be a laughingstock in school, but the only thing that kept me going was my American dream, and so I prayed to God to make it happen in order for me to have my freedom, and I sometimes imagined the Statue of Liberty that Odoi showed me in his books.

Sometimes I, too, asked God why I was different from other kids who had fewer chores to do and had everything they needed. And though he didn't answer me in person, I found words boldly written on trucks like "No condition is permanent" and "A downfall of a man doesn't mean the end of his life," and so those encouraged me, and I wrote them on the cover of my books as my mottos. Those words really motivated me when I am sad, also because of those filthy insults and bullying, especially by Adjeley. What hurts me more was that it wasn't because of something wrong that I did, but maybe it was because I couldn't finish selling her sardines and matches, for which I walked for miles from house to house for sales every early evening; I couldn't finish selling all the kenkey and the fried fish; or I was sent to buy food for them for lunch and dinner or to fetch water and there were long lines of people ahead of me and I returned back late. And then both Aaatswei and her daughter, Adjeley, rained those filthy insults like "Atswei, come eat my ass," "Atswei, you are good-for-nothing child who was dumped on us," "You are as useless as your dad who left you with nothing." Also, they insulted the soul of my vagina. It was unbelievable to me because I never knew that my soul had a vagina until I moved in with them, and it was a common insult I had repeatedly, and also they yelled at me to walk faster when I was sent because I walked like a penguin, and so they gave me a nick-name: "Atswei abedeikankose!" And I was teased by the neighbors' kids, and they even shortened "Atswei abedeikankose" and called me "Atsweiabedei" all over the neighborhood, and it hurts me so much, because when I thought over and over again about myself, among the neighborhood kids and my mates in school, none of them were humble, respectful, obedient, and hardworking like me, so I deserve a little credit for that and to be treated with kind of a little love and care. I was so depressed, and I cried myself out of the rejections and denials, but I didn't think of returning to Mom or Dad, but rather I decided to endure the pain and focus on my education and learned so hard to be able to go to America to be a classic lady.

Sometimes as a child, I wondered why most Gas don't like to cook good home-cooked meals to eat with their families like break-fast, lunch, and dinner, from what I saw when I lived with Grandma Kai and then when I was living at my family house Aberewankowe. They like to share money for their kids in the morning hours to buy, and they themselves also bought breakfast, lunch, and dinner, which are sold at every roadside, like all sorts of tea like Milo, Horlicks, cof-fee, Lipton, and they were served with milk, sugar, alongside either buttered bread or bread with sugar inside, and they also fried eggs, preferably, and then they sell to costumers who have their cups from homes, and they also served workers or passersby with their own cups. And aside from that, some people also sell types of porridge like plain corn porridge with no pepper or salt added to it; hausa porridge, which is corn mixed with hot peppers, ginger, and herbs called "so" in Ghana language; and also millet porridge, also mixed with hot peppers, ginger, and so. And they are served with sugar, milk, alongside two types of bread. And some people prefer kenkey and fried fish with hot peppers for breakfast, lunch, and dinner, which is also sold at every roadside, and then "watse," which is rice mixed with pea beans and cooked and served with spicy steamed hot peppers with shrimps, smoked herring, salt and oil and stew prepared with meat, fish, and wele, and there are chop bars also at every corner where fufu, banku, and konkonte are prepared with different types of soups, and those sellers make more money because there are lines formed to buy food. But when it comes to the Adas, Ewes, Fanties, Ashantis, etc., they prefer preparing home-cooked meals. And so a few months later, Mom came once to visit me for a few hours, and she brought Adzoa to spend vacation time with me, and she brought me clothes and provisions, and I didn't tell her anthing about what I was going through, but Adzoa returned back to Lagos Town in a couple of weeks' time because she couldn't endure hardships and pains.

It came to a point where I couldn't stand hunger anymore, and so I joined some of my mates who, after school, in the farms, went from tree to tree for mangoes, grapes, cashews, oranges and plunged those fruits in sacks, and they took them home, since there were only a few houses around, with old folks living inside, and the only thing they protected themselves with were power guns. And so the boys climbed some of those trees, and they plunged the fruits, or they shook the trees, and then we girls packed the fruits in sacks in haste, because when the owners heard noises, they came outside with their guns pointing toward our direction, and they asked who those people were. And then we ran away to our special hideout, and we ate as much as we could and then shared the rest equally, and we went our separate ways, and so my friends sold theirs to provide for some of their needs, and Aaatswei also sold my fruits in the market, but she didn't give me any money because she said she was providing for me with that, and so I understood her, and it didn't bother me all, because since then, my belly was full from those delicious fruits before I arrived home from school.

And to be honest, one of the nastiest thing I saw there and though I didn't like and didn't feel comfortable with it either but I coped up with the situation was that, can you imagine that a big bucket which I carried every day to fetch water for drinking and cooking, each night it turned to a peeing container we pee inside and even menstrual cycle blood drops in from some of them and, then in the morning I poured it out into the garters by the roadside and then I just rinsed it to fetch water again like I was told? Isn't that so disgusting? I mean, I was born and raised halfway in a village, but no one did that because those days peeing and bowel movement containers were sold which were made with metals and sprayed in different colors with all sizes and they had name called chamber pots and so all my family at Lolonya had big sizes on their own which were always placed at a corner the bedroom at nights and so if you needed to pee all you is to sit on it and then at daybreak they themselves picked it outside with care and poured it out and then it was cleaned with soap and sponge and then they placed it under the bed.

God did something amazing to me, and after suffering from abuses and rejections, I cried myself a lot during prayers. Though they continued to do it, that didn't hurt me anymore, but rather whenever Aaatswei and Adjeley insulted me, I just laughed at them so much that it hurts them more, and then they asked me why I laughed. "But is it because they have had feces all over themselves?" And then they said, "Ooh, now we realize how stupid you are, because only foolish people laugh when they are insulted." That calmed me down and gave me hope to continue dreaming of America, and I was smarter at school, and I had good grades in class 6, more than Boley, who was eating well and treated like a princess at home by Aaatswei and Adjeley. I zipped my mouth and didn't share my American dream with anyone at school or the kids in the neighborhood, in the family house. People living there were all grown-ups, and only Boley and I were in our early teens, but I kept my dreams a secret from her too. And so surprisingly, whenever Adjeley calls Boley or talks about her to her friends, she would be like, "As for my only daughter, Boley, as soon as she completes her college, she will be leaving straight to overseas." The Gas called "Abolotsiri" to stay there for good and married a white person. And then she gave her a nickname: "Boley, white man's wife." And so Boley got so excited about that, and as Adjeley continued to boast of the great future of Boley, I laughed, and I told myself that soon I will also be leaving for America to enjoy American dreams where honey and milk are. And so you know, it's amazing and funny to me now when I think about the toughest situations I was in my early teens at Labadi. I was almost five tall and taller than my mom, Aaatswei, and her baby daughter, Adjokor. I had smooth brown skin, and meanwhile, I was the only one in the house who bathed with Keys soap bar and used it for washing clothes, and the rest of them bathed with Lux and Rexona deodorant soaps. And I rubbed my body with shea butter. Those days, only the most poor used that, but the rest preferred made-in-Britain pomades for hair and skin, and Mom was one of those people that used pomades. And also I have a long face, medium-sized eyes, a small nose that is in between flat and pointed, a small mouth, and I am beautiful and well shaped by God because I have a flexible body, sizable hips and butt, nice thighs and legs, big voice, a great sense of humor, and much more, and because I stretch my left hand more, I am noticed to be left-handed. But Boley, known as white man's wife, was about four feet and four inches tall, fat and ugly, not properly shaped. She had broad eyes, chubby cheeks, black skin color, big flat nose, and a big mouth. And maybe that was some of the reasons why Adjeley didn't like me, because if she had to choose a daughter, she would have chosen me. And because Homowo festival is celebrated yearly and another festival was a few months away, since I moved in with them, Auntie Adjeley decided to shop early, because in Ghana, when it comes close to celebrations like Homowo festivals, Christmas, New Year's Day, and Easter, everything becomes expensive in the stores and the markets.

When she invited me and told me to carry her youngest child on my back, I got so excited, thinking that I won't be left out, and then we picked a lorry at the station to Accra, the city, and we first went to the store where her husband worked, and he gave Adjeley enough money before we went to Kingsway shopping mall, which was the biggest shopping center in those days. It was a huge-story building, and each floor was fully loaded with different items, all made from Britain. Adjeley, Boley, her three brothers, and I went straight to the children's department, which was filled with ready-made clothes, like dresses for all ages, both shorts and long-sleeved shirts for all ages, shoes, sandals, socks, all accessories, etc. And because it was made in Britain, it was expensive, and I realized that only rich people could afford to buy things there. Adjeley helped her kids to fit in clothes and shoes. Boley also chose a couple of nice dresses, shoes, and panties. Before she paid for them, including toys, she said that we should leave for home, without buying me a pantie. And so instantly, I was sad and emotional. I couldn't hold my tears anymore, and it was flowing through my cheeks. I had flashbacks of all the bad things I went through and what she also just did to me, because I happened to be her maid. She would feed me, and at each month, she would pay me and much more. She would give me gifts, occasionally, though I took all horrible treatments like bullets in my soul, but this is my life, full of suffering, and "it is what it is," wether living with my parents or family. And here I was, being loaded with work, like a donkey, and being fed like an African prisoner, and aside from those terrible treatments, I was faithful to her by keeping her akpeteshie money without taking a peswa from it. And in fact, it was one of those worse days of my life, because I am a human with feelings, and I wasn't a stupid fool like they thought, to rejoice in situations like this. But God, being so kind to me, did it again for the second time. When I lived with Grandma Kai, a stranger was sent by Mom to bring me beautiful sewn dresses, wrapping cloths and same blouse, slippers, and gold jewelries a few days to the Homowo festival, and then instantly, I was in happy, good mood again. And so on the festival day, I wore one of my beautiful dresses, and I wore makeup. Adjokor borrowed me, for the first time, and my jewelries and slippers, and I looked divine and so prettier than Boley in those Britain-made clothes, and like my mom's mother used to say, "When you are already beautiful, anything you put on, you look amazing inside, but if you are ugly and will be dressed up with all diamonds, gold, and most expensive clothes in the world, nobody notices you."

During Homowo festivities, something else is about twins' celebrations, and so I was told by Grandpa, who also had twin daughters and had cow horns displayed in his room, that some Gas thought twins were spiritual cows with horns, and so for each twin, Dad, in those days, had two separate cow horns displayed in their rooms, with a bottle of schnapps beside them. And so during the festivities, in those twin homes, a medium-sized wooden basin is placed in front of their voodoos and filled with water halfway, and hyssop leaves are added inside it, and then they slaughter goats or chickens, and they sprinkle the blood on the cow horns and inside the wooden basin. And then the fetish priests in the house pour libations, and thereafter, family members that needed a child or had some problems put a number of coins inside and then fetched some of the water to wash his or her face and make their declarations to the twins about their needs. And then mashed yams and boiled eggs, "oto," were also prepared for the twins, who were dressed in white clothes, and the family members also dig hands inside and eat with them, and then the meats are used to prepare dishes like soup and fufu and also boiled rice and stew. And they also provide nonalcoholic and alcoholic drinks, and they play music, and they also invite friends to celebrate the twins, and then the main ritual part of it is, some had to carry the wooden basin, or "sese" as it's called in Ga language, and then that person claimed to be in motion, and she holds the edge of the sese with two hands, and she shakes herself, and she moved here and there like she was going to hit someone with the wooden basin, so someone had to hold the side of her waist, and some family members followed her to direct her movements to either the riverside or a bush area to dump everything there, except the wooden basin she returned back home, because as soon as she dumped it, she came back to her normal self. And so when those rituals (called in Ga language "sese teremo") are done and they returned back home and then the real party continues with music and dancing, from my observations, the Gas worship twins more than the Adamgbes. And so though we kids were warned not to touch any of those money, because it's forbidden and it brings bad luck, so I haven't touched the money before, but some of the kids rushed to collect that money at every point they were dumped and spent.

And so another celebration, after a few days of the Homowo festival, was called "Kpele" drumming at Lakpaanaa shrine, where the chief fetish priests called Lakpaa Wulomo lived with a bunch of voodoos, and so fetish priests all over Labadi and surrounding towns and the linguistics were invited to the celebration, and they arrived with their own stools, carried by their helpers, so the day after the Lakpaa Wulomo poured libations and then, they slaughtered a cow, and the blood went to a wooden basin; the Gas called it "sese," and so they fetch some and sprinkled on their voodoos, and then they marked the right foot of all the fetish priests with the blood. And then most of them claimed to be in motions when the fetish's cultural music and drumming were played, and so during those periods, some men also cut the meat into small portions, and they wrapped them with empty cement papers in one of the rooms, and so the interesting part was that the new female fetish priests who were under training dressed halfway naked with just two yards of cloths wrapped from the side of the waist, but all their breasts and the rest of their bodies were showing, and they danced around, and those who already graduated, though they also wrapped from their waist side with two yards of cloths, their breasts were covered with another two yards of cloths, and couple of the fetish priests in motions claimed that there were foreigners, and so they wore long gowns and spoke broken English. Some, too, claimed they came from Tamale, upper region of Ghana, and they were traditional dresses called "patankari." And so because Lakpaanaa ground was so small and hot for big crowd, a couple of the curious kids like me who went for sight scenes fainted, and instead sending them to the health center, rather they took them to the shrine, and they revived them with hot pepper on fire, which made them sneeze, and water was given to drink. Some was poured on them, but the sad part was that the fetish priests claimed that the poor kids were married by the voodoos, and that was why they fainted, and so they were forced to be fetish priests for the rest of their lives. And so at the end of the celebration, they shared the wrapped meat for the fetish priests and the chief's linguistics. And so I had a chance to go see things for myself, after I said not to go, but deep inside me, I know that I am untouchable, and maybe God encouraged me to be there to have a story to tell someday.

And because of not getting enough food, especially meat, to eat, I ate "fotoli," the meal prepared with goat meat for voodoos at their yearly celebrations in several shrines at Labadi, just to keep on surviving. I ended up watching few fetish priests, who graduated from boot camps.

And so a couple of weeks to graduation, posters were posted on walls, especially public toilets and bathrooms. You know, watching those tricks of the fetish priests, also distractions, was entertaining to me because I was so sad, and I secretly cried mostly and much more because of depression and the anxiety I had from my past and how I was treated there, so sometimes I felt overwhelmed in that house, and if I rather stepped outside, I felt safe and like a bird freed from a cage. I didn't care about what would happen to me if I returned home, but I tried to enjoy the moments by watching them and laughing. What a couple of my friends and I normally do was that, because those ceremonies took place on Fridays at a particular big park about a block away from the house, we faked malaria sickness from school on Thursdays, and so we collected sick forms from the headmistress. So early Friday morning, we were the first patients to be attended to at Labadi Poly Clinic by the doctor, one after another, and he signed the forms, just to indicate that we were cared for, and then after we had our medicines from the pharmacy, we went back to our houses to meet at the ceremony grounds. When I returned back home, I made sure I filled everything with water and helped by buying them food from outside, in the afternoon, and then when I was given money for lunch, I stepped outside to buy food, and then I went straight to the grounds around twelve noon, where benches were packed until canopies and only a few kids were sitting and waiting, until the ceremony started around 2:00 p.m., and that gave me the chance to the front roll to see things into details. And so the invited fetish priests arrived one after another with their helpers carrying their stools and also a couple of clothes they changed the bags into, when they were in motions, and so just like in churches where women are the majority, it was same thing to fetch priests; there were just a few male fetish priests. And so my best motivational part was that before the ceremony started, they poured libations with a bottle of schnapps, and the most high God comes first, before Mother Earth, their voodoos, and then their ancestors, and the fetish cultural music and drumming went on. The funny part, to me, was how they all started shaking one after another, claimed to be in motions, and each of them were singing their songs, and then they were sent to the fetish graduate's house, and on their return back to the grounds, they changed into their different costumes, and their bodies and faces were powdered with a white rock called Ayilo in Ghana language, and so it was the start of speaking different Ghana languages like Ga, Adamgbe, Fanti, Twi, Ewe, and some too-broken English. And each language came with different dances, music, and drumming, well rehearsed like choir members, and thereafter, the new graduate came from the house, well dressed in her costume. She also claimed to be in motion, and then she had the attention by choosing her own songs, and she danced when music and drumming were going on, and then she ended up changing to a few nice, different costumes, before the end of the ceremony around 6:00 p.m. And so before the fetish priests all came to their normal selves, they sat back on their stools, and then they washed their faces with water and wiped them with their towels, then they became calm, and so before they leave back to their homes, they were served with dishes prepared from goats slaughtered, and the blood was sprinkled on the voodoos of the graduate, and then she wore their normal cloths before they left. And when I returned back home around 6:00 p.m., "Ooh my goodness," Aaatswei and Adjeley continued yelling at me, followed with insults, and they were on my nerves, asking me where I came from. Because I claimed to be sick and I went to the clinic and then disappeared for over six hours, I just looked at them and smiled and said nothing back to them. But I asked myself, if I skipped having to sell sardines and matches, why didn't Boley do that? And if I skipped selling akpeteshie, why didn't Boley sell it? I ignored them, and rather all funny and interesting things I watched remained in my head, and then I went to the roadside with kenkey and fried fish and peppers to sell, and by the time I returned back from the roadside, they were all snoring, but I woke earlier than all of them, because it was how I was trained by Mom. And so as a curious child, I didn't stop watching all about fetish priests, but I watched a couple of them who died in the neighborhood and were laid in state, and so instead of their corpses to be laid in bed in a room for families and well-wishers to pay their last respects, rather they were all dressed in their fetish clothes, and their whole bodies were rubbed with perfume herbs called "krobo" and white rock called "ayilo" in Ga language, and their hair were styled the fetish way, and they sat on their own stools, with their backs leaned on the wall to prevent them from falling, and they made them look like they were alive and just sitting down for hours, and fetish priests, families, and friends came to pay respects, and they put coins in their white handkerchiefs on their laps, which they should pay to cross the river, because they believe when people die, they pay money to cross river to life.

A couple of kids and I watched those interesting things through the opened windows, and so after libations were poured and goats were slaughtered and the blood was sprinkled on their voodoos and meals were prepared from the meat, it was time for them to be put in the coffins. Those windows were closed, and so after they were placed in coffins, fetish songs and drumming continue, and they were carried by six strong men, followed by songs and drumming, and the chief fetish priests carried two full bottles of open schnapps, alcoholic drinks in both hands, and he poured libations at each junctions around the whole town, and the female fetish priests also claimed they were in motions, and they also followed the corpses and the rest of them, and then they were sent to the cemetery for burial. And so after they arrived home, they celebrated with food and drinks. And much more, they know that the most high God doesn't drink or eat. Though we all watched and read Cinderella stories and felt sorry for the bad things that happened to her, but mine was horrible and worse than her, and she had happy ending when she was still young, but mine was just the beginning of my story.

I was finally in class, and I was graduating in three months time to Form 1, which is junior high school. I decided to go to boarding school in order to focus well in my education. Lucky for me, my teacher's daughter, who was my classmate, was about to go to boarding school at Kukurantumi in the eastern region of Ghana. And I requested for requirements and admission forms of the school from my teacher, and then I went to give it to Dad at Cantonment Police Station to buy me all the things and to fill the admission forms, and because it was free education, Dad wouldn't pay fees for that but just the boarding fee, things needed like two school uniforms, two housedresses, sandals, slippers, exercise T-shirt and shorts, panties, student mattress, pillow, bedsheets, provisions, my spending money, etc. After Dad read the forms, he smiled at me, and he was like, "Wow, Atswei, don't you worry at all, because I will provide you with everything, before the due time." And I got so excited for that, for the fact that soon I would be leaving the house-hell and be freed like other normal kids and focus on my education, because I learned couple of meanings about education and also what Nelson Mandela says: "Education is the most powerful weapon which you can use to change the world." Education is the key to eliminating gender inequality, to reducing poverty, to creating a sustainable planet, and to preventing needles and death and illness, and to fostering peace. And so I put in all my best regards to chores and anything I was told to do, and I tried to ignore abusing and bullying, and rather I counted down on my days full of hope, until two weeks to the time. I still hadn't seen Dad, so I went to his place one afternoon after school, and I waited for hours before he came, and then I asked him if he had everything ready for me. In fact, his words were like gunshots through my heart, because he told me, "Sorry, I had other responsibilities I had to take care of, and so for that reason, I can't afford that kind of money for you to go to boarding school."

Immediately I was filled with more anger and rage for him for the first time, because he received enough bribes from drivers when he became a motorcycle rider in the police, during those periods, and so money wasn't an issue to him again. And so I couldn't figure why he refused to invest in my education, the only thing I depended on to be a great lady in the future like Mom told me. It was Mom who provided everything for us when they were a couple, but he rather prefers to spend money on other women for his own selfish reasons. And so though lots of things went through my mind, which I had to say to him, about his heartless behaviors, I couldn't say anything, because I was also shocked, and so I cried myself out, and I told myself that if I knew that, Dad would disappoint me. I would have asked Mom instead to sponsor me, and she wouldn't deny me that, because she was giving her siblings great education, and so how much me? And so I walked away, and on my way back to Labadi, I was hurting so badly, and I felt worse than ever and more rejections, like I was a mistake to my family, and he didn't even give anything to be given to her mom, who was caring for me, and so I arrived back to the house-hell, which was also like a valley for me, and I pretended nothing happened, though I was in pain. I told Ms. Dora about my dad's behavior, and she felt sorry for me, and two weeks later, sadly, Ms. Dora's daughter left for boarding school without me. After my graduation, because I scored high marks in the promotion exams, I was the only girl enrolled by the school management to a new nice middle school built at the beachside, in between estate houses of Osu, which was the next town before Accra, called Osu Fisheries Girls Middle School, and it was newly built with cement blocks, with enough space in the classroom, a table and a chair per student, a nice table and chair for the teacher, a large cupboard filled with books, a library, few separate bathrooms, and latrine toilets, and it also had a hallway straight from form 1 to form 4. I was like, Wow! Because I haven't studied in such a beautiful school with those facilities before in a good neighborhood and also because of the sea breeze, I felt like I was in an air-conditioned classroom.

One more thing about that school was, the school district selected smart kids from different surrounding schools, and so my new mates were also smart, and then my old classmates went to a different middle school. We had a tough lady teacher called Ms. Patience who came from the Volta Region. She was so strict, and she gave us lashes with special flexible canes that were used to weave baskets, chairs, tables, etc. But Ghanaian teachers adapted those canes to lash us in schools as a form of punishment whenever we had some class exercises wrong, were late to school, or tried to be disrespectful. At first I thought she was the most wicked teacher of teachers who taught. And so my first time at school, I was thankful to God for replacing boarding school with a beautiful, comfortable daytime school, though chores, insults, and bullying were still waiting for me at home every day, but I tried to get used to them and just take my education seriously. And so surprisingly, Ms. Patience shared dozens of exercise books, big notebooks to write our notes inside for different subjects like mathematics, instrumental set, pencils, erasers, pen, black ink set, etc. She also gave us enough brown papers to cover our books and to write subjects on each cover like math, English, dictations, history, geography, science, Ga language, biology, religion, etc. And so my jaw dropped afterward from all those miracles. I never thought of the government, and so I didn't have to buy anything else to study because I had no idea how to get the money, and that would be a setback to my education. And so my new school was about two miles away, and I was supposed to be given money for transportation, but because it didn't happen, I fetched water during evening hours instead of early mornings, and I walked as fast as my legs would carry me to school every day without being late. And one more thing was that the upper back of my school uniforms got torn, and Adjeley refused to sew me a new one, and my sandals got ruined, so I used black thread from hair braiding and a piece of old uniform to sew with a needle to patch the holes, and I wore it to school, and though I was embarrassed and mates gossiped behind my back and laughed when I was approaching them, that didn't stop me from going to school every day to learn.

I saved some of little peswas given to me, and then I went to Accra Makola one day after school, during evening time because we spent eight hours in school every day, to buy local ready-made school uniforms that were below the knees, with orange color and blue color, band of the short sleeves, sewn for girls. The boys had khaki color, and it was cheaper, and they economized the material the way it was a little differently designed, and everyone knows that was one of those uniforms hanging on the shelves in Accra, and they made fun of me because of that too, but I didn't pay any attention to them, since I was smarter than most of them, and later I went to my dad's place to collect the Achimota sandals that Mom bought me long time ago at Lagos Town, and it was bigger than my legs by then. And it fitted me perfectly, so I liked my sandals that; I kept them clean at all times by polishing them, because they were pure brown leather sandals, made in Britain, and it was named Achimota sandals because Achimota was a new township by then, and that was a rich neighborhood, and they have a private school which chose those expensive sandals as one of their dress codes in the school. And so I washed my uniforms, and I added cooked starch to make it shine and stiff, twice in a week, which was Saturdays and Wednesdays, and then I ironed it well before wearing it to school because we had inspections by the teachers regarding uniforms, sandals, socks, hair, and fingernails at the assembly ground on Monday and Thursday mornings, to make sure that we were neatly dressed up, and with a little fault, that person would be lashed with a cane for the others to learn from that. And when it comes to the school bag, all my mates had new leather ones, but I couldn't afford it, so I used a material bag, which l made at sewing periods with tread and needle when I was in class six at my former school.

I stopped begging for food in my new school, and rather I fasted in the mornings, and then in the afternoons, I bought food like konkonte, banku, with either okra stew or peanut butter soup prepared with fish, meats, wele, and crabs and also boiled rice with stew. Since that, a woman who came from Ada found out that we spoke the same language on my first time, and since then, she favors me by adding more food to mine, and she gives me either meat, crabs, or fish for free because she realized that I didn't have enough money like the other kids, and I knew that was divine intervention, so I thanked God for that, and I learned he doesn't blink his eyes from me. Because I hate being lashed, I focused in class, and I did well too, and I took my homework also seriously at the roadside, selling kenkey, with fried fish, and it worked for me because costumers came to buy with some intervals, and it gave me a chance to study too, under locally made kerosene lamps. And so I know I was glad to have a tough teacher like her who pushed me so hard and made me smarter besides all that was going through in the house. All the while, my American dreams were my main concern and the only way to be successful.

3
CHAPTER

One Saturday morning, an unbelievable, terrible thing happened to me, and that turned my whole life upside down, so I was standing in front of the door, and then I saw Mom approaching from the entrance of the house, and for the first time leaving home, she had no makeup on, and her wrapped cloths were on just below her knee, instead of it being wrapped a bit down to her feet like she does always, and her hair was somehow scarfed. And she also looked traumatized, and then instantly I knew something awful was wrong, and she hugged me so tight, and she started crying out loud, and she was like, "Your uncle Odoi is dead!" And immediately, I was in shock, and then I moved a little bit backward, and then I was like, "What? What did you just say? I mean when? And how?" And then I cried, and I rolled myself on the floor, because Odoi was my gateway to America, and that dream was what kept me going and continuing to survive all insults, bullying, and also being their slave, since I knew that it was a temporary situation, and so it would change soon when he goes to America, and then I would be next.

When Mom sat down, with Aaatswei and Adjeley also by her side, she said that Odoi was complaining of severe stomach pains a few days ago, so she took him to the health center, and after he was examined, the doctor prescribed some medications for him. So she got them from the pharmacy, and then they returned back home, and she started treating him like she was told, but rather it was getting worse, and he couldn't eat or slept. And so on the third day, she sent him to Ada Foah, my grandma, to help out with his healing, and rather she invited a fetish priest, and he charged her money to buy things needed for rituals to heal him, so he brought all those things, like two fat chickens, food ingredients, bottles of schnapps, and some fresh herbs, and he did perform the rituals, but unfortunately, Odoi fainted, so at his point of death, he started speaking different languages, including English and French, except Ada, so none of them understood his last words, because they were illiterates. Then he vomited some stinky fluid from his system like a dead rotten anima, with awful smell, and he died, then the fetish concluded that he was poisoned by his friend at school. She told me to collect my few clothes because we were going right away to Ada for his funeral burial, so we picked a truck to Accra and we picked another truck at the Aflawu lorries station heading for Ada Foah, and then we picked another truck to Pute Village, which is couple of miles away from Ada Foah, where part of the families of Mom's father came from. And so when we arrived at Pute in the family house, Odoi's corpse was laid in bed, and he was dressed in white jonpa, a traditional shirt without bottoms, and from his chest down, he was wrapped in four-yard kente cloths and two different kinds of a traditional scarf called "wudasubo," which was braided like a crown around his head in one of the rooms, and the family members were around crying, including Grandma and Adzoa, and he didn't change a bit, but he was the same way he was, just like he was sleeping. And then a few of the high school choir stood by his bedside and had Methodist hymnbooks, and they sang hymns like "Blessed Assurance," "When Peace Like a River," "Rock of Ages," etc.

Surprisingly, I completely ran out of tears, because I was so shocked, since I didn't see this coming at all. He was young and so handsome, smart, and full of great dreams and life. That was the end of his and my American dreams. I was overwhelmed about that, because I lost not just an uncle and a friend but also my dreams of living in America and being a great, successful lady.

After all those thoughts, I was in tears, and I asked myself, "Why is my life such a mess, and why do bad things continuously happen to me?" And also "Why do bad things happen to good people?" And so I did say something silly, and I knew God forgave, because I was thirteen years old, a depressed child with anxiety, and so I was like,

"God, why does it have to be Odoi?" He was so smart and full of dreams and goals in life, and rather, why not my mental retard aunt Ofliboyo? And so during those periods, Mom's shock, depression, and anxiety were so serious that she fainted a couple of times, and water was poured on her before she revived, and one of the emotional moments for everyone was when Mom carried his big suitcase, full of text and exercise books at the funeral grounds. She was like, "Odoi, here are your books, and I have also invested in you so much for nothing." And so a couple of hours later, he was placed in the coffin, though we asked to step outside, but I heard the sounds of the hammer that was used to nail the coffin and there realized how nothing human is on this earth, and then he was held by four men with their hands to the nearest cemetery, and though Grandma went with the family members, Mom was kept in a room in order for her not to go because she was more traumatized, and I wasn't able to go either because kids were not allowed in cemeteries in those days. And so after they returned back home, Grandma, Mom, Adzoa, and I walked by the beachside, about four miles away to Lolonya, for the final funeral rituals, because he was irreligious, and so we stayed there for a week, also to be consoled by family and friends.

Grandma Anumokuor and Ofliboyo moved from Adokope with all her voodoos a little after I got healed from guinea worm disease back to Ada Foah, and she built three rooms and a small hallway with palm branches, and it was roofed with thick dried grass in order for her to be safe during the rainy season, and she fixed the wooden door on the entrance, part of her family property. She continuously worshipped and celebrated them, though she went on market days of Ada Foah on Wednesday and Saturday mornings to sell smoked fish in big baskets and large trays to provide food and other needs for themselves and the voodoos too. She poured libations three times a day for the voodoos with schnapps, which was an expensive foreign drink in those days, and she bought akpeteshie alcoholic drinks made from pineapple juice, which is more expensive than the one made out of sugarcanes, which is so common, and thereafter she slaughtered chickens and some other stuff to celebrate them periodically. Because Grandma was an experienced fetish priest with also a lot of voodoos than any of her colleagues, she was well respected, famous, and known as Masekinye Anumokuor in the whole Adamgbe District, and "Masekinye" means "Maseki Mother" in the Ada language.

And though Grandma's mother and the rest of her siblings are Christians, she rather made fun of them whenever they talked about Jesus Christ being our Lord and only Savior, but on her father's side, her half sisters are also fetish priests, so they supported her all the way. Christians name their kids with names of good meanings to bring them great luck, and some even give angel names to their kids like Michael, Gabriel, and names of saints and prophets in the Bible, and so fetish priests also do some things, and they name their kids after their voodoos, and unfortunately, Grandma was one of them, and so Mom's name, Maseki, was one of her voodoos. Odoi was one of her voodoos. My uncle, who was a trained teacher, Fulani, was one of her voodoos. My other uncle called Vodu was one of her voodoos, and Ofliboyo was also one of her voodoos. And so Grandma proudly named her children, whom she loved so much, after she voodoos to protect them, but rather she destroyed them all one after another with those names.

After Odoi's death, Mom and I weren't the only ones who suffered most from his loss, but Grandma did suffer too. She was also shocked and depressed, and she became so disappointed in the voodoos. She cherished her, and she completely lost the desire to worship them again. She was so brainwashed in her early teens about voodoos being like saviors, healers, and protectors more than anything else, though God comes first whenever they poured libations; they give him due respect. He deserves it as Creator of heaven and earth, and so they asked permission in everything they do. And after she returned from Lolonyah to Ada Foah, when all final rituals were made, she rather hated the voodoos, because she said that, since she gave them her lifetime, sacrificed so much for them, and also served them with honor and dignity, they were supposed to protect her son from being poisoned or dying, even if he had any poison inside him, and so it was pointless to continue serving them, and then she decided to give her life to God and to be a good Christian and win souls of Jesus Christ instead. And so what Grandma did was that she packed all her family voodoos and the pots in a bigger basin, and she wrapped the whole basin together with the voodoos, and she tied them with four yards of cloths, so none of them could fall and break.

With a helper, she carried them on her head, and she walked for a few miles from Ada Foah beachside, straight to Lolonyah, and though she got so tired, she also felt neck pains on the way, but amazingly, she made it home at the shrine before she was helped to lifting them off her head. And right there she aggressively told the chief fetish priest in the family that she was done with serving those generational voodoos, who could have saved her son, Odoi, from dying, and so for that reason, he should count all the voodoos and make sure some weren't left out, and also he should check the pots if there were any damages. He tried to persuade her not to give up because death is unpreventable, but she told him her mind was made up, and so with shock, he checked everything she brought over, and he said everything was well-kept and nothing else was left out, and then Grandma left his sight to the family house of her mother's side, and she announced that she is a Christian from now on, and so she returned those generational voodoos back to her father's family, and as soon as she returned back to Ada Foah, she would ask the Church of Pentecost pastor to burn the rest of the thirty-seven voodoos she bought with her own money, and rather she would serve God and be a living testimony for the rest of her life like them. At first they thought it was a joke, but they all rejoiced when they realized that she meant what she said, and they prayed together and thanked the Lord Jesus Christ because they waited for so long on God to turn Grandma into a Christian. And so she chose to carry those voodoos and walk, rather than to pick a truck, to Lolonyah, because the roads were rough and filled with potholes, so she feared that if a voodoo got damaged or there was a small crack of a pot, the family's chief fetish priest would hold that against her, and he would reject the rest, and she wouldn't be able to become a Christian like she wanted, and that showed Grandma's smartness. And she returned in couple of days later for Ada Foah, and she actually told the pastor about everything, so he came to the house with a few church members, and then they prayed over those voodoos before they brought them all outside in the middle of the compound, and they poured kerosene on them, and then the pastor lit the matches, and he threw on the voodoos. And they were all in flames and burning, so they continued to sing and prayed to God to cast all demons in those voodoos into the sea. And after they burned in ashes, the pastor collected it into a cement paper, and they went to the beachside just a few yards away and baptized Grandma in the sea after she accepted Jesus Christ as her Lord and Savior in her early fifties, and she was given a Christian name: Mercy. Then those ashes were thrown in the sea, and the pastor told her to buy a Ga Bible, and he blessed it by praying over it. And since then, Grandma saw the Bible more than her voodoos, and though she couldn't read, it didn't leave her sight, because she opened it and placed it under her pillow. She didn't pray without kneeling on the ground and holding the Bible. She really prayed so loud and with sincerity to God, and because she heard that she can pray to God at anytime, she prayed more than necessary a day, especially in the middle of the night, since, according to her, the forces of darkness are at work, except when she stepped out to the market side.

She also went to Church of Pentecost every Sunday, Wednesday, and Friday, and what she even enjoyed most days was fasting, and so it became part of her, and she fasted mostly, and she ate after 6:00 p.m., when she breaks her fasting with prayers for a while, and she liked to testify how God was so good to her at the marketplace, for people to give their lives to God, who is even simpler to worship than those graven images. And she took tithes and offerings too seriously and gave more than the one-tenth of her profits, and the interesting thing about her tithes is, she tore a small size of cement paper, and she put the money inside and wrapped it, and she put it in the offertory box with no name written on it, but she said God, who sees secrets, knows that was her tithes, and also she bought new white cloth, and she wrapped her Bible inside whenever she was going to church. There was something funny about her tone of singing Ghana gospel songs; it sounded like the same tones she used when she was a fetish priest. A few days later after Odoi's burial rituals at Lolonyah, Mom, Adzoa, and I returned back to Accra, and Mom sent me back to Labadi to continue my education, since I was doing well in class, and she promised to give me her sewing machine, for me to learn how to sew as soon as I complete form 4, and she told me that because her favorite little brother, who put the American dream in my mind, was gone for good. And to be honest with you, form 4 certificate, in those days, was equal to college degree nowadays, because we had devoted teachers who really forced us to learn in the hard way, with severe lashes that gave us wounds on our bodies and no parents to walk in to attack or to have the teacher arrested. Since my return back to Labadi, I was still grieving for my uncle Odoi's death, and I cried secretly when I was alone, and I asked God multiple times why he had to die. And I wouldn't be able to go to America again, so I told myself that, well, at least when I complete form 4, I will become a seamstress like during the essays period, when I wasn't having American dreams, and the teacher asked us to write about ourselves. I wrote that I would like to be a seamstress in the future, and Mom also confirmed it. And so Mom still didn't know my living situation in Labadi because I didn't tell her, and also nothing changed after I returned from Ada, but I was facing those same challenges, and whenever she mentioned about her daughter Boley traveling to overseas, that also added to my depression, and I cried because of that and much more how she treated her, like a toddler. If she had malaria fever, she would send her to a private health center to be well examined and given malaria drugs, and what even made me imagine myself being sick and how I would be treated was how Adjeley prepared either Milo or Horlicks, tea with sugar and milk, served with buttered bread, and sometimes she spoon-fed her until she got better and with love and pampering. A couple of months later, Mom came over to let me know that she and Adzoa were moving out from Lagos Town to Ada Foah to be with Grandma, because life there without Odoi was unbearable no matter how she tried.

I asked her how to reach out to her in case of emergency. And so she told me that if I picked a truck to Accra Aflawu lorries stations, where different trucks and buses, almost all over Ghana, Nigeria, Togo, and Ivory Coast, are located, then I should ask for Ada Foah bus, and they charged six shillings straight to Ada Foah, so I should ask the driver to drop me off by the roadside at a neighborhood called Fiegbedu, and then I should keep on walking on the gravel road toward the beachside, and if I asked for Salem We, then I will find her and Adzoa. And so one day, I had severe malaria for real, with headaches, cough from mosquito bites, for the first time in a year and a half, and also lost my appetite completely, and rather my situation got worsened after I walked a mile away to the La Poly Clinic and returned back home, so I couldn't eat or drink water for twenty-four hours, and I felt like vomiting, so I was just lying on the mat on the floor, so weak, and then I looked up at the ceiling, and I asked God, *Why do bad things happen to me, and why does nobody love or care about me?* And I wasn't given anything to try to eat, but what Aaatswei did was that she came to the room and just threw coins on the mat for me to go get something and eat, and there I know how worthless I was to them, and they didn't care even if I died, including my own family, because Adzoa was always their priority. And so I couldn't reach out to Mom or even Dad and I just lay in the room with all those symptoms, and I was so helpless and thinking that I will follow Odoi in his next world, and they still refused to contact any of my parents, but in case I died, they would have figure out how to get them right away. Then an idea suddenly came to my mind that the only way for me to survive was to escape to Mom, but I asked myself how. I had no money, and even if I did, how could I make it to Ada Foah with this kind of weakness and dizziness?

The little voice inside me said to take only the lorry fare out of Auntie Adjeley's money I saved for her from the akpeteshie sales, and so miraculously, I felt energized and then got up. I took the money I saved in a scarf she gave me to keep it inside, and I took up only a couple of peswas to pick a truck from Labadi to Accra and six shillings for a bus to Ada Foah, and I hid them in my dress pocket, and then I placed the rest of her money under her pillow on her bed, then I stepped out and told Aaatswei and Adjeley I was going to use the toilet. And so I went straight to Labadi lorry station to pick a truck to Accra, and then I went to the Aflawu lorries station, and then I picked a bus, in which the driver's mate collected my six shillings before he allowed me inside, and so I told him that was my first time going to Ada Foah by myself and so he should tell the driver to drop me off at Fiegbedu. I asked the mate, "Are we there yet?" for a couple of times because I was so scared that I might get lost before he told me. We finally arrived at Fiegbedu, so I got off the truck and was directed to keep on walking on the gravel road, and on the right side of the road, there is a house, fenced gate, and that is Salem We, which in Ada language means Salem house, and I walked about half a mile, and then I saw the house like Mom told me. Adzoa saw me when I walked inside, and we hugged each other so tight, and she told me Mom had gone for fasting and prayers at Heradura church of brotherhood when I asked about Mom, and I was like, "What? Mom had gone to church? Seriously?"

I told Adzoa about my illness, which forced me to escape from Labadi, and it was a miracle I survived, and I was able to make it safe and sound over, and so immediately she prepared me Milo tea with milk and sugar, and she served me with buttered bread, and I drank it all and didn't vomit, but I started sweating. Then I slept unaware for hours, until Mom came home late evening, and then Adzoa prepared banku, since they had leftover okra soup cooked with fresh fish. And so I told Mom about all I went through at Labadi, and if it had not been for God, I could have been long dead, and so Mom was emotional, and she blamed me for being in such horrible situations. I told her nothing about it, but she thought I loved my school the way I talked about it, and that was why she allowed me to continue living there. And so we both thanked God for uniting us, and so Mom promised, since then, she wouldn't let me go and that we would live together forever.

Mom lived in one of the rented medium-sized rooms in the center of the two plots of land, and the homeowners lived in a self-contained house on the other side, and so Mom, like a lady born and raised from a foreign land, furnished her room with twin beds and mattresses with clean sheets and six pillows. She had a small couch, a drawer, a dresser filled with perfume powder, creams, pomades and designer perfumes, and showcase cardboard filled with provisions. Her floor was carpet, and she had a medium-sized table behind the door with her trunks, box, and basket filled with cloths, and she had her slippers under the bed, and she had clay-made cooler filled with well water from the house with a cup on top of it, and so Adzoa and I laid a mat on the floor, and we slept on it. And so I was thankful to God for making me choose him, at the age of eight, instead of voodoos and then Grandma and, much more, Mom and Adzoa. Mom said, since I arrived on a weekend, that she would send me to the clinic on Monday, but with a warm welcome and with good homemade food, I felt better without going to the clinic. And also because the Bible, in Proverbs 17:22, says, "A joyful heart is a good medicine, but a broken spirit dries up the bones." And so for the first time in my life at the age of thirteen, Grandma, Mom, Adzoa, and I talked more about God and and his wonders, and that made me so happy and my eyes brighten. Odoi had a tragic death, but because of that, it drew my family close to God. On the other hand, he sacrificed his life for Grandma, Mom, Adzoa, and Ofliboyo to become Christians. But it was a great loss to me, because it felt like he died with my American dreams, and when it clicked on my mind, I became sad, and I cried because of that, and I asked God, "Lord, so that's it?" since Odoi is no more. And so two weeks passed since I left Labadi, and Dad even didn't come looking for me, because if he wanted to, it would have been easier for him, because he knew Lagos Town, where Mom lived, and Fulani, Korletey, and his family are living there, so he would be directed to Ada Foah to see if I was there or had disappeared, so Dad proved to me that not only did he not care about me, but he also wished me death, to get out of his life for good. And so I asked myself during that period, "What if I was a victim of those kids who were kidnapped, and they were put into sacks whenever any king or chief died across the country, and they were buried alive alongside with the servants, and so no one cared to look for me?" My dad's rejections hurt me for a while, but the good news was that I was with my family, who loved me in their special ways— talking, laughing, eating homemade good food, bathing with perfumed soap, and also having access to everything I wanted. No more filthy insults. I would be in nice clothes, and I stopped seeing myself as inferior, and that's all that matters to me. And so Mom enrolled at a Methodist Middle School, though Adzoa was in Presbyterian Girls Middle School, which was well-built with cement blocks and some good facilities. But I couldn't be with her, because the management had a number of kids they needed in form 1, and so the bad things about the school was that forms 1 and 2 were in wretched conditions, like my old primary school in Labadi, because it was halfway built with old aluminum sheets and roofed with the same old aluminum sheets. The cemented floor had potholes in which someone can easily fall. They had benches and tables for two students to sit on, and everyone who passed by sees students from the head to the chest, and when it rained, the students got wet. The classes were small, and so teachers had a medium-size table at the corner of the class, with small book cabinets. But forms 3 and 4 had cemented block building with spacious rooms, a table and chair per student, a table and chair for a teacher, and no library in the school, so whenever it was reading time, the class prefect had to collect books from the headmaster's office and return them after they finished reading. The bathrooms were built with palm branches, and it wasn't cemented, and because the whole compound was sandy, it soaked the urine, and for that reason, it smelled bad, like the bathrooms in Lolonyah in those days, and we also had a few separate latrine toilets. It was an unhappy situation for me, because I was in those types of school for a long time, and I just moved to a beautiful school, where I thought I would complete form 4 over there, and not even the end of the first semester, and then I was back to the sort-of-nasty school I disliked, but I had no choice than to be in those awful situations for two years before I would be promoted to the cemented block building. And so days after I started school, the headmaster called; Ocansey asked me to go back to my school at Osu and bring my transferred letter and all my books to use in the class, because exercise books wouldn't be distributed until another semester, and when I told Mom about it, she told me to go to Labadi in the family house and collect those books I haven't used and the valuable things I needed after I received the transferred letter. I was okay with the transferred letter, but I wasn't okay for the fact that I had to go to the family house. They hated me so much, and my disappearance meant nothing to them. Moreover, I didn't know what I was going to get myself into, and that broke my heart, and if I had choices, I would have told Mom I wouldn't be going to that house again.

I cried, and I prayed overnight for God to give me protection and courage to face them and get what I wanted and return back safe and sound to Ada Foah. The next day early morning, Mom gave me lorry fare in and out and spending money to buy food. And so I picked a bus in the next house straight to Accra, and so I was at Osu before Teacher Patience arrived, and she felt sorry for me, and she hated to see me leaving, just as I do, because she likes me, and so she gave the transferred letter with my good conduct and performance, and since I forgot to take a big basket to collect my books and stuff inside, I bought a big white plastic bag and put my exercise books inside and then tied the knot, and then I carried on my head from the school. And then on my way to Labadi, I was so nervous and with anxiety, rather than being happy to see my family, if they were good to me, but I made it to the house, thankfully, and either Aaatswei or Adjeley responded to my greetings or pretended to ask me where I had been or how I was doing just to show a little concern about me, and because I wasn't expecting any of those from them, I rushed to the room and picked my stuff in haste, because I feared for my life that they might hurt me, make me bleed to death, and make it look like an accident, because they were so heartless. They must have been bad people or else they wouldn't have treated me in such a way.

I added my stuff to the one in the plastic bag, and I tied the knot, and then I carried it. When I said goodbye to them, I expected Adjeley to ask me about her six shillings, but she said nothing about it, and then I assumed she had no idea that I even took six shillings from her saved money. On my way, in a truck back to Ada Foah, after I thought about it, I realized that God wanted me to make use of some of her money at the right time, so that was the reason why she willingly gave me the money to continuously keep for her; else I wouldn't have been able to get to Mom in Ada Foah, and I could have died on the mat, like several people who die from malaria fever without proper care.

I arrived at Ada Foah in the evening, and I told Mom about what happened, and she was sad, emotional, and she told me that she had just Adzoa and me as her children, so she wondered why I had to be going through all those terrible things since my childhood. But anyway, thank God it's all over, and that would not happen again because we wouldn't be separated from each other, and so I had my dinner and got myself ready for bed, since I was so tired of the long journey and also from carrying those heavy books.

The next morning, I went back to the school with my transferred letter and some of my big notes and exercise books. I then joined the students' class, and because it was a mixed school, a boy and a girl sat on the same bench and used the same table, maybe to avoid talking in the class, and so I sat with a boy called Nene Oha. There were four boys, with the same last name: Oha. But they had different first names and came from one of the surrounding villages, across the River Volta, as a family, and two of them were in their late teens, but the other two were in their twenties, like most of the students from other classes, and every day they came in and out to school with their small canoe. And so they left it at the bank of the river, because the other sides of the Volta River have strong trees all over the bank, and so they tied the rope hanging on the canoe to one of those trees. And because those trees have strong, flexible sticks, Mr. Ocansey ordered them to fetch more sticks during the weekends, and on Mondays, they brought a bunch of them to school, like firewood, and Master Ocansey told them to bury them on the ground and water those sticks for a couple of days before they were pulled out from the ground to his office. Then he and all the teachers used them to lash at us as punishments, and to be honest with you, those sticks, when soaked in water, were made heavy and more flexible, and they barely break and really hurt more than being lashed with canes, and they easily cut our bodies, like being cut with knife and blood followed. And so no parent reported him, and so he continuously physically abused us, and he preached that he was being strict in order for us to be smart kids.

One more heartless thing he did was that every day we had either math or English mental drills during assembly in the morning hours, and he made sure we had exercise books and pencils in our hands, and still standing, he called either addition, subtraction, or multiplication, in haste, and we had to calculate it so fast and put the answer on our sheets of papers. After he finished with twenty different types of maths, we exchanged papers to mark by numbers, if he mentioned the answers, and we returned them back to the owners. At one mistake, he gave two hard lashes, and it means that if someone scored zero over twenty, then that person had to receive forty lashes on the upper back. Though he was in his early fifties, he was strong enough to lash about one hundred and fifty students by himself. His white shirt and shorts got all wet with sweat, and he went back to change into new clothes and returned back to school. He had two nicknames, which were "my nose," because he had an ugly pointed nose, and also "hold the pillar," because whenever he lashes, he told us to hold the pillar of the school hallway, and he repeatedly told us to hold the pillar, because of how badly those lashes hurt, and so we kept on taking, our hands off the pillar. And so none of the students liked him because of his wicked behaviors toward us and because he was a choirmaster and an organist of the Methodist Church, in the same big compound, and so he formed a choir group in the school, and he thought all parts of the music tones like treble, tenor, and bass on Fridays after assembly, and that also wasn't easy because if someone was out of key, he lashed instead of warnings, and so he added me to the choir group, and I sang tenor well because of my big voice, but I was also lashed sometimes.

One more thing he disliked about me was that no matter how painful his lashes were, I didn't move my hands from the pillar or move my body during singing time until I received all the lashes. I thanked him up top, and then I sat and cried for a while, and for that reason, he said I was a stubborn girl, and so instead of giving me like four lashes, he doubled it, but that didn't change me to be like the rest of the students who cried out loud like toddlers and begged him, but he still lashed them. And in my case, the terrible things I went through, which didn't kill me, made me stronger, as little as I was, and I learned how to endure pains rather than those lashes. And though his actions weren't easy for me to deal with at all, because I was recovering from long-suffering, he also turned out to be a hindrance to me when my family and I just reunited. And one more thing, since it was a small church, he used force to let the whole school attend church on Sundays, and names were written, and on Monday afternoon, he went to class and lashed the absentee, so I tried so hard to study and to take his orders, to make sure I didn't fall in his traps. And he went too for that; he sent strong, grown-up students to go to the house of the absentees to force them to come to school, if only they weren't sick to be lashed. He got married to a nice young lady, but because of his bad behavior, that marriage didn't last long and the woman disappeared to Accra for good and for real. He was a disgrace to Christians because he was also mean to his neighbors and of how he treated them so badly, and he controls them like they're his properties, so they didn't talk well about him. My lady teacher was called Mrs. Amegachie, who was short and slim like Mom, but she was black in skin color, and she happened to live in the same house with me because her Grandma was the land lady.

One thing also about Ghanaians as far as I know is that they don't mind about long distance relationship even if married because they understand that they have different jobs, and so as far as there is love and honesty and support in the relationship, that's all matters. Both she and the husband are Adas, and he was also a trained teacher, but he was transferred to another town, and so he came to visit her and her three-year-old-son on holidays and vacations, and she also visited her husband on some weekends. Mrs. Amegachie is a Christian who worshipped at a church that has the same doctrines like other doctrines like Herradura Churches, and they wear long white gowns, scarf their hair with white cloths, and band their waist part with badges of different colors, and she even invited me over a couple of times when I was a fresh new girl in town, until Mr. Ocansey forced me to join the Methodist Church choir. And so Mrs. Amegachie thought us well and with patience, but she also lashed us with the least mistake in classworks, and because our class was too small, with the heat of the aluminum sheets, since the school was situated a mile away from the beach, we didn't have any fresh air in the classroom, and we felt like we were steaming and filled with sweat all over our bodies, and also whenever someone passed gas, it circulated faster, and then Mrs. Amegachie held her nose, and she ordered all of us students to step out of the class, run, and circle the compound about six times, and she stood in front of the entrance, and she watched us and smiled at us. And in fact, those were tough punishments, more than lashes, because as we kept on running under the hot sun, the sandy grounds were also so hot, and the heat and the sand penetrated inside our sandals and slippers too, so we ran out of air, and we felt like fainting and also panting heavily like racing dogs. Before we returned back, when time was up, we drank water from the bucket fetched from the well in the school and placed in the classroom, with two cups on top of the lid for the class, because there wasn't tap water or electric in Ada Foah like Lolonyah and the surrounding towns and villages of the Adamgbe Districts. And the bad news is, my class was that some students kept on passing gas in between during teaching periods, and so we kept on taking breaks and also running, like, a few times in a day, and that was also new thing, tiring and frustrating for me because already I had enough of Mr. Ocansey's mistreatments, and I was stressed with that type of awful class I studied in compared to Adzoa's school and the Catholic schools in the town, and if anyone passed gas, then we all had to be punished for that.

That disturbed me emotionally for a while, and I couldn't fare well in class, but aside from Mr. Amegachie's bad punishments, she had a sense of humor when teaching, and she advised us how to learn hard no matter what to achieve our dreams and goals in life, and she also advised us girls not to wear makeup frequently, unless we are going to functions to make us look different and more beautiful. And thankfully, I made it to form two, which was just next to form 1, with the same structure, and though a couple of teachers were transferred from other towns to teach us, they couldn't stand the heat of the class and the passing of gas, so they all left as a result of that, and so we were left without a teacher in form 2 class for almost all the semesters. And so those smart form 4 students were instructed by Mr. Ocansey to take turns, and they taught us in different subjects, and they gave us many homework and notes to learn at home. And luckily, none of them lashed us, and that was really a relief for us, and so I took advantage of the situation, and I focused in class. I listened to the seniors, like I listened to teachers, and I took homework and studying at home seriously, and I made it look like I was having fun, so if I was cooking, washing dishes or clothes, and ironing too, I had my notes or poems right next to me, and I learned the same by looking through my books and reciting them. And so it rather helped me continue being smarter than Adzoa, and I had good grades as a result of that.

What I learned at Ada Foah market days was that it's one of the largest market in Ghana, so traders come over to buy and sell food ingredients like goats, pork, chickens, guinea pigs, fresh and smoked fish, yams, plantains, corn kernels, cassava, konkonte, cassava dough, sugarcanes, bananas, oranges, grapes, tomatoes, onions, hot peppers, and local alcoholic drinks like palm wine and akpeteshie made out of sugarcanes and pineapples, sodas like Fanta, Coca-Cola, Lamle, and Asanaa, which is a local nonalcohol drink, and all these are brought in large quantities, also different items like cloths, materials, scarfs, sandals, slippers, pomades, powder, cakes, doughnuts, meat pies, ice cream, etc. And so as always, Mom (I knew that she was a hardworking, independent woman who would do anything to provide for herself and her family) had a medium-sized shed inside the market, and it was roofed with aluminum sheets, and the ground was neatly cemented because the whole market, too, is sandy. And she also had couple of long woods attached to the shed, and she displayed scarfs and assorted color materials for sales, and she also had a large table where she displayed her different items on it, like different sizes of China plates and local metal plates, all packed in the first basin, and then different sizes of aluminum cooking pots, medium and small bowls for stew or soups dishing, and packed in the second basin, so full, and she covered the whole basin together with them with a medium-sized net to prevent them from falling, and so the third basin was filled with cosmetics like both pomades for hair and body, perfumes, powder, lotions, perfumed soaps like Lux and Rexona, antiseptic soaps, etc. She had a chair for herself and a long bench. And so on Wednesday mornings, she had a helper to carry those things to the market, and Adzoa and I would leave straight to school, since we had breaks from noon until 1:30 p.m., before returning back to school, and so Adzoa normally comes to my school, since we were a few yards away, and then we left to the market to meet Mom, and so she gave us money to buy the food of our choice. And that was my favorite part, because I saved some of the money for vanilla ice cream I had only once in a week with different shapes, and I liked ice filled in small plastic balls with a little lid and served with plastic spoons, and so I played with those balls when I finished eating ice cream. And then the hard part was after school around 4:30 p.m., when we returned back to the market, and then Adzoa, Mom's helper, and I had to carry those things in the basins, and then we followed Mom to the market side where cassava dough sellers in large groups were situated, and then we were helped to lift those heavy loads off our heads.

I had a small notebook to record those villagers' names and how much they bought and their down payments, because Mom sold to them on credit basics in higher prices to make more money. And so we spent hours there, since each of them took their time to search for what they needed, and also I felt stressed about that because they had complicated names. I had to think about the spelling, since they were all illiterates, so they couldn't help me with the spelling, and so I figured out something to write. And so we went home late in the evenings, and I had to cook for dinner, and after that, Adzoa and I had to spend a couple of hours with counting those coins with zero note, and thereafter, because Mom also started frying doughnuts for sales as another source of income in order for us to live comfortably, because Dad completely vanished from our lives, she was the only provider of the family. And so Adzoa and I took turns in mixing measured sizes of sugar, salt, vanilla flavor, butter, flour, yeast, and then we mixed it together until the flour dough softened in the basin, then we covered it with a lid in the kitchen, and this was done under Mom's supervisions, and thereafter, we had our homework done before we lay down on the mats on the floor covered with sheets and pillows as usual. And the next day, early morning, around 4:00 a.m., Mom woke us up, and then I filled the firepot with firewood, and then I sprinkled kerosene on it, and I lit matches on, and it burst in flames, and I placed a big frying pan on top of the firepot, and then I poured a gallon of coconut oil inside the pan.

I allowed the oil to heat, then I put a little bit of dough into the oil to make it. It was warmer before I rolled the dough in small balls with my hand, inside the oil, as fast as I could, and I used a two-foot wooden ladle to rotate those balls in the oil to prevent them from burning until they become golden brown, then I used a locally made long metal round ladle with holes in to collect the doughnuts from the oil inside a basket right by my side in a cooking pot in order for the doughnuts not to soak. And so because I was still sleepy, as a result of not having enough sleep, it was my first time of frying doughnuts, and so a few times, the first doughnuts I fried turned white and black, instead of all golden brown, and also maybe because I overheated the oil. But the rest of those I fried afterward turned perfect until I was done frying all. And so Mom took those few days' mistakes seriously out of depression and frustration, and she yelled at me and whined about it for a while, that she didn't have any help in providing for us and all items she sold, including the doughnuts' ingredients, bought them in credits to pay later, and so I should put an end to my carelessness. And so in fact, I didn't take her sudden-change of behaviors well at all, because I found it hard to understand why she also had to yell and whine about my little mistakes, since I was still recovering from all the bad things that happened to me, and so I was sad for a while, and what embarrassed me most was that Mrs. Amegachie and his two nephews of my age group lived in the same house. But I tried my best to correct my mistakes to prevent those doughnuts from burning, and I also obeyed her instructions, and then all those things stopped late, and so though Adzoa wasn't told to try to fry doughnuts, she swept the whole sandy big compound with a broom, and she bathed and dressed up in her uniform, and then Mom counted some doughnuts in a medium-sized tray, and she carried it and followed our neighbor who sells "akasa" (which means *porridge* in Ada language), and they went from home to home to sell. And so as soon as I finished frying them, around 6:00 a.m., I packed everything in haste to the other side of the compound, to be washed later after school, then I poured water on the firewood, and

I went straight to bathe and all dressed up in my uniforms, and by then Adzoa returned back with an empty tray, and she accounted for the doughnuts she sold, and then we had breakfast. Together, Mom gave us money to buy food break periods, and then we left for school.

Mom had customers who came to buy the doughnuts in big quantities in basins, and they sent them to the beachside and sold to the fishermen, and Mom gave those women interest on a certain number of doughnuts they bought as their pay. And one more thing, Mom changed a bit in sharing some of the chores with Adzoa, unlike those days in Accra, though I did more chores than her, and Mom also waited for me to return back home in the afternoons and evenings to cook before we all eat, instead of her doing nothing really at home, unless she was craving for fresh fish and shrimp in okro soup, and then she prepared that herself as a surprise for lunch, but I still had to prepare cassava dough banku to serve with that. And so years passed by, and Dad refused to pay Mom in installments of the car he sold, and so a couple of times, Mom told me to write letters she dictated to Dad in insulting manner and with threats, because if only Dad was kind enough to pay the money, Mom wouldn't have been buying things on credit to sell, since they cost more than buying with cash. But my great-grandmother told me when I was little at Lolonya, "Whenever you are sent with insulting words, and you say it exactly to the person, it means you rather insulted the person." And so I actually couldn't use those words in the letters, but I wrote them in polite words, and then I mailed them through his police address, and I used my school address in case he would reply, but he never replied or came to visit us even once. Mom was still beautiful and classic, and so several men wanted to marry her, but she was still hurting and couldn't trust any man, but one kind guy persistently came after her, and they dated for while. She didn't marry him, because he had two other wives. And during those times, since he was the manager of the post office close to us, he visited Mom when we left for school, and a little after, we returned back home, then he left to his house. And Grandma, who lived just a few yards away, was so supportive, and she provided us with different sorts of fresh and smoked fish and ingredients and fruits like mangoes, oranges, pineapples, etc.

on market days' early evenings. When she finished selling smoked fish, what I liked most were doughnuts prepared like a human shape. And also we couldn't visit Grandma frequently because of chores and school, and so she rather came to visit, especially on Saturdays when we pounded fufu with peanut butter soup.

On Saturdays too, Mom didn't let us rest or play a little after chores; we had to focus on math and English homework and poems and Bible verses in the book of Psalms to learn and to recite on Mondays, but if there were leftover doughnuts, then Adzoa had to carry it, and if not, then she had to carry aluminum cooking pots in a basin, and I carried either cosmetics or china plates in basins, and then we left home with the neighbors' kids, and we walked miles away from village to village, like Otrokpe, Ocansey kope, and Pute, to sell for the villages in their houses. And so Mom gave us a fixed price to sell on each item, and because of my smartness, whenever we arrived in a house with many women and asked for prices, I mentioned higher prices on the items, and then I bargained with them until we agreed on a certain amount of money. They paid in cash, and at the end of the the day, on our way home, we sat down to rest, and I checked all the items we sold, and then I dedicated the exact money we were supposed to give Mom, and then we gained some profits because of the bargains instead of just telling them the actual prices, and so Adzoa and I shared the money right there, and we kept it to buying little things like panties and other stuff we needed on market days, and to me, that was also a relief to Mom. And then I gave Mom the rest of the money, and she checked all items we brought back home. And as usual, she was like, "No problem at all. Just keep one time, when we were on a long vacation in August, which was Ga Homowo festivities, and Adzoa and I asked permission from Mom to go to Accra to visit Dad and to give him lists of things we needed for school, especially our school uniforms, sandals, new clothes, and shoes for church and Christmas, which was a few months away, and also to be able to go to the Homowo festival. Mom wasn't sure if Dad would provide us with that, but we convinced her that maybe he would feel a little guilty about not supporting us and provide us with those needs. And so she gave us lorry fair, and then we packed a few things and left to Accra and went to Labadi in the family house to look for him, and we were told he was living a few blocks away with another woman called Helen. He lied to me years ago that she was a flight attendant, but she was rather an akpeteshie bartender in a small bar at Chorkor, which is a coastal town after Accra. We located Dad and his new wife, Ellen, in a rented single room, with a small porch where she cooked, though Dad was still in the police service as the same motorcycle rider, and according to him, he and a couple of his coleagues made more money from those who smuggled cloths and other things, through bush way, because they didn't want to pay duties on them at the broader. And so they received bribes and expensive Dutch wax cloths from them, and when I gave him the lists we had, I also reminded him not to disappoint us, in order for Mom to freak out, and as usual, he laughed, and he told us that it wasn't a problem at all but that he would make sure we had everything we needed before we returned back to Ada Foah. And so Helen wasn't working, and she tried to be nice to us, and she fed us well, and since she cooked different dishes in a week, I helped her with cooking, filling her barrel with water, and Adzoa also washed the dishes, and she also cleaned. During the Homowo festival, we stepped out to watch a little bit because it was Adzoa's first time witnessing the festival. We returned back because of the huggers, and so being away from Mom was a good break for especially me because of those tough chores and because I didn't trust Dad, so I reminded him every day after work about those items we needed, and he kept saying that he would definitely buy us everything and be spending money to take with us, and I also begged Helen to talk to Dad to buy us those things.

In two weeks, it was time to leave, I reminded him again, and he said the same thing. I even told him to give me the money to go buy them at Accra since I had the listed items, and he told me not to worry. Just two days before we were to leave, we haven't seen anything yet, and I asked him about it, and then he told me the same story I heard from him a couple of years ago about the money he was expecting from somewhere else. He was finally disappointed, and so for that reason, he couldn't get us the listed items we needed, but he had only six yards of cloths to take with us and a lorry fare to return back to Ada Foah. And so I was shocked, speechless for a while before I asked him, "What am I supposed to tell Mom?" She knew this was what would happen, and she tried to discourage us from coming over, but I persuaded her, and now I didn't know how to face her. Aside from his rejection toward me after he dumped me at Labadi, he also disappointed me, and I couldn't go to boarding school as a result of that—and now this. I instantly realized that he wasn't the good, caring, loving dad and husband I thought he was when we were little, but he was a fake. And so Adzoa and I were crying, and Helen said nothing to encourage him to at least give us money to buy a couple of our needs, and so the next morning, he gave us the cloths and the lorry fare like he said but nothing else, and though we arrived at Ada Foah safely, facing Mom wasn't easy for us because of how I confidently told her that we would return back with our needs in order for her to be a little relieved. Mom was so mad at Dad, especially about Helen, his new wife, who wasn't working but was provided with everything and also was not being supportive to us, and then she warned us not to go to Dad's place anymore on vacations and that rather we should help her out by hawking to sell her stuff in order to continue providing for us. And so I agreed with her, and so since then, as a fourteen-year-old child, I pretended to have no dad but had only Mom, and if he was a super dad, then he should come looking for us. And so we continued helping Mom in the best way we can with no complaints, and on Saturdays, as usual, we walked from village to village and from house to house to sell, and because we prayed before leaving home, we made good sales, and the more we sold them, the more profits we had to buy the petty things we needed. And so on Sundays, early mornings, I woke up, and I washed Mom's and my clothes, and I added cooked starch to her cloths and sheets like she wanted, and I also started adding starch to my school uniforms, house and church clothes, so they should look stiff and shiny when I ironed them, which was fashionable in those days. When I was back from church in the afternoon, I prepared fermented cassava dough called "agblemaku" or dried cassava powder called "konkonteku," which is the Adas favorite food, and we normally had a small amount of hot peppers, onions, salt, and more tomatoes, and we grind in earthenware bowl called "kan," in Ga and Ada languages, and the locally made wooden ladle, which is used to grind the ingredients together in the "kan," which is called "tsi" in Ada language and "ato" in Ga language.

After I grinded them together, I then added either smoked fish, grilled fish, fried fish, or grilled salted tilapia called koobi in the most Ghana languages. And then Mom, Adzoa, and I sat around the same medium-sized table with stools, and we ate with our hands. And then I had to prepare the dinner of Mom's choice, and after we had dinner, I ironed both Mom's and my cloths, sheets, and clothes with box iron, since they weren't electric, and to make it a little easier for me, I borrowed a neighbor's box iron, and I added to Mom's, so if one fire turned cold, I then used the reserved hot iron, and at the same time, I set another fire on the charcoal pot, and so I kept on switching irons until I finished everything. During those hours of ironing, as usual, I studied at the same time with my exercise books by my side and homework, and when I was in form 2, we were given Mark Anthony's speech, which was my favorite among the poems ever given to us. And the first sentence was, "Friends, Romans, countrymen, lend me your ears." I tried to keep wake until I learned the whole speech, and I recited it the next day on Monday in the classroom, and I was clapped for, because few students didn't come to school as a result of that, and even though some of them came, they couldn't finish reciting it and were lashed because of that. And I felt so excited and felt in love with that speech since. And so though years had passed by, since Odoi died, l thought my American dream was over, but no matter how much I tried to forget him and my dreams, I couldn't, but rather I cried whenever I was sent out by myself, and I wished he was still alive to let my dreams come to reality, and then one Saturday early evening, when we went to collect ingredients from Grandma in the market, I was on my way home, walking in between bushes, and I was so emotional and asked God, "And so does it mean I won't be going to America again, since Odoi is dead?" And then I heard a voice inside me that repeatedly told me not to worry about it, because someday, I would actually go America and achieve my dreams. And because I doubted that, I asked myself multiple times,

"How am I going to be able to go to America?" And that would happen, maybe in my dreams or my thinking, because none of my family members have a desire for traveling, especially America, aside from him. And so one more thing I took after Mom, apart from her beauty, smartness, being hardworking and a great cook, I also had her neatness and her cleanliness, and that made me so unique, especially with my hips, and Mom also didn't mind if we wear her roll deodorant for our armpits to smell good and to stop perspiration, as well as her designer perfumes to school too.

Boys from our school and neighborhood wanted me to be their girlfriend, but I wasn't ready for any relationship yet. Rather, one of my principles was marriage before sex. Adzoa already had a boyfriend, but Mom didn't know about it. Even one time Mr. Amegatse, who was our form 3 teacher, a married man with kids, told me that he was walking me home because he was going to the same direction, and as he kept on praising me for my great performances in class, he changed the subject by asking me if I had a boyfriend. And so I told him, "Nope," but I had a crush on one of the form 4 students called Ebennezer Kugblenu, who liked me and wanted me to be his girlfriend, and then he tried to discourage me by telling me that he wasn't serious about girls and he was a womanizer and he didn't actually know who his real dad was, so he would end up breaking my heart. And then he told me that he wanted to be in a relationship with me because he liked me and that if I needed something, I shouldn't hesitate to ask him.

I didn't have any respect for him since then in the class, and I stopped smiling back at him like I used to because such teachers are disgraceful to society. I kept it a secret from Mom and Adzoa because Mom wouldn't mind to attack and disgrace him in front of the students, and I didn't want that to happen, since he would victimize me in class. And something else Grandma repeatedly says, since she became a Christian, and it can't leave my mind, was, though Christians have God in Trinity, which is the Father, Son, and the Holy Spirit, she served over sixty voodoos at once for over three decades, and she learned that a lot of people are afraid of fetish priests, so they are well with respect and dignity, because they think, if they take them for granted, they will destroy them and their families. And rather mostly, people take advantage of some men and women of God and Christians, and they disrespect them; they steal from them and treat them so badly without thinking, because they know that God is merciful and compassionate. And so serving God seems to be easier like some pastors say in their sermons, but it's complicated than serving voodoos.

Grandma also shared a story about her and a couple of friends when they were fetish priests in their late teens, and during those days, there weren't trucks available, so they walked many miles away to sell different kinds food from village to village, in their houses, and she carried a big basket full of smoked fish, with a wooden tray on top, and the other friends carried fried fish and "abolo," which is also the Adas favorite food, prepared with corn kernels, sugar, and salt. And they walked barefoot on the hot weather, and so if they ran out of homemade food and water, they carried with them, and they needed something deliciously prepared apart from abolo and fried fish, with hot peppers, they carried. Then before they approached the next village, Grandma had an idea to trick those villages for them to be treated exceptionally. Because those villagers were pagans, voodoo followers, and fetish priests, Grandma took off her blouse, and with her breasts on, she unbraided her Afro hair, and she powdered her face with "ayilo," like a crown, and then she started singing fetish songs, and so as soon as they entered the village, her basket of fish was lifted off her head by her friends, and Grandma would pretend to be in motion, and she moves here and there. And then they were surrounded by the villagers, who were willing to do anything for them, because they thought that their voodoos have sent other fetish priests to visit them and to bring them good luck, and so someone would volunteer to send them to their house, and there when Grandma sat down, she washed her face, and then she pretended nothing happened, and then the house owner prepared food with either slaughtered chicken or duck, and they were served with konkonteku to eat, and they were given reserved rainwater to drink instead of well water the villagers had. And then they bathed, and they were offered to sleep in the house owner's bed, and she rather went to sleep with her children on the mat on the floor in the other room. And so the next morning, they bathed, and they had good breakfast like porridge sugar, served with bread and boiled eggs, and then Grandma and her friends sold the rest of their food to the villagers, and then, before they left the village, their water bottles were filled with rainwater, and they had leftover food to take with them to eat on the way, and they walked back home, with great joy, because their tricks worked. And so Grandma's story gave me confirmation of some of the fetish priests' crafty behaviors, and they rather treated fairly. And Grandma also told me that she was sent to different bushes and she was shown different kinds of fresh herbs for healing, purifying and poisonous ones too, but because she became Christian, she didn't want to use herbs in any way, since mentally, she would feel like she was still a fetish priest.

Though Grandma helped us with groceries, Adzoa and I also helped Mom to continue to provide for us, because aside from God, she was all we had, but her trade wasn't going on well, since the villagers owed her a lot of money, and they gave excuses that their sales weren't going on well whenever we went to the market to collect the money, and some of them also didn't show up at all. And so it came to a point where Mom couldn't provide simple things like magazines called *Challenge*, which was educational, text or exercise books for us, though we were given some by the school district, but we weren't provided with all. And most times, as a child, I asked myself, "And so what does Mom do with those many coins we counted each market days for her?" And also Mom's whole mood changed, and she was depressed more than ever, and there I knew something was wrong with Mom, but I couldn't ask her because she didn't talk to us about her private issues, and we moved out from Salem We to a chamber and hall in a compound fenced home, which was spacious enough for us, and she made new friends there, but she pretended to be the rich, classic woman with no problems at all. One Saturday afternoon, a stranger walked inside the house, and she said in an angry tone that she was looking for Christie, and I told her she was my mom but that she wasn't around, because she stepped outside since morning, and she said, "Well, don't worry about me, but I will sit and wait for her." And then she sat down on a bench outside, not knowing Mom overheard us, and so her heart was beating so fast when I went to the bedroom to tell her about that woman, and so I saw Mom jump through the window, and I didn't know how she did it, but she climbed about eight-foot-tall cement blocks, unplastered walls, and she jumped out of the house. And in fact, I was shocked and so worried that she might get hurt badly, till I heard her voice, and she told me she was at Grandma's and so I should notify her as soon as the woman leaves. And though I was a little calmer, I wondered, *What if she broke her legs and her neck bones?* She could have been dead, and so for her to survive was divine intervention, and I thanked God for that, then I figured out that she owed the woman a lot of money, which she couldn't pay. And so the woman waited, until late evening, and still she didn't see Mom walking in, and she didn't hear me talking to anyone in the room, but rather I was preparing dinner, and then she stood up, and she left a serious message to tell Mom that if she refused to pay money she owed, then next time she comes over, she would fully prepare with food and pillow to sleep on the bench outside and wait until she arrived from wherever she went. And so after the woman left, I was emotional, sad, and I felt sorry for Mom with what she was going through, all because of Dad's betrayal and heartlessness toward Mom, Adzoa, and I; else we would be at Accra, where Mom would be doing her chop bar business that gave her enough money, and even at Ada Foah. If he was supporting us, things would have been different. And so that lady waited for hours till evening, and when still no sign of Mom but I was the only one who stepped in and out of the room, and so I started cooking dinner and then eventually she stood up, and she left serious message that I should tell Mom that if that debt wasn't paid then in her next time visit, she will sleep over by bringing along her own pillow and mat, and she won't leave this time till she had her money back before she walked out.

After I finished preparing the dinner, I then walked in the darkness for about one quarter of a mile to Grandma's, and I whispered to Mom that the debt collector was gone, and so we said goodbye to Grandma, and we left, and so on our way back home, Mom told me about her difficulties, which I already figured out myself, and she thanked me for being so smart enough, saying that she wasn't in the house when the woman asked me about her, but if it were to be Adzoa, she would have welcomed her to the living room, and she would call her that she had a visitor, because she wasn't all that smart and also had a loose mouth. And so Grandma also started supporting us financially also because things were getting worse with Mom's work, and so her depression, stress, and anxiety worsened, and then she had malaria fever, and she went to the clinic, and she was treated with malaria drugs, but it didn't work; rather, she continued having headaches and weaknesses, and so she returned back again to see the doctor, but no tests were done on her to see the actual illness, and all those while she had been going to church, and the pastor prayed for her, and things remained the same.

She was persuaded to see a particular herbalist because maybe it was spiritual attack, and that herbalist came to the house to see Mom in the living room, and he was so crafty, also confirmed it was a spiritual attack called "dadikojo" in the Ada language, and it means that spiritual bad things like broken pieces, bottles, and needles were placed in her blood, and so it moves in her body and causes, headaches, body and bone pains, and also weakness, then he asked Mom to provide a bunch of things like goat with ingredients and two bottles of schnapps and a fixed amount of money, but she should give him money for those items to buy everything himself to perform some rituals and she would be well in no time. And so if Mom were to be in her right mind, she would have known that was all lies and to trust God only, but sometimes in situations like that, you get confused, and so because of that, Mom borrowed money, and she gave it to that crafty herbalist, and so first he brought fresh herbs for Mom to put in a small bowl, and she added water to it and covered it up, so whenever she was ready to bathe, she should add a small amount of that water to the water in her bucket and bath.

The second unbelievable thing he did two times in a week during evening hours was that (I had no idea how he did that) he gave Mom a small cut in her body parts with a sharp razor like in the chest, neck bone, upper back, elbows, and her ankles, and he sucked a little blood from that part of her body, and he spat the blood mixed in pieces of broken bottles in Mom's chamber pot, and then he would show it to Mom, Adzoa, and me that all those came from Mom's body. And thereafter, he used the black powder he brought from home and applied it on the wounds, and so he made Mom believe that those broken pieces of bottles came from her body, but her illness didn't change a little because she was still in pain, and she cried a lot, especially at midnight, and I cried too. I was also worried that something bad could happen to her.

Later on, we found out that those pieces of broken bottles were already in his mouth before he even placed his mouth on Mom's cut part, and so it was a trick to get money from Mom, because how can someone spiritually place those things in a human body? And if he was telling the truth, why didn't Mom get better? And to be honest with you, this "dadikojo" trick still exists in some parts of Ghana. And so the herbalist disappeared, because he didn't do anything to help Mom, and so Mom was sent to Grandma's relative, who is a prophetess called Maami, like Mom, and she prayed, and Grandma fastened, and she also told Grandma to buy Florida water perfume and olive oil, and she added a small amount of Florida water perfume, and she mixed them together in a bottle for Mom to rub her body with after she blessed the water, and she added a small amount of Florida water to bathe. And so she stayed in her house, and she slept in her prayer room for weeks, but Mom didn't get better, and she was still weaker, and she walked slowly with a stick, instead of Maami asking Mom to see a doctor, and at the same time, she would be praying for her. And so someone also told Grandma that a most powerful prophetess was at Krobo Odumase, a town in the eastern region of Ghana, and Mom would be healed just like that, so Grandma and Mom went right away, because Grandma was so concerned, wanted her to get better, and she always says Mom should live long and healthy enough to bury her, but rather she buried a son just a couple of years ago. And so we lived in the same house Mom left us, with not enough money, and so Adzoa and I tried to survive on it, and sometimes the neighbors gave us some leftovers, and so I saved the lorry fare no matter what in order for us to get there immediately after school vacation, but my main concern, which stressed me out more, was that all my life, up to in my middle teens, I haven't really spent much time with Mom or Grandma, and now that we were united and Mom promised not to leave me again, she wasn't getting better. It was so overwhelming for me.

We left Ada Foah on the same day after vacation, and I had the address written down before they left, and so we took two different trucks, and thankfully, we arrived at Krobo Odumasi, and so when we asked for Prophetess Martha, we were directed to her house, and so we arrived at her self-contained house, with a couple of canopies fixed and long benches packed under the canopies for church services. And so when I mentioned Mom's name, we were shown where Prophetess Martha's patients lived, and it wasn't too far, but it was on top of the hill in a few brick-built small rooms, with two patients in a room, and the ground wasn't cemented, and they slept on a mattress made out of local dried grass called "tsatsa" in the Ada language with sheets and pillows on it. So Grandma and Mom were excited to see us, just like us too, but their living standards were too poor and filthy. Mom tried to stay strong for us not to worry about her, but I knew that nothing changed toward her healing, but she was still suffering and in pain, and she was still walking slowly with sticks if she had to bathe, but she had feces in the chamber pot, and Grandma poured them in a scary manhole toilet coupled with thick sticks that were just placed on the hole, and the feces were covered with worms and flies, and those same flies stepped in the food they ate. I was so scared when I had to use it, and I asked myself, "What if the stick broke and I fell in this deep hole?" Then that will be the end of me, because the toilet was in the bush and there wasn't even a ladder around for someone to help me or anyone get out of that hole. And so part of Odumasi I saw was filled with gravels, mountains, hills, and also mango trees at every corner and filled with bats, and they made most noises, especially in the middle of the night during mango seasons. And some of the patients' families, Grandma, and I went mango hunting with baskets in the middle of the night, and those mangoes were so ripe, and they fell under the trees on the grounds, and so with our local lamps, we checked if those bats had eaten part of them before we threw them in the baskets, and then we carried them home, and in the mornings, Grandma carried them to the market to sell, and she bought food with the money. And sometimes too Grandma's other relatives came over with provisions and money to support them. And also the tough part for Mom and te other patients was climbing the hill up and down to morning devotion, Wednesday and Friday evening church, also Sunday church, and much more every end-of-the-month vigils, and other people all over were invited. They kept awake, and they prayed for miracles, which I didn't see happen because Mom wasn't getting better and also none of those patients, according to Grandma. And Grandma had extra strength to carry Mom on her to church and back home, and during services, I heard Mom speak in real tongues, not what she learned and recited, and that gave me hope that God would work through her to get better. And so since I was not used doing nothing, I asked Mom permission to go help Prophetess Martha with chores, and so I helped her maid to prepare light soup with fresh fish, served with fufu, and so after we cleaned dishes, I shared the food I was given with my family. And one time, Adzoa and I accompanied a few of Martha's helpers to the farms on the mountaintop, four miles away to harvest food ingredients like cassava, corn, tomatoes, onions, peppers, etc. in baskets, and we carried them on our heads back home, and we were so tired, and there were some to take with us to live on for a couple of days. And so in few days for school reopening, Adzoa decided to stay with Mom and Grandma because she was the lazy type who couldn't live with someone else aside from Mom, but I decided to return back and complete my form 4 education at Ada Foah, and it didn't matter whom I lived with because there wasn't any tough task I couldn't face.

And so in a couple of days for me to return back to Ada Foah, the only relative of Grandma wanted me to stay with Prophetess Maami, also known as Kakinye. Kaki is her older daughter's name, and "nye" means "Mom" in the Ada language. And so leaving Mom in such condition was a sad moment for me, but I had go to continue my education, because I was in form 3 in my last semester and going to form 4, and Mom also tried to encourage both of us to leave, since she valued education, and she repeatedly told us that if she didn't go to school, we should, for her to be a proud mother. And so Mom told me to hang in there but that she would be back home sooner than I thought, because Adzoa insisted she wanted to stay, and so I left the next alone and so sad back to Ada Foah, thankfully. And one more thing, those days, I had much respect for every man or woman of God, for the fact that they preach the words of God and they also acted so perfectly, and so I believe that doing anything for them, God will bless me, multiple times. I told Kakinye that Grandma said I should stay with her. She was living in her rich younger sister's one-storey building, and she had the first floor, which had three bedrooms, empty storage, bathroom, separate latrine toilet, and a hallway for herself and her two daughters. And in the next compound house, she rented three rooms, and two rooms were for her maids, and the other was her kitchen, and her rich sister lived in Accra Dansoman in her own double-story building, and she sold cloths in large quantities for retailers because she was the only supplier and distributor of Akosombo and Tema Textiles Limited, so she really supported Kakinye financially, and Kakinye also had a shed at Ada Foah market, and her maids sold her sugar and other things on market days. Kakinye had a husband as a pharmacist, who lived a mile away in his own one-plot fenced house with his other wife and young kids, and his phamarcy store was right in front of his house, and he sold different kinds of malaria drugs, pain pills, etc., and he had a small room where he caused abortion, and he charged money for it, and every day Kakinye's maid cooked and sent it to his husband, and he also came over to Kakinye's place. And so financially, Kakinye had no problem at all, but what she told me was that if I wanted to stay with her, then I had to sleep on the hallway, but she wouldn't give any money for school or anything else, no breakfast, but if any homemade food was available, then I would eat. And so I smiled at her and said, "No problem at all," and so I went to our rented house to pick my personal effects, and then with help from neighbors, I moved all our belongings on pushing a big truck to Grandma's place, since she didn't pay rent.

I returned with my stuff in a basket and my books too back to Kakinye's house, and she told me to keep them in the storage. Her daughter Kaki stole money from her mother and her dad for her boyfriend, and so Kakinye kept her bedroom door locked at all times, and she had her keys tied on a little rope on her waist so she didn't lose it. And one disgusting thing about Kaki was that she still peed in her mat at the age of sixteen, at all times, in the middle of the night, and she kept it well from everyone except me, because I woke as early as 4:00 a.m. when she also woke up, and she sent her mat, sheets, and cloths to the balcony. She already had buckets of water fetched from the well house. And then she washed them, rinsed, and dried on old woods at the backyard, instead of the drying line, and then she returned back to the room and mopped the floor with soapy water, and she disinfected with Pine Sol, and she opened both hallway doors to bring in fresh air to the house; that was the only chore she did. I really felt sorry for her because she had a huge problem, and she refused to share with her family and get help, and there I realized that even rich people also faced challenges in different ways, and so I am not in this alone, and so I kept her secret safe, though she didn't ask to because she was too embarrassed.

I wondered why Kakinye, who claimed to be a woman of God who had no issues with money, refused to help me financially, and she knew what was going on in my life, but I tried my best to respect and obey her instructions, and so each early morning, I sent my mat, cloths, and pillows to the storage room, then I cleaned all the hallway, the other rooms, including her bathroom because she gave me the keys. But something unusual happened in her room since day one when I started cleaning, and that was, whenever I entered her bedroom, big notes of money were spread all over the floor and also on her bed too, and she normally left home as soon as she handed me her keys, and she was all dressed up, and for real, it didn't occur to me it was a setup to test me if I was a thief. And so what I rather asked myself was, "Why is Maami so careless that she leaves money on the floor?" And then I picked those notes on the floor, and I arranged them together with those on the bed, then I left all right on the bed. I cleaned in haste, but thank God, it never occurred to me to steal

149

from her, because she refused to give me spending money, and when I was done, I returned back the keys to her, since I didn't keep them long. I bathed in the next house in a nasty bathroom fixed with palm branches on the sandy ground with a medium-sized rock in the middle to stand on, exactly like Lolonyah. When I was ready for school, I rushed to the kitchen to heat leftover soup, with the leftover cold agblemaku I saved from dinner, which I prepared the previous night, and I ate my breakfast before going to school, which, luckily, was five minutes away, and also because I like cooked beans, with palm oil inside and served with ripe fried plantains during breaks, and I didn't have money anymore to buy, and it stresses me out especially when my mates bought and they were eating. I mostly made friends with boys in my class than the girls, because they gossip, and since vernacular was strictly prohibited from school by Master Ocansey and anybody reported for speaking would be lashed, and I took advantage of that, and those boys who liked speaking vernacular, I threatened them to tell Master Ocansey about it. And then they begged me, so I told them that if they buy me beans and fried plantains, then I would keep my mouth shut, so actually, they bought me what I wanted each break at 10:00 a.m., so I was glad about it, and I told myself, *This is better than begging directly.* And so every evening I fetched well water in her containers and buckets in her house to drink and bathe, because there was no tap water, and we used kerosene lamps since there was no electricity, and on Saturdays I washed the clothes of Maami, her six-year-old daughter, and her two maids and their kids and also mine as usual, though her maids didn't ask me to wash them, but I deliberately asked them, just trying to kind. And then on Sundays, after church, when I was done cooking, I ironed her starch cloths, like Mom's, before I also ironed my school uniforms, and so I used the same strategy, to learn at the same time, whether cooking, washing, or ironing. And so since working hard is part of me, and also since Maami didn't abuse me in any way, I prepared much more plenty agblemaku or konkonteku every day, and the maids and I ate at the same table, and I even saved leftovers, so I had a belly full at all times, and so I gained a little weight for that reason. And I was more beautiful, with my shaped body, than before, and so Maami's womanizer husband took advantage of me, and he tried to rape me one time when I was sent to give him his dinner. And what happened was that he told me to send his food to the bedroom instead of his living room, where he had a medium-sized table he could eat on, and I would have naively listened out of respect, but thank God, I learned that he was a womanizer who took advantage of some Ada Secondary School students who got pregnant because of unprotective sex when they came over for abortions. He charged them big money, but he had sex with them before he caused the abortions. And because of that, I boldly told him "no" in a rush, and I placed the food at the usual place, and I ran out of the house, so scared and shaking, and I was grateful that man was not able to destroy my life. And so I was sad, and I felt exposed to danger, but I couldn't tell Maami or anyone about it because that might break their marriage, and so I came with different excuses, like my headaches, my legs hurts, etc., and I stopped sending him dinner, and so rather one of her maids did.

I was used to studying when lying in a mat and with a kerosene lamp close to my pillow, out of exhaustion from chores and school activities. One day I slept without noticing that instead of me pushing the lamp away from the the pillow like I used to, I felt sharp pains on the other side of my cheek, and when I opened my eyes, I saw the lamp on the side of my cheek. I panicked and pushed the lamp off my cheek, and the lampshade broke, and my whole hair and the pillow were soaked with kerosene, and so I moved everything to the backyard, and I quickly stepped out to the next house to bathe with soap, especially my hair, multiple times before I wiped myself, and then I changed to new clothes, and I mopped the floor, and I opened both hallway doors for the kerosene scent to leave the hallway before daybreak. By the grace of God, I didn't have serious burns when I looked at my face in the guest room dressing mirror. I used to rest of my time to pray in the prayer room and to thank God for saving my life, and in the morning people were amazed about what happened to me, and I had a slight burn, because a lot of people completely burned before they were found, some died, and some were disfigured for the rest of their lives.

Since I went to stay with Maami, I was more spiritual than her, from my observations of how her hope and trust were in her rich sister and her husband, who provided her and her children with all needs, and so she wasn't so prayerful like me, with God being my only dependence, and so I am prayerful, especially in the middle of the night, and I sometimes fasted, and I prayed for Mom too always, and I believed in him, trusted him, and kept him completely, because, though I was born and raised among voodoos, I was smart to choose him over them, and I never regretted a little bit, since no matter how much challenges I have been through, he keeps on protecting and providing for me. Since Maami claimed to be a prophetess, sometimes people came to her for healing and other problems, and I was the only one she chose to set charcoal fire, and then I poured it in an empty Milo can, with holes drilled underneath and a little metal wire attached as a handle, to prevent me from burning. And then I poured a small amount of dried skins from different trees and some herbs called incense, or "ohe" in the Ada language. In her little prayer room, she had a medium-sized table, covered with white cloths; she had bottles of Florida perfume, olive, a candle stand with lighted candles, a Bible on the table, two benches too, and then a gallon of water to bless for the patients. The patients also had a bucket of water to bathe afterward, and when I shook the Milo can, the room was filled with smoke and strong wired scent at the same time, and before she started praying, she told me to pray too, and to be honest with you, sometimes I felt suffocated, and I can imagine those patients did feel the same, and Maami also, because she stepped out for a while and returned back when the room turned so foggy from of the smoke.

None of those patients had miracle healing, she said, like Mom, and some self-claimed prophetess and prophets called those rituals as points of contacts, in order to increase the patient's faith in God and to be healed. One day, Maami's fetish elderly mother came to visit from another village, and she had her things packed in a medium-sized plastic bucket, and her money was tied in her white handkerchief, and she placed it in the bucket. Her things were in Maami's room, though she spent the night in the guest room, and as usual, I cleaned all the rooms, including Maami's bedroom, and I got ready for school. During my absence, her mother went through her things and changed her cloths after she bathed, and she mistakenly dropped her handkerchief with her money on the floor, and she placed the bucket on it. And so later, when she went back to pick her money, she found out that her money was not in the bucket, so she told Maami, and she also looked inside, but the money wasn't there, then she jumped to the conclusion that I took her handkerchief with her whole money. But Maami told her mother that they should take their time to search for the missing money before I returned home in the afternoon, because I haven't touched her money. Her mother asked her why she was so sure I didn't steal the money, since she couldn't trust her own daughter with money. Then she told her how she was trapping me with money on her bedroom and I never stole a penny from it, though she didn't give me money for school. And then both of them started looking through things in the room, and then when Maami lifted up her bucket, she found the handkerchief containing her money. When she counted it, nothing was missing from the money, and so her mom was so shocked and told Maami that I am an extraordinary person. Because if I returned before the money was found, she might think I returned it back, and so Maami kept on laughing at me when I returned back to school, and I smiled back at her, though it was unusual, but I couldn't ask why she laughed at me.

After I had lunch with her maids, I went to let her know I was going to school, and then she asked me to sit down and told me everything, and in fact, I was shocked, because I had no idea it was a trap, but I was glad to be saved from it, and she told me to continue being who I am and I would be richly blessed someday. And so I thanked her, and her mother liked me since then, and she invited us to her village one weekend, about six miles away, and I didn't want to go because she was a fetish priest and I didn't want to go close to those voodoos again, and so I decided to give Maami a reasonable excuse to stay. But on the same morning, her womanizer husband came around, and we bumped into each other at the entrance of the house, and he smiled at me and told me in the Ada language, "You child, I will rape you at the least chance I get." And I mean, he told me point-blank before he entered the house when I was on my way out, and I was so scared more than ever. I had a boyfriend, but we hadn't kissed before, and if this filthy middle-aged man happened to rape me as a virgin, I will be hurt for the rest of my life, when I think about it. And so I decided to go with Maami rather that day, because he would definitely know where her wife might be that weekend, and Kaki would spend the night with her boyfriend, since her mom wouldn't be available, and since he had the spare keys to the house, he might come around to open the main door and rape me in the hallway where I sleep and threaten me to keep quiet; else her wife would get rid of me from the house.

We left that Friday afternoon, and we took a truck, and we got dropped off at some point, and then we sat in a rented small canoe on a river, a couple of miles to that small village surrounding the river and bush, and so Maami, her six-year-old child, and I spent the night in one room, since she had two and a hallway, a separate kitchen, and a bathroom, but we had feces in the bush. And so I helped her mother cook, since she wanted us to eat her homemade food, and so I took that weekend as my break from tough chores, and so we returned back home on a Sunday morning. And so for different reasons, when I went to form 4 in my first semester, as a smart kid, humble, respectful, and a good listener, and also as a result of my great academic performances, I was made the school girl's prefect, which was unbelievable, and it really blew my mind away, because of those poor grades I had previously. That nearly made me quit school, and after a long persistence, I turned out to be a genius. And so I was thankful to God for everything, and that position came with huge responsibilities, because I had to be at school by 6:00 a.m., since I had keys to forms 3 and 4, including Mr Ocansey's office, and I cleaned and arranged all kinds of books and files and dusted off the dust before he came around at 7:00 a.m. I made the compound, bathroom and toilets well cleaned, and I was told to let some students secretly write names of vernacular speakers, and they were being punished by the teachers at assembly to encourage English speaking, rather. Because of Mr. Ocansey's bad behavior toward the students, the students saw him like a kind of beast, and I was the spokesperson in case girls needed something from him, and there were so many sacrifices and insults from some of the students. Some girls were jealous of my position, and they wished to be girls-school prefect, but they didn't have what it takes to qualify for that. It wasn't an easy task for me because of the hard work involved in the school and also chores I had at home, but being the whole girls-school prefect was a great deal those days, and I was honored and grateful to God for me to have that position, which I will cherish for the rest of my life.

4

CHAPTER

I was in school, and I was doing good job in my new position with gladness and hope that no matter how tough the challenges were, I would complete form 4 and be a seamstress, for Mom to be proud of me, because that was what she wanted me to be, and that was common in those days, and parents decide their kids' career against their will, and if you refuse, then they disowned you.

With a couple of weeks, before the end of the first semester, I had a message that Mom was transferred to the Tema General Hospital, which is part of the Greater Accra Region, because Prophetess Martha and her family just disappeared and she left her patients without saying anything to them. Though I was sad and emotional about Mom's situation, I was also angry for the fact that Martha, who claimed to be a woman of God and a healer, who couldn't even heal Mom or any patient after all those months, didn't even suggest they should see a doctor to be treated, and then she also prayed for them, and rather she used crafty ways to collect money from them, and finally she left them, heartlessly. I was depressed about the sad news, and I kept on praying until the end of the first semester break, and then the next day, I took my few clothes, and I asked Maami lorry fare to Ashaiman, where Grandma's half sister, called Maa as Grandma and also known as Amarkinye. Grandma and Amarkinye had the same father but different mothers, and she lived in the house of her older daughter called Amarki with her other children, who were called Amarkuo and Emma, her daughters and a son called Afohame, his wife, and her grandkids. And they were all traders at Accra Makola Market who sold koobi, or salted tilapias, in large quantities in large baskets for retailers, but Afohame worked as ship cleaner at Tema Harbor, and also Ashaiman is in the Greater Accra Region, and it's a fifteen-minute drive and thirty-nine minutes to walk to the Tema General Hospital. The family of my mom's side, in those days, were so caring and supportive, and when I arrived at Ashaiman, I had warm welcome for the first time. We had good food and loving conversations. They passed good comments about how beautiful I was and all grown since the last time some of them saw me when I was a toddler and so close to evening visiting hours. The whole family members joined Grandma, Adzoa, and me. We walked to the hospital. We all went inside the big ward with the other patients in bed next to one another, and so we went around Mom's bed, and her leg was in stiff thick bandages and hanging. And though I can see from her red eyes that she cried out of pain, she faked a smile, and she talked with us, and she also said that part of her thighs and leg got swollen, but I assumed that she might have fallen from Grandma's back or she tried to walk with her long stick and then she slipped and fell. So for real I felt sorry for Mom, but I was also glad that she was brought to the hospital to be treated to get better, rather than being in Odumasi with that self-claimed prophetess.

And also apart from those of us who came to visit Mom, her extended family from other parts of Accra were also there to support her, and everyone had provisions and money to give her because they knew she needed it, and I was able to meet my other family members and my cousins. And then saying goodbye to Mom after visiting hours, we returned back to Ashaiman, and every evening, we went to visit her, but her condition remained the same. Though x-rays and a couple of tests were done on her, they couldn't see what went wrong except her leg fracture, because in those days there wasn't much technology. And many more doctors really didn't explain more to patients about what was actually going on with them, but all they did was, they focused on their treatments; they prescribed you medications for them to take or shots to be given to them. To be honest with you, that bothered me a lot, not knowing what was wrong with Mom a long time before she hurt her leg, and I felt like they controlled them, and they also owned them, and as a result of that, patients are scared and nervous around most doctors, and they couldn't tell them details about their illnesses. And so Mom told me how she was loved by the nurses rather, and they braided her beautiful hair and then cleaned her wear, and they tried to cheer her up and also some even brought her homemade food to eat. She was in pain, but if she got a little relief from painkillers, she made jokes out of her sense of humor.

There wasn't enough space for Grandma at her sister's place, since they rented a couple of rooms in the house, and so Grandma, Ofliboyo, and Adzoa moved to stay with her young brother who was in agriculture and a retired brigadier called William Dzeagu, and his family lived on the other side of Ashaiman, a mile away from Amarkinye's place. William and his family owned two plots of land, and they built three bedrooms in self-contained house on the other side of the land, and they also had six wooden rooms which they rented for tenants, and so they gave one room for Grandma, Ofliboyo, and Adzoa to live in. I also moved to live with Grandma and the rest of them at William's, and then he started to make comments about me, which weren't funny, in front of her wife, which made her a little bit jealous of me: "Look at those beautiful hips and that well-shaped body of yours. Someday, a stupid person rather would enjoy it." And so I took it as a joke, and I smiled each time, though he wasn't the only one to talk about my beauty, and I realized more how prettier I was. But later on, I didn't like the last sentence of her comments, saying, "Someday a stupid person rather would enjoy it." It wasn't a good thing to wish for your grandchild at all, because everyone wished nothing but the best thing for his or her family, and so instead he should have wished that "someday a great person would rather enjoy it."

He didn't stop those bad comments, and he kept on saying that as soon as he laid his eyes on me, until her wife could not take it anymore, and so she asked him, "Why do you keep on saying that? Do you want to marry her someday yourself?" Maybe she asked him those questions because she thought, since an arranged-marriage system is in Ghana, he might marry also. There is cash-and-carry system in Ghana when it comes to going to hospitals whenever you fall sick, and Mom's families also contributed to pay for all bills, and I needed money to buy a few things to school, and since I had no one to ask, I worked as a salesgirl in a hardware store at the Ashaiman market by the roadside. And in front of the store, both owners, who were couples, had a big wooden box with a cover, which was cemented, including the whole inside of the box, and they sold bottles of sodas like Fanta, Mirinda, and Coca-Cola, and they also had bottles filled with water with caps placed on them, and then they bought big blocks of ice sold in trucks around the market, and then they broke them into medium sizes and then put them inside the box, and they added empty corn kernel sacks and large white plastic bags to cover them before they closed the box. Everything inside the box turned cold for people to buy, drink, and leave the bottles, including water, but if you want to take out, then you need your own cups to pour them inside, unless you have the same bottles for exchange, because those bottles are returned to the factories for refills, and those bottles with water were washed and refilled too. The couples used that box as refrigerator, because in those days, refrigerators were expensive and they couldn't afford it, including a lot of people in the same businesses, and so those blocks of ice sellers too made good money out of that. I sold both hardware items in their store, and at same time, I sold the drinks too, but I was told not to collect money from customers, because the woman sat by the entrance, and so I made sure they paid the exact amount of money to her, and she gave them change if she had to and placed them in paper bags for customers before they leave. And so they made good sales during those periods because I used my sense of humor in convincing customers to buy, and I was respectful too, and so the store owners liked me and wanted me to come by anytime to sell for them, and aside from the sales, I also cooked for them, though it wasn't part of my job, but I told the woman that I would cook for them one time when she was about to prepare food, because they returned home very late, and so they had charcoal pots, cooking pots, plates, etc., and she just brought everything she needed to cook in the market, and so I cooked outside near the store, and they had food before they returned home. And I also had my share of the food before I rushed to the hospital to see Mom. But one time I was slapped in the face when I fought back by another

Ada salesgirl who was there before I came, and she pretended to be nice to me, and when I mentioned her name to Grandma, she told me that her parents were her distant relatives, and so she changed her good moods toward me, and she tried to be mean to me because the store owners liked me more than her because of her disrespectful behavior and she was also a thief, and she was rude to me, and when I got mad, I talked back, then I had that slap from her behind me, so since I was paid and I left, I didn't step my foot there again. And so before the beginning of the second semester, I had to say goodbye to Mom, though I hated to leave, and so I had enough money to buy a few things I needed and some for my lorry fare, and I saved the rest for school. Since I turned girl-school prefect, I stopped tricking the boys from my class for cooked beans and fried plantains, and I would use the money for that. I returned back to Ada, thankfully, to continue my duties in school, and also resumed my house chores and my studying, too, and so I was seventeen years old at that time, and I was still a virgin, who wanted to complete my forms 4 education, and then I learned how to sew and made living out of it and then married before kissing or sex. And that was something the girls from my class disagreed on, and they thought it was bad idea. They had boyfriends, and they already had sex anytime, and even one of our mates my age called Grace had a baby boy from another school before she came to the school, and she was lucky to have her mom to babysit her child who was a few months old. And so the boy I was few months older than, he was a year ahead of me in school, and he was one of the students' substituted teachers who taught us in form 2. He was same height like me, handsome, he had brown skin color, he wore lens glasses, with broad eyes, and actually he looked different from his mates, because he was quiet, humble, and respectful, called Ebennezer Kugblenu, so he was the one I fell in love with for the first time in my life, and I accepted to be his girlfriend as soon as he asked me through a love poem.

That was common in those days when someone loves you. He had to write a sweet love letter expressing his feelings toward you, and then he gave it to a mate to give you, and then after you also reply, you sent it to that same person to deliver it, and those people were called "betweenness," and so since then, we didn't talk, like, face-to-face or walk side by side after school, because it was even against school rules for someone to talk to someone he or she was in a relationship with, because they would be punished if they were be reported. And so some of those love poems were like "from the sugar mountains and across the milky oceans" and on and on, and trust me, after I read those letters, I felt like my world was filled with a sugar mountain and milky ocean, and so for that reason, nothing else matters. Rather I read through multiple times, and I placed it under my pillow before sleeping, and then the next day, I also thought of sweet words to write back to him, and Mom even advised me to wait and get married before sex when I mentioned him to her on the vacation in the hospital. Both Ebennezer and I loved each other, but because of his good behavior, girls gave him scholarships, like gifts, just for him to become their boyfriend, and so he also accepted those gifts and was in relationships with them, and some of them even visited his place, which wasn't fancy but just a small room in the family house, with a student bed, a chair, and a table to study on, and he had protected sex with them, and so when he told me about that, I was a little disappointed in him for being a womanizer, and I wanted to stop that relationship, but his sweet letters telling me that they meant nothing to him, that I was the one he loved, and that we would spend our lives together, also because he was my first love, I couldn't leave him.

He went to Ada Secondary School. After he completed form 4 just a few yards away from the school, we still communicate through letters, and then one time, my best friend Eva stayed late one evening, and we studied in the house, so I went to see her off, and because she and Ebennezer lived close to each other, I was tempted to visit him for the first time, when I said goodbye to her. And so as we talked face-to-face alone in his small room, he kissed me for the first time, then I felt some kind of awakening inside me and my whole body for the first time, then I kissed him back, and then we went on and on kissing, and we ended up in his local mattress, "tsatsa," and then he pulled off my panties, and because I was a virgin, he couldn't penetrate him penis inside me, and so he had to rub it with ointment before slowly, and we had sex, but he made sure he came not inside me but into his towel. And so I left for home right after, and I felt pain in my vagina, instead of enjoying it, and so I asked myself, "If this was how sex felt like, then why do people like to have sex continuously?" And at the same time, I felt content to have sex with someone I loved than to be raped by someone I didn't love, also the feelings and kisses that came out from losing your virginity to your first loved one. And so I was so worried that I might get pregnant if a little sperm gets inside me because my underpart was a little wet, and I showered before going to sleep, and so luckily, I had my menstrual cycle, and I promised myself that, though I broke my promise (maybe because Mom wasn't around to protect me) that wouldn't happen again.

The last time I saw my uncle Fulani was a couple of years ago, when he came to Ada Foah to introduce his girlfriend to Mom a little after I arrived from Labadi, and they were given a warm welcome and then left back to Accra in a couple of days' time. But since Mom got sick, though he was told, he didn't visit her at Odumasi or at Tema General Hospital, and the next time I saw him, he came to see me at Maami's house, and so I was glad to see him because I thought he came to visit me and to support me financially. And so when he asked how I was doing and how my studying was going on, then he told me that his wife needed a sewing machine to learn how to sew, but when he asked Mom's for hers, she said that it was already mine, and so he should ask me first, and he needed it right away, for a couple of months, and as soon as he bought her one, he was going to return it over. And so I told him, "Uncle Fulani, you knew that Mom blessed me with this sewing machine, and in a few months' time, I would be needing it after my graduation." And so he smiled at me and told me not to worry about it because he would surely bring it back to me before I finish my forms 4 education.

My instinct told me that he didn't even bother to visit and to ask Mom about it, but he used wisdom to fool me because he took advantage of the respect I had for him, but anyway, I reluctantly went with him to Grandma's, and then sadly, I gave him the sewing machine. I felt like I lost it, and he just gave me his little pocket change, and then he left. And so I was emotional for a while because I lost two dreams in life, my American dreams and then being a seamstress, and that really hurt me. And so I was depressed and confused about it, and I felt like I needed to talk to someone to encourage me a little bit from what I was going through since Fulani came for the only property left for me, and so I went to see my boyfriend, Ebennezer, again in his place. And so after he encouraged me a little bit, he walked me home around 8:00 p.m. under a bright moon and stars, and so we sat down at an isolated place on a huge sand surrounded by cement blocks, to protect it from spreading, and because of the brightness and it looked like early evening, we were looking at each other's faces, and through the eyes, were were kind of admiring ourselves, then once again, we started kissing, and then we lay comfortable, like on a soft mattress, we romanced, and we had the most passionate sex ever for the first time in my life, because I felt extraordinary sweetness throughout my whole body. Unfortunately, he came inside me this time, but I ignored it, and rather we had a goodbye kiss, and I rushed home, bathed, and changed my panties and clothes, and then I went to lie on my mat, and those periods were like I had nothing else to think about than my enjoyable sex, and I felt like I won a lottery. And so I had sweet dreams, and I had no idea that I could get pregnant because it was unprotected sex, and I was doing good job with all my tasks in both school and house, and then for the past five weeks, I didn't have my menstrual cycle, and I went to tell Ebennezer, "I think I am pregnant."

Since he had experience with that, he encouraged me not to worry about it and then gave me some four abortion pills to take and I would menstruate, and so I took it with water right there without thinking, *What if I bleed to death or it didn't work?* And so two passed since I took those pills, and I still haven't menstruated, so I was more depressed, stressed out with anxiety, but I was still healthy, and I was moving on with my normal duties, and I faked a smile, like nothing was going on with me, though I secretly cried, and I prayed to God to help me terminate the pregnancy and to move with my life; else I would be in big trouble. And if only Mom wasn't sick, no matter how mad she would be at me, she would encourage me to have the baby, and she would take care of him, and she would encourage me to go back to school, like the mother of my mate Grace did. And so during Christmas break, I went back to Ashaiman to visit Mom and to spend Christmas holidays and New Year's Day with her, but I saw her rather in William's home, and she told me that her doctor discharged her because they couldn't find what was actually wrong with her. And she still walked slowly with a stick from the room to sit outside, or she moved a little bit around the compound, but she was still in pain, and so she was under herbal treatments, and the herbs were grinded by Grandma, and she mixed it with small water, and I applied it to the affected areas, and she was taking pain medications too. And so I brought her some money I collected from the villagers, who still owed her. She told me to get from them, but she told me to keep it and not give it to Grandma. And so that day was December 20, 1973, which was my birthday, but I didn't notice, because I haven't celebrated my birthday before, and so during that late evening, Mom, Adzoa, and I went to lie in the "tsatsa" mattress covered with sheets and pillows, and Mom was in the middle, and Adzoa and I lay by her side in a mosquito net. And so in the middle of the night, she was crying out loud from the unbearable pain, and she was having fever with high temperature, so I panicked and started crying too, and I kept on asking her if there was anything at all I could do to help her feel a little relieved. And all those while she didn't talk to any of us, and rather her voice changed, like she was crying through her nose, then she cried like she was whispering, and so when I touched the leg part that hurts the most, she couldn't scream anymore, but she whispered in pain, and then she gasped for air.

Instantly, I had a hard feeling that Mom wouldn't make it. She was dying, and I felt so overwhelmed, and I cried out loud, and I repeatedly begged Mom not to leave us because we had no one else in the world. And so Grandma told us to stepped outside for some fresh air, and so we went outside, and I was just strolling around the house and crying about Mom, who promised me we wouldn't be separated from each other in our lives again but that we would be together forever. She was leaving me when I was just seventeen years old and also pregnant, and I didn't even have a chance to tell her. And so it was like my world was shattered, and I wished we all died together because I lost my American dreams and my sewing machine, I was pregnant, and if abortions didn't work, that means I wouldn't be able to complete my forms 4 education, and then much more, I was about to lose the most precious thing in my life: my mom. And so I continued to check on her, and it came to a point where she couldn't whisper anymore and was just gasping for air, and so around 8:00 a.m., a kenkey and fried-fish seller came around at her usual time, and Grandma bought some for Adzoa and me to eat. But I refused to eat mine at noon because I lost my appetite, and also Mom refused to drink her favorite Milo and milk tea when I tried to spoon-fed her, since her teeth were stuck together. And so I couldn't stop crying and checking on her to see if there would be a miracle for survival, but nothing changed, and no matter how many times I prayed, I was so depressed and also had panic attacks.

Grandma stepped out, and she sent a family member to inform all family members at Ashaiman and Accra that Mom was dying, and so around 2:00 p.m., I returned to the room, and I kept on tapping her to talk to me because it was like she was in a very deep sleep. And then she suddenly opened her eyes, and she looked like me, and she said that "Mankpa" means, in the Ga language, "big mother," like she used to call me since childhood. If she was in a good mood, she asked, "Have you had something to eat?" And so I burst into tears, and I said, "Mom, how can I eat when you refused to eat something?" And then she told me to prepare her some tea, and so in a rush, I poured warm water from the flask inside her cup, and I added four tablespoons of Milo, a small amount of sugar, and a good amount of evaporated milk, and I mixed it together, and I sat by her side, and l spoon-fed her until her cup was empty. And then she whispered to my ears and told me, "Now it's your turn. Go get something to eat." And then she closed her eyes again, and so I was motivated to eat a little bit of food because I thought that if she was able to talk to me and had a cup of tea, it means there was a chance for her to get better. And so in about two hours later, some of the family members came around, including Grandma's stepsister, Amarkinye, and so Mom stopped breathing when they checked on her, and so they laid a mat on the cement floor in the side of the compound, and she was laid on the mat, but her face wasn't covered. And then something unusual happened, something I had never seen before, though I saw many dead bodies at Labadi in the family house, and that was when Mom's eyes opened, and she was crying, and I saw nonstop tears flowing on her cheeks. And so I was crying out loud, and so were the rest of the family members, but Adzoa couldn't cry out of shock, and though she was fifteen years old, maybe she still didn't believe Mom was actually dead. And so I saw Amarkinye with a calabash with water in her hands, and she poured libations, and she said, "Maseki, I know you are crying, because of your two young daughters, but you don't need to look behind, when you are already dead, because they are in good hands, and they will be well taken care of, and so stay far away from them, and rather pray for their protections in order for you to see your generations." And thereafter, she used her own white handkerchief to wipe her face, and she closed her eyes with her fingertips, and then Mom stopped crying; she shed no more tears because she heard Amarkinye, and so she covered her face with Mom's cloths. And so Mom's death took me by surprise because I didn't see it coming, since some people were in sick beds for a few years but eventually got better, and so I isolated myself from everybody and went to Uncle William's backyard and stood there for a long time.

And many thoughts came through my mind, and the first one was, I realized how much Mom loved me, because she knew she was dying and so told me to keep the money I brought to her from her debtors and spent with Adzoa and not to give it to Grandma, and so it means, if she had anything else precious, she would have definitely given it to me. And the second one was, she could have died without me being around, before I would be informed later, but she wanted to say goodbye to me, and so she waited for me to come, and that day she smiled good, and she had conversations with me when we strolled in the compound before she died the next day, and that means the world to me. And the third one was, I was the only person she was so concerned about, and she asked if I had eaten something. And she found out that I hadn't eaten because she refused to eat, and so for that reason, she allowed me to spoon-feed her, which was her last food on earth, to encourage me to eat something, since she knew how much I loved her and so I wouldn't be eating for a while after she died and because she taught me the hard way in doing chores in order to face any tough obstacles that came my way, and also because she knew that we had no one else to count on aside from God, and her, she was really hurting to leave us orphans, and if she could stop death, she would, and that was her reason for sharing tears, though she was dead. And so after more family members arrived during nighttime, they hired a big Toyota passengers bus called motorway, and Mom was wrapped with both her four-yard men cloths and bedsheets together with a brand-new mat, and she was put in the back seat, and I sat by her side by the window, and the family members, Adzoa, and Grandma also joined the bus for her to be sent to Lolonyah for burial. And so we left Ashaiman in December 21, 1973, late night. Mom's corpse could have been sent to Tema General Hospital mortuary for a few days, and the family would have received her death certificate, but Mom's dying wish was, she didn't want to be frozen after she died before buried. And so because of a couple of police barriers on the road to Ada, they checked death certificates before corpses are sent over to Big Ada and Ada Foah and its surrounding villages, and so my family members were smart enough to buy tambourines, and they shared for the women to sing gospel music, play tambourines, or clap hands, whenever we get close to any barrier.

On the way, if they asked us where we were heading to, we told them that we were going on church convention, and so they just flashed their flashlights to check inside the bus, then they told the driver to move the bus, and so thankfully, we made it safely to Lolonyah; else, if they find Mom's corpse, the officers would return us back to bring the death certificate. And so Korletey and her family were informed, and he promised to buy a coffin and bring it over to Lolonyah in his own passenger truck, which he did, but Fulani was told about Mom's death, but he didn't show up. And so before we arrived at Lolonyah, my family members and almost all the villagers, including the Church of Pentecost members, were all sitting in our

big compound house, and they were singing songs of praises to the
Lord, and they kept awake, waiting for our arrival. And so Mom
was bathed. She was dressed up in her Heradura white long gown,
with her blue cotton material band around her waist side. Her head
was scarfed with "wodasubo" traditional scarf, and she was laid in
a state in bed in one of the rooms, with the Ga bible she cherished
(though she couldn't read) by her bedside, with a small wooden cross
inside. And in the traditional way, the family went through Mom's
cloths, and they picked two yards of two different cloths, and they
cut them into pieces, and they tied it on their wrists. And so in the
late morning, Adzoa and I were told to go say goodbye to her before
she was put in the coffin, but when we went inside and I saw Mom,
dead for real, and that would be my last seeing her, in fact, I felt like
I was trapped in another world and there wasn't a way out, and so
I couldn't cry anymore, like I ran out of tears, though I was hurt so
badly, and I wished we were all placed in the same coffin to be buried
together, so no more sufferings for me, and things turned quite opposite for Adzoa, and she was shouting and crying and asking Mom not
to leave her. And so I overheard one of the elderly women in the
room said it seems her baby daughter felt her mom's death than her
oldest with the way she was crying, but I said nothing to them, and
I told myself that if only they knew what I was going through, they
wouldn't have passed such comments. And so around 11:00 a.m., in
December 22, 1973, Adzoa and I were told to step outside, and then
the pastor of Church of Pentecost and a couple of members, including some family members and Grandma, went to the room, and the
door was closed. So after they prayed, the next noises I heard were
sounds of the hammer nailing the coffin, and I felt sharp pains in my
heart and my stomach. And thereafter, her coffin was brought outside on a bench in the middle of the gathering, and the pastor said a
few words of encouragement for the family, and then she was sent to
the cemetery, which was a few yards away, but we kids were told not
to come to the cemetery, and Grandma offered her cement blocks for
her monument, but it was done, and so I took her Ga Bible and the
cross, but my great-grandma's baby son called Love, who was known
as "Lofuy" since they couldn't pronounce it well, took the Bible from

me, and I was left with the wooden cross. And so the first Sunday, in a week's time, she was buried. We went to church for thanksgiving, then the next day, afternoon, a few family members gathered in the room where Mom's boxes of cloths were, and they opened them in front of Adzoa and me as an old-fashioned way to reading a will and also to see how hardworking Mom was, affording those cloths.

They went through all these cloths, one after another, and they made good comments about Mom's hard work, and then I was told to pick as many cloths as I needed, since I was the elder, but to be honest with you, I didn't want anything else, except Mom, and so I stood there for a while, and I touched nothing. But they insisted that if I refused to pick something, Mom's ghost will feel rejected, and so I chose her two yards each of two pieces of brown cloths and with peacock designs inside and a matching blouse. And so Adzoa was also told to chose, and she chose, like I did, and the rest were kept for both of us to get whatever we needed, but Adzoa, being selfish, went behind my back later to collect the rest of Mom's cloths. I didn't care, even though I wasn't having any, because where is Mom, who worked so hard to buy those cloths? And so why do I have to fight her? And there was one more heartless thing Dad did. His family was told right after Mom's death, and Dad was telegrammed in Tamale, where he was transferred to, and instead of him taking a few days off to attend Mom's funeral to perform traditional rights, he rather sent only six yards of Holland Dutch printed cloths, which was yellow in color with blue butterfly designs inside, and a mat to his two half brothers to give to Mom's family. And so when his brothers brought them, it was rejected by the family, and they were told to return them back until they added the rest of the items, like coffin, white gown, six yards of three different white cloths, another six yards of three different kinds of assorted color cloths, two bottles of schnapps, brooms, and a fixed amount of money, which is commonly done in Ghana for both sex, which is either way. And that gives respect to the corpse, because the items are announced in the gathering for the public to hear. And so Dad's brothers begged the family to give them just a week after Mom's burial, and they would accompany Dad to bring everything, and they left the cloths and mat, and so they asked how we were doing. And they told us Dad was in Tamale Police Station, and he said, before he received the telegrams, that Mom already told him in his dreams that she died and so he should attend her funeral, and so truthfully, since then, Dad or any of his brought those items. And so as a seventeen-year-old child, I was so hurt about how Dad treated Mom terribly all those years, and from the look of things, though no one told me the actual causes of Mom's death, I kno, it was out of suffering, from depression, stress, and anxiety. I told myself that disgracing Mom's corpse in front of her family and friends was unforgivable, and that if Dad dies, I wouldn't go to his funeral, because whenever I thought of that, it really bothers me.

In two weeks' time, I returned back to Ada Foah to face another terrible, unsolved problem with my pregnancy, because now more than ever, I had to terminate my pregnancy, even if it would cause me my worthless life. And so I decided to leave Ebennezer out of it, because should anything happen to me, he would be held responsible, though he didn't rape me, and so I didn't tell him anything after I returned to Ada Foah, and I told full responsibility for my life. And so I couldn't focus in class anymore, though I tried my best to do my school duties and house chores, because I was grieving over Mom's death and then my pregnancy too, and I kept it a secret from the girls in my class girls, I didn't tell Eva too, since they knew me as marriage-before-sex person. And because I overheard one of the girls say a box of blue dye for white clothes and enough sugar, mixed together, cause abortions, I went to buy a small box of blue dye. So since Kakinye had bags of sugar for sales, she had some in a big basin. She sold them in small portions, with medium and small sizes, empty margarine cans, and so I took a big cup with some warm water, and I poured about a medium-sized margarine can of white sugar inside, and then I added two packets of blue dye in, and I stirred it until it all melted into thick liquid. And then I prayed over it, and I asked God to bless it so as soon as I drink, I would start bleeding and have an abortion, because he knew all about me, that he is all I have spiritually, but in physical, I had no one else. And then I had cut lemons by my side in case I felt like vomiting. I was alone in the house because Maami stepped out, so I closed my eyes, and luckily, I drank everything in the cup in an empty stomach for it to work fast, and I had the lemons too. And then I returned to the next house to wash clothes and cloths, prepared lunch, so hours later, when I was expecting, like, cramps in my abdomen, to give me hope that things would work out, I felt nothing but noises in my belly, and that was it.

I cried secretly, and I was so frustrated than ever, then I also remembered another girl in class mentioned to her friends that Nestle coffee with plenty of sugar also helped cause abortion, and so I went to buy a can of Nestle coffee, made in Britain, a week later, on Saturday, which was Maami's busy day of going to events, and so I took the same big plastic cup, poured the amount of warm water inside, and doubled the amount of sugar. Then I added the full can of the coffee in, and I stirred it until it all melted. And so again I prayed the same prayers over that thick liquid in tears, and I closed my eyes and held my nose as a result of the strong scent, then I forced myself to continuously drink it in an empty stomach again until I emptied the cup, and I had the lemons too, and so in fact, it wasn't easy drinking all that, but I have to do what I have to do and move on with my life. And I was grateful for not vomiting, and with great expectations, it would work, and I had no doubt that mixture would melt that tiny thing inside me, and I would be able to complete my forms 4 education and to see what my future holds next. And so I waited the whole day, and I was doing my normal chores, at the same time expecting a little sign of abdominal pain, but I felt absolutely nothing, and it scared me to death, and I was wondering what was going on with me. And why does my life have to be so complicated? I heard many girls causing abortions with tiny, little things. They drink, and they successfully move on with their lives, and some people also have natural miscarriages, not doing anything wrong to hurt those babies. But look at me and all those dangerous things I had inside me, and the baby was stuck with me, and I was so perplexed with everything going on with me and thinking for a while about it. Keeping the baby was the last thing to do because I couldn't stand the shame from the girls in the school and the gossip, because I, the girls-school prefect, should have shown a good example to them and much more. Grandma was so hard to deal with most times, and she wouldn't be able to care for my child. And so I was more determined to cause the abortion no matter what. And so the third chance I took was, I went to the market on one Saturday morning, when Maami stepped out, with money I still had from Mom to buy six thick pieces of six-foot-tall sugarcanes sold in the large quantities in the market for retailers, and they also cut them foot long in basins for hawking, in house-to-house sales. And so I carried them to Maami's backyard, and l had my knife, well sharpened by a professional, who carried local small knife sharpeners, attached to a medium-sized bench, from to house to house, and they charged for it. And so that wasn't an easy work at all, because I had to cut the sugarcanes into pieces, about an inch, in a big basin, and then I also cut those small inches that I couldn't take a bite at once into tiny pieces, and I chewed it, then I swallowed the juice, then I threw the peels off my mouth. And there, you know how desperate I was, and so I went on and on for hours, and though my belly was full and my jaws were hurting and I was so tired more than from my whole day chores, I didn't stop there because I needed that baby out from my life, and so I went on until I finished with them. And that also didn't work because there was no sign of any cramps, and I was so depressed. I felt like I was better off dead since this baby wanted to ruin my life, and I cried myself out, missing Mom more, because if she were alive, I wouldn't be stepping out to get myself pregnant.

So I started thinking about suicidal thoughts because my life was worthless without Mom and God, the only one I had to refuse to help me get rid of the child to be free and to pursue happiness, but instead he wanted me to continue suffering. And so the last thing I did was that I went to the pharmacy store a couple of blocks away, and I bought a full bottle of APC painkillers, which contained one hundred pills, and I bought a bottle of Fanta too, and then I went to see my best friend Eva, and we talked a little bit, but I couldn't tell her about my plans. To me, it was my way of saying goodbye to her, and so she walked me home before she returned. And so as usual, it was Saturday morning, and I went inside the house, then I closed the door halfway, then I laid my mat with my pillow on it, then I sat down, well prepared, and I took the white sheets I brought from school and lay on the floor, and I poured the whole one hundred painkillers on it, and then I covered it with another sheet, and I ground them with a grinding stone until they turned to powder. And then I poured it in the same cup, then I opened the Fanta, and I poured all into the cup, then I stirred it with a spoon until it was well mixed, and though I wasn't happy with God, before I drank it, I said my last prayer: "Our father in heaven, hallowed be your name, your kingdom come, your will be done, on earth as it is in heaven. Give us today our daily bread. And forgive us our debts, as we also forgive our debtors. And lead us not into temptations, but deliver us from evil one. And the power and glory are all yours in Jesus's name. Amen." And then I was crying all the while, and thereafter, I placed the cup on my mouth and drank it so fast until the cup was emptied, and I had lemons too, and so I was still sitting, and I felt dizzy, so I lay down, and my head was on the pillow, and the whole ceiling started spinning, and I was expecting to die right away, to meet Mom and Odoi in the next world; maybe I would be happier. And then I totally passed out, and I couldn't remember anything anymore, then all of a sudden, I woke in a sitting position and started vomiting all over my clothes, the mat, and I was still dizzy, then I cried out loud and said, "This can't be happening." I mean, why do I have to survive, since I was so close? And so I was so disappointed to be living again and not dead, and I felt worse, punished in my entire life, and so I asked myself, why do I have to continue suffering? And I thought living was torture to me rather than dying, because the same words are used for the dead, which are "May your soul rest in peace," and so that means life after death is nothing else but peace, quietness, and happiness. And so why can't my soul also "rest in peace" once and for all to be happy? And I still had no abdominal cramps or any pains at all, then I was still crying and dizzy, but I had to clean those messes before Maami arrived home, so supernaturally, I had a little strength to get rid of the mat with those stuff to the backyard, then I washed my face and changed my clothes, and then slowly I walked to the next house to heat leftover food. And so the maids asked me if I was okay, because I didn't look okay but so pale, then I told them I had malaria fever with dizziness.

They were concerned, and they prepared me corn porridge, mixed with hot peppers and ginger, with sugar and bread, and after I had some, I started sweating, then the dizziness was reduced, and so I went back to the backyard to wash all those things and dried them before I went to bathe. And I wasn't happy; rather I was mad at death, who should have taken me right away willingly, but for some reason (I wasn't sure about it), I survived and continue suffering, again and again. And so it came to a point in the house where, whenever Maami sees me, she made fun of me and laughed at me, because my heart beats faster than before and it showed on my throat, and according to her, it happens only to pregnant women. And so I knew she noticed I was pregnant, but if I were to be her daughter or she is a good God-fearing person, she would have sat me down and asked if I was really pregnant and if there was anything she can do to help or say to make me feel a little better, rather than making fun jokes about me, and that also added to my depression. And so I attended school every day, including the same chores, and I was left with a few months still ahead of me to write the West Africa Middle School leavers examinations, and I might be so pregnant, or I would have childbirth. And because I was so determined to get rid of that child, I decided to put all shyness aside and asked for professional help, because that child would be a hindrance to my life. And my belly turned hard when I touched it, and my loose school belt tied me when I wore it, and then I realized that my belly was showing a little bit, but I waited until the end of the semester, and then I went to the house at Grandma's stepsister, Ashaiman. I pretended to spend the vacation times with them and for real, so it wasn't easy to break the bad news to someone because I barely knew them, but I was left with no choice, and so I told Amarkuo's son, called Amartey, about my issues, and begged him to send me to a clinic for the abortion. And so I was surprised; he was nice to me, and he told me not to worry about it, because he worked at Tema Textile prints factory, so he would pay for the bills. And so I was calmed because it went better than I thought, so I thanked him, and I assured him that I learned hard lessons from my mistakes and that it wouldn't happen again.

5
CHAPTER

Amartey told me that everyone makes mistakes and then we learn from it. He also confirmed that I can't achieve any dream in life if I keep the child because my mom is dead, and I also asked him for keeping it a secret between us, because I didn't want the family to know about it. And so I had faith and hoped that the abortion would be over with and that I would return back to school to write my exams then receive my certificate, with good grades. And so the next evening, we went to a maternity clinic close to the house, and they also caused abortions too and charged for it, and so after a lady doctor examined me in her office, she asked me to wait in the waiting area. And then later, she called Amartey and me to her office, and she told me that I was five months pregnant and that she could easily abort the pregnancy, but she was having a bad feeling that I wouldn't survive afterward if she went through. And it seems so strange to her because many people came even close to birth, and she did abort those pregnancies without any second thoughts. And so she told me I had just four months left to deliver that child, so I can decide to put him up for adoption then move with my life. And in fact, I had goose bumps all over my body, and I was in tears, because I asked myself many times, "Why am I being tortured in life in whatever I do?" Many people have unprotected sex, but they aren't pregnant, and even if they get pregnant, they abort it so easily with natural remedies or through professionals, and it doesn't matter how many months pregnant. But in my case, nothing seems to help me abort that child. It seemed like I was trapped in a deep hole and there wasn't any chance to get out of it.

I wouldn't be able to step foot in Ada Foah and complete the school by writing the exams because of the bad record I had set, and also Ghana is not like America or any European countries; you can easily walk in class in the school with pregnancy, since, the way students will make funny jokes about you right in your face, you won't like to come back again, and even if you have the child, you better find a new school to continue your education. And so Amartey encouraged me to calm down because having this child wasn't the end of the world, but I wasn't the first person in such a situation, and of course, I wouldn't be the last one, and his family are good people, and they would stand by me no matter what to make sure I need nothing and to help me raise my child, and I shouldn't think of adoption, since, you never know, it might be my only child. And so I thought he was saying things to make me feel better, so nothing changed my feelings emotionally, and so I was more depressed and cried myself out for weeks and lost my appetite for eating. I couldn't sleep, but I wished I were dead to get out of this shameful situation. And finally when we told his parents, they didn't blame me like I thought, but they were supportive, and they offered to let me stay with them, and they would help me in any way, but I still wasn't happy. I thanked them for being so kind to me, and I was grateful to God for opening windows to me when my door was closed, because Mom was my closed door, and they are the opening windows.

They asked me who got me pregnant. And I told them it was my boyfriend and that some of his family are cattle farmers in the south side of Ashaiman, so when I mentioned his name, Ebennezer Kugblenu, Maa then knew the family I was talking about. And so she sent her two daughters and me one Sunday to their farmhouse, and they informed them what happened, and so Ebennezer's grandma, who was in her late seventies, said that she was the only one taking care of Ebennezer and his education because his dad denied him since he was born. And her mom, too, was poor to care for him, and so he shouldn't have impregnated me in the first place to bring more responsibilities to her, but anyway, they would think about it and let us know. And so I was ashamed of myself and disappointed, and I cried on the way back home, but Amarki and Amarkuo encouraged me to stop crying, and I shouldn't blame her grandma because she was frustrated about the whole issue at her age, investing in Ebennezer, then he also brought her another responsibility. And so they assured me that with or without their help, I would be well taken care of and would need nothing.

A few weeks after I moved in with them, I had the worst nightmare of my life I never thought would happen to me, and the thing was, I wanted to sleep on the mat on the floor, as usual, with Amarkuo's kids in the hall, where Amarkuo slept in a twin bed, because in the chamber, Maa and Amaki slept on the same queen-size bed, and so in between the separate latrine toilet and bathroom, Amartey slept in a small storage room. And he had a student bed with mattress, a small old-fashioned couch, and a little plastic wardrobe. And so he insisted that I should sleep on his bed because the floor would be cold for a pregnant woman, but he wouldn't mind squeezing in his couch. Though Amaki's son, called Akplehe, had his little room, he could have slept in with him. And so I thought that he was being nice to me like his family and nothing else and also because he seemed to be humble, respectful, the only older guy in the house, though he was just nineteen years old, who was able to complete forms 4 education, and so his family trusted him, and they respected him too, and his words were taken seriously. And then one night, I was halfway sleeping, and because the room was too hot, I had my panties on cloths on the dark room, then I felt some heaviness on me, and then when I opened my eyes, I saw Amartey on top of me, and he pulled my panties, and so I yelled at him, then I was like, "What are you doing on top of me?" And then he was like, "Oh, just watering the child inside you, because he needed that." And so I was shocked that I turned like a statue and couldn't push him from me or yell for help. I told him to stop, but he went ahead and raped me that night. And so I cried in bed all night long, and I felt so depressed and filthy, and I missed Mom more that if she were to be alive, all those wouldn't be happening to me. And I sat on the mat, and I thought of where to go from here. I had no idea, and looking at him snoring provoked me more, so I stepped out and fetched water to the bath, and I stopped talking back to him when he talked to me for a while. He lost the respect I had for him, and his family asked me if I was doing okay because of my sad mood, and I was tempted to tell them what he did to me, but they might rather think I made moves on him, since that normally happened if they trusted a guy who raped you in those days. And so raping me, a pregnant girl, with an excuse that he was watering the child inside me was my first time and, worse, an unforgivable excuse, because who waters a child God has in someone's womb? And it's like saying that you are filling coconut on the tree with water, which was supernatural, already filled by the mighty God. I started sleeping on the floor on the mat with the kids soon after Amaki's daughter, called Adede, came on vacation from one of the commercial schools at Accra New Town to live in that storage room, which rather belonged to her. And I felt more comfortable and peaceful then sleeping in the room. He had everything planned for me to be raped, and he never apologized for his actions toward me, but he couldn't even look at me in the face, but a couple of months later, he brought me six yards of white cloths with green designs inside during evening time when the family was around, which he received free as yearly gifts from his jobsite. And so maybe that was his way of saying he was sorry for what he did to me, but nothing can change my feelings after he raped me. I forgave him years later, but whenever I think about it, it comes with the same feelings I had that night, because for rape, naturally, overwhelming feelings that don't easily go away no matter how long it happened. And so Amarkinye or Maa and her two daughters, Amarki and Amarkuo, left home as early as 4:00 a.m., Mondays through Saturdays, to Makola Market for their koobi business, so Amarkuo took me like her own daughter, and she gives me some peswas every day to buy anything I craved for aside from leftovers in the house. And she also gave me money to buy food for her two young girls, ages three and five years old, and one thing about them was, they contributed money to buy food ingredients every day after sales from the market, and they brought them home every evening to be cooked the next day, and so I cooked different types of dishes every day, either palm nuts soup, okro soup, or peanut butter soup, and it was served with either agblemaku or konkonteku. On their arrival home, by 6:00 p.m., food was ready to be served. And then all the family sat around the same medium-sized table with stools around to eat with rinsed hands. So Maa, being the head of the family, kept fetching soup inside the earthenware bowl, when needed, and either agblemaku or konkonteku was in a couple of big plates, so we kept switching empty plates with plates filled with food until everyone finished eating, one after another, with lively conversations, to which I just listened, and smiled. And they made good comments about the food I cooked and all the good job I do with other things in the house, and I smiled too, instead of frowning, each time. It really made me feel good inside, and it makes me feel appreciated and energized, with less stress, rather than insulted and treated badly. And since there wasn't tap water in the house but a block away, they charged for a bucket, and so it depends on how many buckets of water you fetched. I filled all barrels and pots with water every day, and I washed dishes and cleaned the house, though Amarkuo's older fifteen-year-old daughter, called Felicia, who used to do the house chores when I wasn't around, was there. But since I arrived at the house, she left all chores for me to do, and she stepped out to be with her friends. And to be honest with you, that didn't bother me at all, because I am used to tough house chores; rather I am grateful to have a good hideout from all those at Ada Foah, and also, for the first time in my life, I was living with good people who really cared about me, fed me well, gave me good spending money, which I saved because the leftovers were enough for me, and much more. They appreciated me in all things I did for them. And what surprised me was that they were pagans who believed in voodoos, but they treated me like the Good Samaritan. And also instead of buying prepared food for Amarkuo's kids by the roadside, I rather walked to Ashaiman market, half a mile away, to buy simple food ingredients to prepare lunch for them to eat, and I got a little change out of that, and they also had homemade food they really loved. I bathed them twice a day, and I changed their clothes, then washed them right, and much more. I braided their hair nicely. That made Amarkuo like me more. And so he told me that Mom really helped her when she was facing financial difficulties at Lolonyah, and so she would repay her by treating me like her own, and so if there was anything

I needed, I shouldn't hesitate to tell her, and she also said, you never know, maybe someday, I will help her children too if they are facing any challenges.

After I started thinking straight, because of the good treatments I received, I realized that was God's idea to bring that child to the world, no matter what, though it was bad timing to me, and what blows my mind away is that many women wanted a child so badly that they spend months on bed rest, and they still had miscarriages. And some get pregnant, get sick, and end up dying, and some also end up paying big money for adopting a child, but look at all those dangerous efforts I made, including suicide, and even a doctor who would be paid for her services also refused to terminate the pregnancy. And so I finally told myself, "Atswei, just keep on keeping calm, because in four months' time, you will have this child, get your life back, and see what the future holds."

Because Sundays were their rest days at home, I asked each of them to give me all their cloths and blouses to handwash, so there were lots of cloths and matched blouses. Because koobi stinks, they changed cloths and blouses every day. Also, they had special cloths and blouses they wore to occasions like funerals or babies' outdoorings. And so the three of them brought me those cloths and blouses, and they added more of sunlight, Lux, or Rexona soaps and also perfume water in a bottle to rinse them again before I dried them. And so as a pregnant girl, Sundays was my busiest day, so I woke up early morning to fill barrels, big pots, and buckets with water, and then I cooked starch, because they liked their occasional wear cloths starched and ironed. And so after I had either tea or porridge with bread, then I started washing those cloths first, then I starched and dried them before I continued with those koobi stinky cloths and blouses, and those took more washing in about four different soapy water before they smiled good, and then I rinsed them in the perfume water before I dried them too. And so I took just lunch break, and then I started preparing dinner, though they encouraged me to rest, but I felt energized by God's grace, and so I told them I wasn't tired at all until I finished preparing their favorite meals. And so after dinner, I ironed their occasion cloths and blouses, but they told me just to fold those koobi cloths and blouses and put them in their big baskets, because they weren't important.

Each weekend I got a couple of leftover soaps, and I kept in one and their empty boxes because I would need them after my child was delivered. And though they were pagans who believed in voodoos, I didn't see any voodoo in the house, but Maa had bottles of schnapps in their bedroom and occasionally poured libations, especially when they were traveling to someplace with them, or she used calabash full with water. And I heard her mention Tsatse Maawu, which means, in Ada language, "Father God, have a drink." All of her father's and mother's voodoos should have a drink, and then all ghosts should also have some and help and bless them in all things. I am a secret Christian in the house, and I prayed for God's protections on both me and my child, and during those times, I still miss Mom, and I thanked God for all the toughest chores she put me through, and I thought she hated me that much, and she did it as a result of that. But now I know how much she loved me, and it was like she had my future in the palm of her hands, and she knew what would happen if she died. And throughout my pregnancy, God was so good to me. I never felt morning sicknesses, I didn't napped, and I was healthy to to do anything for them, and they even saw me more as a blessing than I did, except what Amartey did to me. The only thing was that I felt the child kicking, and my belly was also showing at my eighth month, but I didn't take any vitamins, so they encouraged me many times to go to Tema General Hospital to see a doctor; else I wouldn't be accepted if I was in labor pains, and those maternity clinics around charged big money after delivering. And something funny about me was that I had enough strength to step out of the house and joined neighborhood kids in playing games like "ampe" and skipping ropes in early evenings, even when I was eight months' pregnant. And so I walked to the hospital, and I was examined by the doctor, and both I and the child were doing well, so he prescribed the same iron vitamins for me to start taking, and he asked me to see him every two weeks.

A block away, there was a hotel called "Mexico Hotel" owned by an Ada middle-aged man, and with his two wives and children, they lived in the next house, so at the end of each month, they played live band musics, like high life and reggae. And he had a good crowd of people because it was one of the nicest hotels in Ashaiman in those days, so because of loud music from the speakers, we felt like it was played in our house. And so we couldn't sleep for that reason, so rather we teenagers sat in front of the house and enjoyed the music, and we sang along until they closed around 4:00 a.m. before we went back to sleep, so Amarkuo leaves spending money under her pillow for me to collect when I found some difficulties in waking up when they were about to go to the market. And so during those periods, reggae-style gospel music played, among other songs, which touched me and stuck in my brain since 1974 and motivates me to pray more, and that makes me feel God's presence to keep on surviving. And here it goes: "At night before I sleep, I beg the Lord my soul he keeps. With a little prayer to my God Father, my sweet Lord, Jesus, Jesus, Jesus, keepeth my own soul. He keeps my soul. My Lord desires few words at the end of the day. I'm tired, but I have to pray. I can't help it in my soul. He is my savior. I was told to medicate in his day, saying, we walked together side by side. Through my soul, he replies, 'Ooooh, glory hallelujah.' At night before I sleep, I beg the Lord my soul he keeps. With a little prayer to my God Father, my sweet Lord Jesus, Jesus, Jesus, keepeth my soul, he keeps my souls. He leads me through the green, green valley. I never feel lonely. I felt all my story. I worship him every day in my prayers everywhere. Through my soul, he replies. We walked together side by side. Ooh, glory hallelujah, at night before I sleep, I beg the Lord my soul he keeps. With a little prayer to my God Father, my sweet Lord Jesus, Jesus, Jesus, keepeth my soul. He keeps my soul." And that gospel music touched me, and I knew God used those musicians to play that music of hope, to motivate me to pray more, because I lived with pagans who talked about nothing else but voodoos, and I couldn't visit any church to listen to preachers, also because Sundays were my busiest days, from morning till late evening. And so since then, I sang that music more like my prayer especially when I was busy, and I saw that music record plate put in YouTube in 2010 by Kaibara City after thirty-three years later.

One more thing which happened in my family was that I wasn't the only pregnant teenager, but Akplehe, an eleven-year-old son, impregnated his thirteen-year-old teenage girlfriend, who was in form 1 in the same class with him. And so when her family came over to inform my family, he was asked. He denied, said that he wasn't responsible for that, and so Amaki, his mom, and Amarkuo believed him because they said, "There is no way an eleven-year-old can impregnate someone." And so that teenage girl's parents, being pagans, said they were going to their hometown at Krobo Odumasi at their shrine to curse or cast a spell on Akplehe for denying the pregnancy because they believed in their child. And then Maa put her foot down, and she encouraged them to accept the pregnancy and perform all traditional rights and to accept Julie in the family because she already lost some of her children and she didn't want to lose a child anymore. Cursed words, in Ghana, means that spells cast at a shrine for someone to die or for something terrible to happen to that person and his or her entire family if found guilty, and that is for real and not a joke out of my experiences. And so they listened to Maa, and they went to Julie's family with acceptance drinks, which means they accept the pregnancy, so Julie moved to our home, to live with us, and we all slept on the floor, but I didn't allow her to do anything because chores means nothing to me. And so we became good friends. We braided each other's hair and shared our feelings. We ate together during daytime before the family arrived for dinner, so knowing that I wasn't in this alone really calmed me down, and we attended doctor's appointments. But Akplehe couldn't look at her in the face or come close to her and asked how she was doing, though they were in the same house.

Since she was a couple of weeks ahead of me, Julie's parents sent her to their hometown in order for my family to get all traditional rights to perform their duties over there. And in two weeks' time, we received a message that Julie had a beautiful baby girl and my family was supposed to be there in seven days to perform the child's outdooring. And some of the family members contributed money to help at Accra Makola, then they bought baby's clothes, disposable diapers, shoes, towels, mat, bucket, basin, feeding bottles, SMA baby formulas, etc., all for the baby. And then four different types of African textile prints, which were two white cloths with different black designs and two other cloths with assorted colors, all six yards each, slippers, jewelries, four different kinds of wudasubo scarfs, two bottles of schnapps, etc., for Julie, and then a fixed good amount of money for her, called "sunueici" in the Ada language, means "under pillow," because she just had a child, so she wouldn't be working for while. When food had to be prepared for her, all she had to do was lift her pillow and pick some money. And so on the seventh day after her birth, Amarki and Amarkuo traveled to Odumasi with all those items, including the money, to perform all traditional rights, and the child is named Grace, and so Maa stayed at home on Sundays because she said, "Dudo ye pah se bue le yaa pah," which, in the Ada language, means that largest pots aren't carried to the stream to fetch water but that the medium-sized pots are carried to the stream or riverside to fetch water, to fill the big pots in the house.

During those days, largest pots are equivalent to the size of big barrels, and they remain in the kitchen, at the corner of the compounds and rooms, so medium-sized pots are used to fill those pots, with medium-sized calabashes in a tray on top of it as a cover. And so what Maa wants to say is that she is a largest pot and her children are medium-sized pots, and so they had to go to the riverside and fetch water to fill her. And so she waited all day long for them to return back from Krobo Odumasi to give her some feedback. The only way to found out if baby Grace is Akplehe's child is the resemblance, since there was no DNA test available in those days, so when they eventually arrived there in the night and sat down, Maa and the children also sat by their side anxiously to hear the news about the babies. And so according to Amarki and Amarkuo, when they arrived to Odumasi, they were offered stools, to sit, water to drink, and then the Julie's mom brought a beautiful week-old Grace, and as soon as Amarki held her in her arms, she was covered with goose bumps all over her body, because, though Grace is a girl, the resemblance was unbelievable. She and Akplehe are like twins when Akplehe was little. And so both of them regretted that they made a big mistake for denying the pregnancy, and if Maa hadn't used common sense, their family would have been destroyed. And so after family members of Julie came around, then Amarki and Amarkuo, presented all those items to them, and they were happy about every-thing provided, and Julie, too, was around, nicely dressed in white cloths with matching blouse, with slippers and silver jewelries on, and she seemed so excited to be honored by her boyfriend's fam-ily though she was a teenage mom. And then the baby was named Grace Ocansey, since Akplehe's last name is Ocansey. Then tradi-tional beads were put on her right wrist, which was a fashion and a big deal in those days to prove that the baby really had the name of the father's side. And so Maa and all of us were so happy about the great news, and in two weeks' time, Julie, her mom, and Grace returned back to Ashaiman, where she lives with her older daughter and Julie in a rented compound house, which had a small kiosk where she sold akpeteshie for a living.

All the children in the house went to visit Julie and Grace, who lived just a couple of blocks away, and later, Maa, her children, and Akplehe were really encouraged before he went with them to see his child for the first time, and so afterward, Julie and her baby frequently came around to spend time with us, and she looked so excited because she told me that when Grace turned few months old, her mom would babysit her in order for her to go back to complete her education. And though I was happy for her, at the same time, I was sad, because if only my mom was also around, I would have had a second chance to go back to school and write my exams and then complete my form 4 education, and I also was jealous at her for hav-ing my good, supportive family, since the Ebennezer's family denied me and my child like his dad did, and they didn't come around or send any money to support me. My family encouraged me to go see her mom, who lived across the street of Ashaiman market, and in fact, she lived in a very poor neighborhood known as "tuutu line," which means, in Ga language, "prostitution neighborhood," because prostitutes lived there, and those buildings were built with aluminum sheets in smaller rooms. They were sitting on stools by their door entrances. And so I was directed to the place of Ebennezer's mom when I mentioned her name, and I was surprised to see her so pregnant in her middle forties, and she also had a four-year-old daughter in such very poor condition. And I asked myself why her family lives in such a nice farmhouse and why she was living in such an awful way. Was it because those tiny rooms were cheaper or she was one of them? She welcomed me after I introduced myself. She offered a stool to sit on. She asked me about my family, my background, how many months pregnant I was. And I said, "Nine months," then she offered me food, but I told her, "No thanks," because I wasn't hungry, so she gave me some fresh herbs to grind, mixed with water, and insert into my butt with a syringe, which was squeezed for the herbs to go inside me for about ten minutes, after which I should use the toilet and the liquid would come out together with feces, and that would strengthen the baby more to move faster inside me, with my head down to be born. And so I asked myself why she was still in her forties and pregnant, because women got married in their early ages, then they started having babies right away continuously and still working hard, so in their forties, they already had many children, and so they stopped having more babies with some natural herbs. They grinded and mixed with water and then inserted them into their butts with syringes, or they stopped getting pregnant naturally.

Though she told me to visit her anytime, she couldn't give me anything else, like money or provisions, so since then, I didn't visit her again, and when I told my family about those herbs, they said it was okay for me to use because she wouldn't harm me or her own grandchild. And so I was tenth months pregnant, and I haven't had my baby yet, though it still kicks, and I wasn't having any symptoms, and Amarkuo told me one time she was a Christian before she moved to Ashaiman but that she was discouraged from going to church because her family were pagans. And since she realized that I am a Christian and she heard me sing gospel music and I also prayed, she took me one time to see a prophet at Mexico Hotel, who came from the Volta Region called Tagbolu, who travels all over Ghana to pray for traders, businessmen, farmers, fishermen, and their wives, and he blessed water with Florida water perfume and olive oil for anointing. He charged them, and some gave big donations too. And so when he prayed for me, he told me that he saw me with a nice rooster, and that means I would have a son and he would be richer than the other kids I would have in future. He anointed me, he also prayed for Amarkuo, and she put offering in a small bowl on a medium-sized table in his hotel room. And then I knew I would be having a boy, because in those days, there wasn't any technology showing babies' genders or ultrasounds, and I came home also expecting to deliver the child right away, but that didn't happen.

Four days after we visited Tagbolu, it was Sunday, so I went back to my normal chores. I washed the same number of clothes. I cooked, I cleaned, I ironed, and I also stepped outside to play and skipped rope with the neighbors' kids as usual, but after I bathed and laid myself down for another day, I started having some contractions with intervals, but I tried not to be noticed, and so I stepped outside for fresh air, and the contractions increased with bitter pains on my lower back and abdomen, then I felt the movements of the baby. I couldn't sit down or stand at one place, and I was just crying and moving here and there for hours. I was snapping my fingers and feelings pains I never experienced before. Then all I kept on saying was "Yehowaeeee, naami mobo," which means, in Ga language, "Lord, have mercy on me." And so I called Amarkuo when my water finally broke, around 11:00 p.m., and I told her what was going on, because we were told at antenatal class to wait at home for our water to break before we come to the hospital. And so I had all things needed for childbirth ready for the hospital, like a couple of babies' clothes, disposable diapers, used cloths to wrap the baby after birth, perfume soaps, sponge, towels for me and the child, my night wear, etc., like we were told at antenatal class, which I bought from the money I saved, since the hospital doesn't provide those for patients. And so Maa, as usual, fetched water in a calabash, and she poured libations, especially for Mom's ghosts, that as I am going to fetch water right now with my pot in the riverside, she should help me carry it back safely home without being broken. And so she made that statement in her libations because some of the Ghanaians believe that childbirth is like carrying a pot to the riverside to fetch water, and so in case, you die during the process, it means that your pot fell and got broken. And so after she finished her libations, Amarkuo already instructed a taxi to be called at the roadside, and so I kept asking God for help in the taxi on the way to the hospital, and I was still in severe pains, so after I was examined by the midwife, I was then admitted right away.

I was encouraged by Amarkuo to quit worrying and rather hang in there, that soon, this would be over and I would start smiling again, and then she told me she was going home but she would check on me in the early morning before she leaves to Makola Market. The ward was large and spacious but had few beds with mattresses on and rather plenty of pregnant women in labor pains, and so the rest of us were given blankets, pillows, and sheets to lie down on long benches, and because we were all in painful situations, some of us were crying out loud and moving here and there and snapping our fingers. And some of the midwives were so mean, and instead of them calming us down, rather they blamed us, that it wasn't their fault to get pregnant in the first place, and that we should be quiet and continue moving around for the babies to be born faster. And so I started enduring my pains by sharing tears and snapping my fingers and calling God in my mind to help me. Nurses checked on us periodically if the babies were ready to be born right away, and if they were ready, then they were taking them to delivery rooms a few yards away that were divided with curtains, and then they gave birth. And so in my case, at 12:00 a.m., after a nurse examined me, she told me that I was ready, and then she sent me to one of those delivery rooms. To be honest with you, it wasn't easy for me to move my steps, and nobody helped me too, but thankfully, I was able to climb that high small bed, and then both of my legs were tied with a belt to a pole by both beds. I pushed when I was asked to, but there wasn't enough space for the childbirth, and so the doctor cut a space between my vagina and anus before. When I pushed, the baby's head came out, and with my third push, the child was born, and I heard him crying, then the midwife said, "Wow, congratulations. What a cute little boy."

The more I heard him cry, over and over again, my heart was filled with joy and happiness, and that's all that matters, and then I said to myself, "This is my real forms 4 leaving certificate, which wasn't just a piece of paper, but thank God, I had a live one," and that was in August 4, 1974, just a couple of seconds to 12:00 a.m., and that is my memorable day, even if you wake me up from my sleep, because of the deadly process I went through, and also it was supposed to be my forms 4 after-exams certificate. And just after a few seconds, he was taken from me to the nursery, and I was told to go back to the ward and get some sleep at my post on the benches, but I couldn't sleep out of anxiety and also was not feeling comfortable. And so in the morning, I joined new moms to bathe in the same bathroom, like the old times in Labadi, when I was living in my house, and so Amarkuo came to visit me with a flask and Milo tea inside and buttered bread, and she was so happy for me, and she told me that she saw my handsome baby in the nursery. The doctor said I would be discharged that day, so on her way home from the market, she would come over and take us home, and we spoke in brief because it wasn't visiting hours, and she left. And so I was doing okay until I was called again to the delivery room, and my legs were separated and tied on those poles, and the doctor gave me a few stitches, which was another painful thing I didn't think of, because I thought I was out of severe pains for good. I had injections in the thighs to reduce the pains, but it didn't work. And so in the evening, Amarkuo came to the hospital, and she paid all the bills, and she hired a taxi, and I sat in the front seat, and she held the child in her arms, and she covered her whole body and his face with her cloths, and we arrived home. And so I had a big welcome back home, and everybody wanted to see my handsome, healthy baby, and so Amarkuo, being so kind, put brand-new sheets in the bed with pillowcases, and she told me to sleep on with my child, and rather she joined her kids in sleeping on the mat on the floor. She said she didn't want the baby to catch a cold. And so that evening, palm nut soup was prepared with smoked fish from the Akosombo River, mixed with meat and served with konkonteku. This was what I had for dinner, and then I was told by Amarkuo to sit on big chamber pot filled halfway with warmer water, and mothballs, ground into powder, were poured into it for about thirty minutes.

I stood up in between for a few seconds, then I sat on it again because I can't stand the painful heat that came out of it straight into my body. And so she said if I continuously do that twice a day for seven days, the wound I had for the cut during childbirth would heal. So I did exactly what she told me to do because I was in pain, and I couldn't sit on the stool, and I sweated during the process, so as soon as I finished, I went to bathe, and thankfully, that old-fashioned remedy worked, and I was completely healed. And one more thing was, I had severe sharp cramps in my abdomen for a week after I had my child, and so Amarkuo gave me codeine painkillers to take after meals three times daily for those days before it stopped hurting, and so she didn't send me back to the hospital for the doctor to prescribe medications for me, because most Ghanaians are used to self-medications and natural remedies. Amarki's only daughter, who is Akplehe's big sister, who is well educated in the family, did a good job to help me, which blew my mind away when I was in pains, and the family weren't around those times, and she was on school vacation. She got up every morning to wash my clothes, Amo's clothes, and used cloths I wrapped him with, and I kept on changing them when he peed or had feces inside. Because I didn't have enough disposable diapers to change him during nighttimes, he rinsed them with Pine Sol disinfectant, and she dried them all on the drying lines, which was a surprise to me, because she didn't wash her own brother's baby clothes, and she is the only classic young lady in both her father's and her mom's sides of the family, and I never thought she would help a poor person like me, and so I felt myself more blessed in that house, and that joy suppressed the rape feelings in living with them. Because it took days before I had breast milk to feed Amos when he cries after we arrived from the hospital, Julie breastfed him for a couple of days, which is commonly done if two women have babies in the same house and one person's breast milk delayed for some reasons.

Amarkuo bought him feeding bottles and Nestle Lactogen baby formula to drink, and she didn't stop buying even after I had breast milk to feed him, so I was grateful and was contented, and it was unbelievable for me to be treated with such respect and honor. No one would do that except Mom and much more. I wasn't having a boyfriend who was supportive in any way. And so Maa informed the other family members at Accra, including, my mom's mother who didn't know our whereabouts after Mom's burial, and Ebennezer's families also were told, and they said we would hear from them, like the first time, and one of them came to visit when he was couple of days old, but they denied my son, just like Ebennezer's dad also denied him, and he grew up without knowing his real dad, and so he was named by the family on his mother's side. And so thank God, I didn't only have Maa and her family's support, but my other family members also came to visit me, with provisions, food ingredients, baby's clothes, dresses for me too, and also money. And my grandma also came to visit me with lots of food ingredients, and she also spent a few days with us, and then I prayed for a Christian name, and on the seventh day, like history repeated itself, I named my son Amos, which means "borne by God," because God wanted him in the world at his own time, even when I wasn't ready yet to have a child, and also both Amos's and my survival was a miracle from God. And even though it wasn't a real fancy outdooring like what Julie and her baby had or any other outdoorings I witnessed, his poor mom came over to visit us once, with eight yards, her used cloths, in two yards each, for the child to be wrapped inside, and also two bars of Keys soaps, and that was all she could provide for her grandson. She couldn't come back again because of shyness, since she had no money or something else to give, and so my family and I pitied her rather than blaming her. But I was grateful to God, for me to be able to give him a perfect Christian name, and also having my family's support means the world to me because it was incredible, a divine intervention. And so for the first time in my life, I felt like a princess surrounded by people who loved and cared about her. Thereafter, when Amos was a couple of months old, Amartey called him Salifu whenever he was playing with him, and I hate him calling him with that name, which he normally does when my family was around, and because I didn't want to create a scene in front of them, I ignored him, but because that wasn't designed for him, Amos is the name everybody calls him.

When Amos was two months old, Maa told me to go to Kasseh with a nickname, Ada Junction, which was a new township by then and surrounded by villages, and it's about a forty-five-minute drive to Big Ada to visit Grandma; else she would be jealous I chose her over my grandma. And so I wasn't happy with that idea, because she was quick-tempered and got provoked easily and yelled and didn't care if people were watching, and also, if she really care about me, she would know where I was living, because she introduced me to Kakinye as her family, but she didn't even visit me once and support me financially, so if she hadn't received a message that I had a child, she wouldn't have known where I was. And for real, I chose Maa over her because she is so easy to deal with and slow in anger. She was funny, and she had a great sense of humor. Even when you were wrong, she talked to you in an amicable manner, and her own grandkids gave her a nickname, called "kusii," which means "basket" in the Ada language. I had no idea how she ended up with that nickname, but she chewed tobacco alongside with "kawe." And so with encouragements from my family, I decided to go visit her for a few days, and so I noted her address before she left, and so one time, Amos and I took a straight lorry from Ashaiman market to Ada Junction, which is called "Dzosinya" in the Ada language. And when we were dropped off at the roadside, we asked about Kasseh Chief's house. I was led to the house by someone, and so I entered inside a cement-block house that looked fenced with a gate on a plot of land, and then I realized there were twelve single rooms that were built in a circular way, and those rooms had a hallway throughout the rooms and a sizable compound and a deeper well in the center of the gravel compound, just like the path to the house and buildings around which we covered with gravel dust.

Grandma lived in one of those medium-sized rooms, and some few tenants, including the chief of Kasseh, surprisingly rented three rooms, and he lived in one room. His wife and three daughters and his only son shared a room, and he reserved one room for meetings. And I was surprised because the chiefs and his elders in Ghana have rights to sell lands for others, and so they get more plots of lands for themselves, and they build homes and big palaces with the help of their people, so he was the first poor chief I saw in a rented house, and his family were also poor, and because of the heat in the room, his grown-up daughters slept on tsatsa on the hallway in mosquito nets made out of floor cotton sacks, and they sold smoked fish at the

Dzosinya market for a living. And so I waited for a couple of hours before Grandma arrived from the market, because it was Tuesday, since their market days are Tuesdays and Fridays, and I also went unannounced, so she welcomed us to her room, and after she asked how we were doing and everything.

We held Amos a little bit, and we talked, then we stepped outside to sit down on the hallway, and she quickly set charcoal-pot fire in the compound, and she prepared okro soup with different kinds of smoked fish she brought from the market and served with agblemaku. So we sat and had dinner, and then she told me the Ofliboyo was married with two kids in the next village, and then I had couple of mangoes as sweets after meals. I was an inexperienced mother, so instead of me getting Amos out from my back, as soon as I entered the lorry, rather he was still on my back, and he was sleeping comfortably all those times on rough roads full of potholes that kept on bouncing back the lorry. And so he had chest pains, he was coughing, he was breathing heavily, and he had shortness of breath, with fever. He was crying, and he couldn't even suck my breast milk or feeding bottle. That seems so scary to me, and so Grandma put a warm towel on his chest, and she rubbed it with shea butter. And there we go again.

I was also used to self-medicating, so instead of me sending him to see the doctor in the health center, rather I mistakenly bought him adult Meltus cough syrup because I didn't take my time to read what was on the box. And then I started giving him the dosage, and so I put Amos in terrible situations, but I didn't send him to the health center, and so in three days of sleepless nights, we returned back to Ashaiman before I found out that I should have bought Junior Meltus cough syrup instead, because the adults' cough syrup was too strong for a two-month-old child, and then I went back to the pharmacy store a block away to buy Junior Meltus cough syrup, and I started giving it to him. And I was told to bring him outside in the compound around 3:00 a.m., to sit down and allow him to inhale the dew, and naturally, he would start breathing well because it was a natural remedy for shortness of breath, and Amarkuo also continuously massaged his chest with shea butter, and little by little, thankfully, he got well again.

And so here I was, from wanting to get rid of my child in the womb, I am now begging God to save him because I felt in love with him right in my womb. I did all my best to get rid of him, but that didn't work. I even love him more after he was born, and I decided to cherish him for the rest of my life, more than a diamond trophy. And so when Amos was three months old, one of my former schoolmates at Ada Foah, called Mariama, who was from Tamale, who happened to be one of Ebennezer's girlfriends, came to our house one afternoon on a surprise visit, and I was holding Amos sleeping, and she told me that Ebennezer was just a block away and he wanted to talk to me for the first time since I was five weeks pregnant. And I missed him too, and I really wanted him to meet our son because I still loved him, and I didn't blame him for what happened to me, because true love is uncontrollable, so anything happens as a result of that. And so in haste, I placed Amos on my back, and I followed Mariama, toward his direction, and both of us were shy to look at each other's faces, like when we just met for the first time—to him, it was maybe because of bad treatments, how his family treated me. But anyway, he called my name, Atswei, as usual, and he said, "How are you both doing?"

I also smiled at him, and as usual, I called him Eben. "We are doing well." And to be honest with you, his love was still fresh in my heart, and so at that moment, nothing else matters, not even all hell I went through with him, and because of that, I couldn't complete my forms to receive my certificate, but he did complete, and he was continuing his secondary education. And also for me, true love is blameless, no matter what happens in relationships. And I also knew that he truly loved me, like I did love him, no matter how many girls he hooked up with, just like he hadn't met his dad; before he wouldn't bother to come looking for me and his three-month-old son. And so I truly believed in our love, also for the fact that, when he was asked if he impregnated me, he said, "Yes," and since his family didn't perform the traditional rights, he had no right to give him a name, but he liked the name Amos I gave our child. It is not until he completed his education and got a job to buy all those things that he can add his name to what I had already given him. Though instead of babies' clothes, he had to provide clothes according to his age. And so he asked me if he could hold him. And I said, "Why not?"

He held Amos in his hands for a while, and he told me that he did look for me and he was told I left for Ashaiman, so he couldn't tell me what happened next to him after they found out that he impregnated me, but meanwhile, I imagined that he was still clothed, he was fed, he was given some spending money, and his education also had been sponsored, and so he would face problems for his actions in his family. Then he told me that he was living with his aunt and still in the secondary school at Ada Foah, but he came for a couple of weeks' break, and he thought of seeing us. And so after we had a conversation, about thirty minutes, he told me that he was leaving, but he would be seeing me oftentimes to talk more, and then he left back with Mariama. And from that moment, I felt calm and happier to see the love of my life and the father of my child, and I was content with that alone, even though he and his family didn't give me physical cash or anything. But I kept his visit a secret from my family, though they would be okay with his visit, and at same time, they might have negative ideas that in no time he would impregnate me again, but what they didn't know was, that was the last thing on my mind, because I learned my lesson in the hard way, an unforgettable experience. And so in a couple of weeks in December, before Christmas Eve, the whole family, including those from other parts of the country, had to go to Lolonyah to perform the final traditional rights for Mom and all those who died in a year later from all over the country and were brought in the village for burial, at once to save costsm wehther they were Christians or pagans. And so Adzoa went to live with Grandma's younger sister and her only daughter, at Nima, mainly a Muslims' town, which is close to Lagos Town, and so he came to meet Amos for the first time and to go to the village with us.

I felt sorry for her when she told me about how she was being verbally and emotionally abused by Grandma's sibling, called Awudunye, and that reminded me about my past experience in

Labadi. And so I encouraged her to take it easy and that from now on, it would be just me and her and nothing would separate us again because I would talk to Maa to allow her to stay with us and also because we are safe here and for her to complete her education, since she wasn't going to school when she was with them. But she still cried a lot, and she repeatedly said that she wished Mom's ghost came over to take her with her. And so she refused to listen when I kept on telling her to stop wishing that for herself because I had been there, and I realized death isn't something to wish for herself, then one time, she had a fever, and she was in the room by herself, and she was crying out loud, "Mama! Mama! Please don't take me away! I don't want to die!" And so we all rushed to the room, and I shook her with all the strength inside me because she was unconscious, and so when she came to, I asked her what happened. And then she said she saw Mom's coffin closer to her, and she wanted to hit her, and she was still shivering, and she looked so terrified, and then Maa took a calabash, and she filled it with water, then she poured libations. She was told Mom's ghost to ignore her, because if she tried talking to us with her at any last complaint, she wouldn't have any generation. But rather she stayed far and prayed for us to be blessed with all needs, including children, so that whenever we introduce our children to family members, her name won't be left out. And so I never forget these impressive words in Maa's way of communicating to Mom's ghost, and instantly, she felt better, and so she learned a big lesson from that, and since then, she stopped asking Mom's ghost to come for her, and she never had that experience again.

Amarkuo bought Adzoa and me some dark cloths for those traditional funeral rights, and so a neighbor seamstress had sewn us nice styles when we had a week left to go to Lolonyah, and then Korletey and his family drove from Lagos Town in his big truck to pick up at the village at the due date. And so because it was close to Harmattan season, I bought Amos thick sweaters to protect him from such cold and dry weather, and so the truck was filled with family members, and so we talked, we laughed, and the grown-ups made jokes too. And so we arrived at the village faster, safe and sound, before we knew it, and the next morning, it turned into a big celebration. They fixed local canopies in our big compound, and many hired benches were arranged under those canopies. And all family members from all over filled the big space and cultural drumming, and music was played, and so for rituals like goats being slaughtered in preparing different dishes, they poured libations with schnapps for the departed souls, and their names were mentioned one after another. And then the ritual that I haven't experienced before was that each firstborn child of the deceased heir would be shaved by the elders of the family with blades in the center of the gathering, and so when it was my turn, I boldly told Maa that I wouldn't like my hair to be shaved, and so she told me that I had to pay some money in replacement for my hair, so Amarkuo paid for that, and my hair wasn't shaved. And this type of ritual was so important to the Adamgbes in those days, and so they combined funeral services called "yisemi," which means, in the Ada language, "haircuts," so after all that, names of people who donated money were called and how much they gave, one after another and after another, and then whole crowd being families and loved ones said in the Ada language, "Openoooo," which means "Thanks so much" to everyone who donated money. And then "asana," the local drink, and akpeteshie were served in smaller calabashes to everyone, and food was prepared in big aluminum cooking pots, like palm nut, and okro soups with goat's meat was served with both agblemaku and konkonteku in big aluminum pots to everyone in the audience in medium-sized earthenware bowls, and some preferred to join others to eat together right there under those canopies on the benches. And also for the safety of the family members who came from other places that had tap water, they bought reserved rainwater, which was sold in tanks in the village, rather than drink from the well or pond water.

We stayed for a few days after everything was over, and some of the family members already left back to their destinations, and so after New Year's when decided to leave back for Ashaiman, Maa told me some bad news, and that made me feel so sad and miserable and another worse pain of my life instantly, which I didn't see coming. She told me Grandma summoned her in front of the elders of the family, that either one of us is to live with her at Ada Junction; else Mom's ghost would be mad at her for rejecting us. And so I was like, "Okay then, Adzoa had to go with her." Because I was used to living with her, and besides, I also had some future plans, as soon as Amos walks and I put him in daycare, to rent a kiosk and start selling lottery tickets to the public for a living, and with my sense of humor, I would break through, since people are making good money out of that.

She smiled at me, but unfortunately, according to the tradition, the older daughter had to live with her. There I started crying for the first time in months. Oh no! "That is not fair." They can't do this to me, after all I had been through, and I was trying to pick up the pieces of my life, and now this? In fact, she was sad too, and she said, "You are the best granddaughter I ever had, and I wished you live with me, forever, but my hands are tied right now." And so Maa, her daughters, her grandkids, and Adzoa all cried alongside me, and so I couldn't keep my promise to Adzoa because she had to go with them to Ashaiman. I told them that at every end of the month, I would be there on a visit to spend weekends with them, and I also told Adzoa to come over to visit on vacation periods. And so we said goodbye to each other in tears, then I left on the same day with Grandma to Ada Junction with little Amos, and now the only dream left for me was nothing but being a fishmonger, like Grandma. And also knowing for sure that I would be humiliated by Grandma made me more sad. And so here I was, in a new undeveloped town that had no electricity, tap water, and the room temperature was like that of a preheated oven, and so the more I thought of my destiny, I realized that whenever good things started to happen to me, all of a sudden, something terrible happened to set me back instead of moving forward, and that is something I don't understand, no matter how many times I asked for answers, and I had no control over that, except God, my creator. Sleeping in that room just for few days, Amos and I had heat rashes all over our bodies, which were itchy and made it unbearable to sleep, and so we moved outside to join the chief's daughters to sleep on the hallway, on the stsatsa local mattress, in the mosque net. And we had some fresh air, and we felt a little comfortable, so we applied medicated powder on our bodies, and then a few days later, we had relieved and smooth skin again and so continued to sleep on the hallway since then. And also though we had a small kitchen for all tenants with a firepot, everyone liked cooking in the compound on charcoal pots, having fresh air, unless someone wanted to use the firepot if she ran out of charcoal before she used the kitchen, and we also cooked on the hallway when it rains, and we had two bathrooms but no toilets, and so we go to the surrounding bushes to have feces, and sometimes I forget to take a piece of cement paper with me, and so when I was done, I just picked up a leaf from the ground or used a dirty paper on the floor to wipe myself without thinking about it before I returned back home, and it was all because of depression and anxiety.

My worst fear was to fetch salty chocolate-colored water from the deepest well in the house, and it was deep, like two-thirds of a mile, and it seems more scary compared to those wells at Ada Foah. They had doubled thick long ropes made from a particular plant, and they tied them firmly in a medium-sized bucket, and then they stood on the concrete on top of the side of the well, and then they threw the bucket inside the well, and they started losing the ropes until the bucket touches the water, and they fetched it, and then they started pulling the ropes outside, little by little, until they reached out to the bucket, and then they poured water inside big buckets on the ground and went through same procedure till all buckets were filled. And they poured them in their big pots, and then they returned back to fetch again until they were done. And they thought fetching water from those wells wasn't a big deal at all because some of them were born and raised, there and some, too, live there for long time, and so they were used to it, but I wasn't, so I had buckets packed by the side of the well, and whenever I saw someone fetching water, I begged for my buckets to be filled, and I also watched closely how they did that. And so I repeatedly asked myself, "What if I fall inside the well when fetching water by standing on the concrete. I didn't know when it was built. How am I supposed to be rescued?" If a bucket falls into the water during those periods, it takes days to get a professional to come over with the longest ladder to put inside the well, and then he climbed into the water and dived in to bring the bucket from underground before he climbed back outside together with the bucket, and he charged the service. And so you know how dangerous it was to fetch from the wells, and if someone happens to fall inside, he or she wouldn't survive, because there is a little police station, but no firefighters or any emergency to call, and because of the bucket issue too, they had reserved buckets with ropes on for individuals. "It is what is," and there wasn't any way out to skip fetching water from the well, since people started giving me attitude when I continued begging them to fetch me water, and so with the help of God, I started fetching on my own, though I was so afraid to stand on the concrete or to look inside the well, but little by little, I had the courage to stand tall and long inside the well when fetching water, like anyone else.

I did the same chores at Grandma's place, which wasn't a big deal to me because I was used to it, and even when my lazy aunt Ofliboyo and her kids were around for a few days, I didn't notice her, and I did what I was supposed to do on my own. And one good thing I liked about Grandma was that she didn't like her cloths and blouses to be starchy or ironed after I washed them, but she folded them nicely and then packed them under her pillows, like the oldpfashioned way, before box iron existed, and so wherever she went, she just picked up cloths and blouses under her pillows to wear. And so in Ada Junction market days, just like Ada Foah market days, traders across the country brought items to sell, and they also buy things to sell in their towns and villages, and so I think Grandma couldn't stay in Ada Foah after Mom's death, and so she had Mom's shed, including the aluminum sheets she removed, and she built a shed in Ada Junction in the market, and she hired half to it, and she sold smoked fish in front of the shed on a large wooden tray on top of a bigger basket filled with fish. And so as the fish kept on decreasing, she kept on filling the tray with more fish from the basket until she finished selling all the fish. And also the Kasseh Chief's wife and daughters also sat next to Grandma at her left side, and they also buy smoked fish from the fishmongers, like Grandma, in baskets, and they sold them the same way Grandma did. And so when I went to the market with Grandma, I was under the shed, and she went to buy the smoked fish from the fishmongers, and she brought them over to me, and she placed them on a wooden tray, on top of my basket of fish, next to her on the right side, and she gave me prices on each of them, and she also told me to call high prices first and then bargain with the customers before selling them. And so sometimes I sold everything, and I gave her the amount she told me to give, but I had small profits to buy Amos oatmeal, custard, Milo, and milk and also used cheap nice clothes from Britain for Amos and myself in the market because I went to Ada Junction unaware.

One more thing about Grandma was that she wasn't treating me fairly at all because I had a child to provide for with all needs, and I also had to buy beautiful clothes for myself, and so she was supposed to be honest with me and to give me the actual prices for those fish she bought from the fishmongers in order for me to gain more profits from my sales to even start saving money. But rather she added her own prices to the fish for me to sell, and she was cheating and having my profits for herself. And so I found out myself because the chief's wife and her daughters went together with their baskets to the fishmongers, and she bargained to buy the fish in cheaper prices for herself and her daughters, and they sold them same way I did, but they gained more profits because their mom was being fair to them, and so they didn't have money issues.

My own grandma's bad treatments against me were frustrating, and I cried myself a lot because of that, and it added up to my depression, but Amos gave me hope to continue surviving and also depending on leftovers I was used to having in order for me to save a little money to continue to provide healthy food for him. And so I wasn't only turned into a fishmonger, but because I needed some extra money, I worked at a construction site, and I carried mixed cement for builders in medium-sized pants, and I also carried cement blocks too, and I was paid at the end of the day. And the hard part is that I had Amos on my back, and at the same time, I carried those things, and that made me feel so tired at the end of the day, but God is so amazing that he energized me the next day to work, five days in a week, since I had to go to the market on Tuesdays and Fridays. And one more thing was, though I was living in an undeveloped town with uncivilized people, who dressed anyhow and mostly halfway naked with no blouses on, they had cloths on from their waist down, both grown-ups and teenagers in their late teens, like me. But I dressed differently, like a real lady from the city, in my secondhand, used dresses shipped from Britain. And though I talked with neighbors, I made friends in the house, but my past remained a secret, and I lied to them that I had a husband at Ashaiman, and I begged Grandma not to share my past with anyone, and so they believed me because I actually left for Ashaiman at the end of each month on Friday evenings when I arrived from the market, and I told them that Amos missed his dad, so we would return on Monday morning.

I was able to visit my family, and they also enjoyed Amos for a couple of days before we returned back to Ada Junction. And so though I was still in love with Ebennezer, I knew that wouldn't be possible anymore because we were separated from each other, and we lost contact too. Besides, the last thing I needed was a new relationship with someone else, and that was one of the reasons why I told everyone that I had a husband, because a young Fanti teacher transferred to the Ada Junction school was our next-door neighbor, and since I speak Fanti language with him, he was nicer to Amos and me, but I told him point-blank I had a husband for him to not go any further with his intentions. And so one day, I was at home after Grandma returned back home from the church of Pentecost, as usual, around 5:00 p.m., and I already prepared dinner, and then I saw Ebennezer and his schoolmate approaching me, and so at first I couldn't believe my eyes, then I took a second look, and it was really him, then my heart beat faster, out of shock, and I was speechless for a few seconds. And then I came closer to me, then I was like, "What are you doing here? And how did you find us?"

I mean, I asked him two questions continuously, but all he did was, he smiled at me, and then Grandma asked who they were. And I told her that was my child's daddy and his friend, and then surprisingly, she told me to give them seats and water to drink. Then she asked him his name and a little bit about his family background and also what he was doing for a living. And so he called his middle and last name, "Ngblotey Kugblenu," and then Grandma knew the tribe. His family came from Big Ada, and she mentioned it, then he told her he was a student of Ada Secondary School and that he was responsible for my pregnancy, for which, unfortunately, his parents couldn't help me in any way. And since the last time we talked at Ashaiman a few months ago, he returned back to school without seeing us again, and it came to a point where he couldn't focus in class, and he couldn't sleep too because he couldn't stop thinking about of Amos and me, and so he went to our house in Ashaiman, and he was given directions to our current location, and so since he was scared of her, he didn't know what to expect, and so he brought his friend along with him. And then Grandma told him that he did the right thing to come over to see us, because it takes courage to do what he did, and so he was welcome anytime to see us, then Grandma told me to serve them food to eat separately so they wouldn't be shy. And so I did serve them with okro soup, prepared with beef and smoked fish, with konkonteku and a cup of water and a bowl of water to wash their hands by the table side in the room, before we sat down and had our dinner on the hallway. And so I was surprised to see Grandma being so nice to him at her first time meeting him as a student who couldn't support us. And so after they ate dinner, I introduced a year-old Amos to his daddy, and since he was friendly, he was able to play with him a little, and then the three of us had quiet time alone outside, and Ebennezer expressed his feelings toward me that though there were beautiful girls in the school, he still loved me and he couldn't stop thinking about me, and so after he finished his secondary education, he would get a job, and then he told he would marry me, to be my husband and the father of my children. And so I totally believed him because I knew him as a handsome womanizer who could easily get any girl he wanted in the school, but for the fact that he came looking for me, a school dropout and teenage mom with flat breasts from breastfeeding and a fishmonger, proved he really loved me and our child. And so you know, one of my principles in life, is that the first man I fall in love with should be the only man in my life, because I dislike the way some girls want to be in many relationships before they chose to marry one out of them. And so I thought that Ebennezer was my first love and he was going to be the last man I would be having sex with in my lifetime, until I was raped by Amartey. And so no matter how it hurts sometimes that my wish didn't come to reality, in a Bible verse in 1 Thessalonians 5:18, it says, "Give thanks in all circumstances; for this is God's will for you in Christ." And sometimes I kept asking myself, how can I be raped and feel okay about it and then be like "Thank you, Jesus, for being raped because it's your will"? And though I don't understand why terrible things keep on happening to me, I have to be thankful, since what I am supposed to be thankful for are all the good things he does for me, but maybe someday, I will understand his reasons for saying that when things work together for good on my behalf, because I really love more than anything in the world, no matter what. I learned, since I was eight years old, he is greatest above all voodoo powers and forces of darkness, and their followers know that, and for those reasons, they are so smart and acknowledge God in all things, and they put God first, him for God, in all things, which a lot of Christ followers don't really like to do.

And I also know that after all terrible things, God will really pay me good for all those injustices by turning me into an American citizen someday, which is one of my dreams, since I was ten years old. Since Ebennezer and his friends left back to Ada Foah, he didn't stop visiting Amos and me, mostly on Saturday. He knew Grandma was at Ada Foah market selling, and he spent some time with us, especially Amos, whom he also loved so much, and sometimes too he visited us on market days, in the market, when he closed from school, in his uniform, if he wouldn't be able to visit in the weekend. And so because we learned from our mistakes, we decided not to have kids at all that leads to making love, and also no more sex until he completed his education and married me before we start to continue having sex. And so it wasn't a big deal to me, because, thank God, his resistance spirit is inside me, so no matter how much I love him, whenever I was around him, the last thing on my mind was sex, and if I even tried to think about it, then quickly I remembered all that happened after I had sex, and then I refrained from those thoughts. And so you know, my mom's family came from Big Ada, which is the smallest town of the Adamgbe peoples and where they first settled as their numbers increased, and then they extended to Ada Foah and all the surrounding towns and villages of the Ga Adamgbe District. And so in each first week of August, they had a festival called Asafotufiam, which is somehow like Ga Homowo festivals, but the difference is that they don't cook kpekple; they carry their paramount chief and subchiefs, who are well-dressed in their Ashanti kentey cloths and oheneba slippers in palanquins, around town like in a Elmina bakatue festival. They also have old-fashioned guns they filled with gunpowder, and they repeatedly shoot around the whole town, especially at the first grounds. And I visited with my friends only once when I lived with Kakinye. And so our house owner's brother, in his forties, who was a subchief of the close-by village, because his sister lived in Accra, and he came over to collect monthly rents from the tenants. One day he came around, and he told me that he wanted to talk to me in private. And so I gave him a seat in the room, with the door opened, since Grandma still sold fish on Ada Foah market days, so she wasn't around, and then he told me that he was in love with me, so he wanted to marry me and to cherish Amos and me and he would provide everything for us all so I didn't have to work, because he was rich, with many properties, so I would be his secetary, since he and his other four wives were illiterates. But he talked to my grandma, and she told him to tell me himself, and so I told him that, with all respect, "I have a husband, who is my son's daddy, and though your offer is so tempting, I'm sorry, I can't take it."

He looked disappointed, but he faked a smile, and he told me, "Anyway, the Ten Commandments in the Bible says we shouldn't take something that belongs to someone else, and so he can't take the only thing which somebody has, because he already had four wives." Then I smiled back at him, and I thanked him, and he left, but I was 100 percent sure that when he talked to Grandma about me, he told him all about me, and so he came to me confidently with a great attitude, knowing that it was going to be a piece of cake to win me if he mentioned his wealth, because he saw me like a classic, humble teen mom selling smoked fish, so I needed money so badly to get out from poverty. And anyway, I appreciate his honesty and for being a good person, because rich people, especially rich chiefs, don't give up so easily on someone they love, because they would do anything to persuade that one, and even if they had to kill a man she loved, in order to get her, they will do it.

The thing is that I knew money is good, but to me, I had chosen love and happiness over money, because all I wanted more in life is to be loved and cared for, and nothing else matters, even if both of us had to struggle to become rich. I know we are in together. I knew we will become rich and still love each other and be happy at the same time, and our kids will have great lives too. And sometimes I wonder how some people could choose money over love, and their mentality is that money is everything.

6

CHAPTER

And so in 1975, a few months after I moved to Ada Junction, a lady pastor came from Accra called Ms. Comfort Allotey, who is in her early sixties, who belonged to a church at Nugua called Christ Deliverance Ministry, and her head pastor's name was Michael. And because she was sent to open a church branch in Ada Junction, she rented the three available rooms in the house, and because the Ada language is their first language in the Adamgbes, only the educated ones speak the English language, but Ms. Comfort spoke English and Ga languages. And so for that reason, she faced difficulties in communicating with the people because, unfortunately, they were all illiterates, and so when she found out that I speak both English and Ada languages, she begged me to be her interpreter. And so I told her to give me some time to think about it because it was a long time since I had been to church, though I fasted and prayed to God to bless, protect me and my son, and moreover, I didn't trust her just because she introduced herself as a pastor, from experiences I had from Kakinye—Martha, who claimed to be prophetess. But one about Ms. Comfort was that she knew Bible verses to convince you. She makes sure you read it and understand her points, and so since she was born in Ga, she read the Ga Bible well, and so she invited Amos and me one time to a room which, she said, was the consultation and prayer room. And she convinced me to be a volunteer for Jesus Christ. Aside from my busy schedules, he would bless me and open new doors that will blow my mind away. And so it took me some time before I decided to help in God's ministry, with the interpretation gift I have, and she also encouraged me to buy a Bible at the market, and so in the evenings, I had Bible lessons with her, and I noted some verses down, then later I read on my own, and that really changed my way of thinking negatives things about my life, and I realized that there is hope for me.

I also learned from her in the Bible in Proverbs 24:16 that though the righteous fall seven times, they rise again, but the wicked stumble when calamity strikes. And so I realize that following God doesn't mean bad things won't happen to me, and though I will fall, I keep on rising over and over again. And so I help her to start a small church in the hallway in front of her rooms, and I interpreted to the members, from Ga to Ada, the language at church services, and I turned into her Bible reader whenever she called Bible verses when preaching. I interpreted to her in the Ga language when members were testifying things God did for them and also when people come for prayers too. I was there to interpret it for them to understand. And to be honest with you, Ms. Comfort was like a godsent angel to me, in those days, to increase my faith, to trust, and to hope for a better future ahead of me, but not a fishmonger or a laborer. And so later on, I decided to stop selling fish and start a new life by selling tickets for the market traders, which is done by the state workers, and so with encouragement from a tenant, I went to Ada Foah, to the manager's office, and I applied, but there wasn't an opening at that time, so the manager told me to check on him each month, because there wasn't any way to contact me. But I returned home discouraged, and I also thought of who would be babysitting Amos when I had the job, so I didn't go back to check.

So I continued to sell smoked fish in the market, but temporarily, until God opened new doors for me. And I was attached to her more than ever, and so because some people volunteered to cook for her for free, I also started washing her cloths and other things, and on days we didn't have church service or prayers, we spent more time discussing the Bible together, and I read it, and she explained to me. And so I fasted and prayed more for miracles, and she also convinced Grandma to join the church, and I followed her footsteps by wrapping my tithes in a cement paper and placing it in the offertory every weekend, because I worked every day except Sundays and got my profits and also got paid at the end of the day by being a laborer. And so I became committed. I read the Bible in my free time, and I understood Ms. Allotey more, and I took my interpretation too seriously like I was volunteering for God, because without me, his messages wouldn't be heard. And one more thing I like most in Comfort's teachings is the Bible in Psalm 50:14, which says, "Sacrifice thanks offerings to God. Fulfill your vows to the most high God." And verse 15 says, "And call me in the day of trouble, I will deliver you, and you will honor me." I like this quote, because interpreting to me is like my sacrifice thanks offering to the most high God, though I give my tithes and offerings, and so I know that when I call him in time of trouble, he will deliver me, and I will continue to honor him.

Another quotation of tithing that moves me most is Malachi 3:8–10 says, "Will a man rob God? Yet you robbed me. But ye say, wherein have we robbed thee? In tithes and offerings. Ye are cursed with a curse: for ye have robbed me, even ye whole nation. Bring ye all tithes into the warehouse, that there may be meat, in mine house and proof me now herewith saith the Lord of hosts, if I will not open the window of heavens, and pour you out a blessing, that there shall be no room enough to receive it." And it is my favorite quote because I learned that if I give my tithes and offerings to God, he has windows in heaven, and he will pour blessings over me, and I will not have enough rooms to receive it, so that means if I obey God, then there is a great future ahead of me, and soon, I will get out of Ada Junction and become so rich. And also the "curse" in Ghana language means to cast a spell on someone, which I understand more because I was born by both pagan parents, and I grew up, and I explored voodoos and their worshippers too, and so I am afraid to that word in Malachi 3:9. The first sentence says, "You are under a curse," and so for that reason, I take my tithes and offerings seriously, to stay away from God's curses and rather to be blessed.

And one more thing was, when there weren't any new buildings to be built in the neighborhood for a while, that means my friends and I were laid off from the building sites, and so I didn't sit down and do nothing, since I didn't have enough money, but the rest of the days, I carried smoked herring on a medium-sized tray on top of a basket full of more fish. And I hawked to the surrounding villages from house to house for sales, with Amos on my back, even if Grandma was at home. I walked for miles before I finished selling everything, then I returned back home so tired, and after both of us had something to eat, I had to prepare dinner in haste, especially if we had early-evening church services on Wednesdays and Fridays with her ten members. And what actually saved me from being so exhausted when I went to those villages to sell was that they gave me a stool to sit on. I took Amos from my back, then I put him on my lap, and at the same time, I was selling to them. We talked, and we laughed also. One compound house had more than twenty people inside, and I had water and snacks with me to give Amos.

A couple of months later, four young men and women, their late twenties, went to the house, and they said that they were sent from Nugua, the church headquarter, by the head pastor, Michael, to help Ms. Comfort's church to grow. And they were Solomon, Largea, Jack, and a guy with the nickname "Akronkron," which is a type of worm inside rotten palm nut trees, and it tastes delicious, when steamed, with its natural oil. And the names of those women were Kai and Tsotsoo, and so Ms. Comfort gave them the spare room for the six of them. Besides, they came to help her, temporarily, and returned back to Nugua. And so they started with house-to-house camping at dawn, preaching, then they went to preach in the market days, with help from one of them who understood and spoke a little bit of the Ada language. And so they found out that it wasn't easy to win souls, just like that in Ada, because when they understood one thing, that's it, and also because they are committed to their churches as born Christians, and also pagans, to their voodoos, so their faith lies there. And so those visitors from Nugua decided to use crafty means to win those people, and so they started giving fake prophecies to the traders in the marketplace, one after another, like they saw some thick darkness close to them, and it means that force of darkness wanted to attack them, and some also were told they had dark cloths on spiritually, and that means death was coming in their family, etc. And so they actually put fears in them with those lies, and some even were emotional because of that, and they encouraged them not to worry since there was a way out, and so they should bring a gallon of water, Florida water perfume, and olive oil to the Kasseh Chief's place, where they were residing.

They bought those items in a rush, and they brought them to the house, and then they gave them benches to sit on, then they sent them to a prayer room to pray for them and also to let them give offerings in a bowl they had in the prayer room, and they blessed the water with Florida water perfume, to add a little bit to their bucket of water to bathe at home, rub the anointing oil, and then they told them to continue to come to the church services, and they would be well protected by God. And so Ms. Comfort was so sad because they pushed her aside and they took total control of the church without asking her opinions in any way, or to let her at least preach sometimes and much more. They told her that Micheal, sent them over for just a weekend to help, but two weeks passed, and they couldn't even win a single soul after all those tricks, and they refused to return back to Nugua. At the church headquarters, they struggled to survive, since they weren't working, with excuses. They were doing the work of the Lord, but those ten members Ms. Comfort had were generous givers who served them with lunches, like agblemaku, with peppers and grilled fish or fried fish. One of them, called Bondee, is a cattle farmer who had many properties, and he generously treated them well by providing good dinner for them every day, and Grandma also provided them with breakfast, which was Milo tea, at all times, with milk and sugar, and I served them with bread with butter spread inside. And so they started gaining weight rather and seem happy, and one of them went to tell Pastor Michael to give them more time to win more souls, so Ms. Comfort was mostly in her room with me, if I was available or by myself, and all she was allowed to do was to give benedictions at the end of the service.

Something else was that they paid the chief money, and his gongon player played gongon in the town and all villages when new pastors arrived from Accra, and they had miracle powers to heal patients, like the cripple and blind, or any other diseases, and so they should come over for prayers and anointing, and they asked for big donations, anointed them with olive oil. They blessed water for them to bathe, but nothing happened, because nobody was healed as a living testimony. And so one of them confessed that they used some to those money every late night at the Shell petrol station, which had a generator, and the refrigerator, their small bar, chilled beer, akpeteshie, and Guinness, and so they had more alcoholic drinks inside them, with weed, and they smoked cigarettes, and then they returned back home to sleep, and the next morning, they turned to angels. And so that money stopped coming because nobody was healed and those patients stopped the church. And so now they depended on the church offerings and tithes. Grandma gives half of her weekly profits, instead of one-tenth, which Malachi talks about, and surprisingly, Grandma and couple of her age groups in their sixties left Church of Pentecost completely, and they joined the new church, shortened to "CDC," which means Christ Deliverance Church, and they also convinced three late teens boys, with first names of Emmanuel, who weren't educated or learned trade; they were drummers in the church.

Four girls, in their late teens, who were three of those elderly women, were their parents, called Lehuyo, Elizabeth, Patience, and Georgina, and me of course, and so we were the only youths in the church, and we also helped with worship and praise songs with those early women in the church, without a single man. And so at each church service, after they collected offerings and tithes, they also collected more money from those poor, hardworking, and naive villagers, they named it "an appeal for funds," and so before they started to ask them a specific amount of money, then they read Bible verses, and their favorite is about the widows' mites in Luke 21:1–4, and that was about how Jesus watched the rich people put their pocket changes in the offertory, but he saw a poor widow who put all she had in the offertory, so Jesus commended her for that. And so it motivates them to give more money to those fake men of God, and so sadly, some of them borrowed money for that appeal for funds, for which they thought they would be well protected and blessed, financially, and commended by Jesus like the widow, because of that.

Those fake men of God weren't even ordained by the the head pastor, and so he shouldn't have brought them to Ada Junction in the first place, and I wondered why Ms. Comfort, as an ordained pastor, was watching them, mocking God, and she couldn't even report them or say something to them. And so they went on speaking faked, memorized tongues at each service, and they made us believe with Bible verses attached to it in Acts 2:1–4, and then they told us how crowds of people were all filled with the Holy Ghosts and spoke in tongues in the day of Pentecost as they spun around. Then one of them, who was Jack, spoke a little Korean he learned in school, and he pretended he was speaking tongues to fool us, and so Jack went ahead, and he pretended like God was speaking through him to us, and he told us all to be on our knees, so he said, "Oh, my beloved children, it's me, mighty God, speaking to you," "Don't be afraid," and "Quit worrying yourselves, because I heard your crying, and soon your prayers would be answered," and also "I haven't left you, orphans, but my Holy Spirit is with you always."

And then Jack finally sat down among his coleagues. And to be honest with you, I, as their interpreter, also believed them, especially who played God, because I went to Methodist Church, and I haven't been to Pentecostal Church before, and so it was my first experience, and Ms. Comfort Allotey, I knew, for a few months before they came, didn't do such things, so later on before one of them told me that was all fake, especially Jack, because he attended Muslims' school a bit, primary school. What they did was called wisdom, which was a common sense for them to keep on living. And so you know, since I turned into a committed Christian, my perception toward men and women of God was totally different from everyone else's because of how voodoo worshippers respect fetish priests, and they treated them with honor and dignity, and so I also treated them the same way, and I saw them as mouthpieces of God. And so for the fact that those money collected from those members weren't used for good reasons but for their own selfish ways, they didn't perform a single miracle, and they didn't win a single soul to add to Ms. Comfort's souls after all those pretending. Sometimes, Bondee provides us his truck to spend weekends in other villages for church services to win souls, and during the process, I saw them laying their hands on people's heads and pushing them backward to fall and pretending that was because of the holy Spirit.

And they spoke their memorized tongues, like "Alabalabalaba," "Shedededede," and then those fake men of God continued to spin those poor villagers' bodies until they fall out of dizziness, just to prove to the so naive crowd that it was the Holy Spirit that made them fall. But to me, who now realized what was going on, it was sad for me watching how their heads and bodies hit the hard ground. And I should have left the church as soon as I found out that everything about them was fake, but Ms. Comfort encouraged me to continue my duties as an interpreter so God will reward me in secret. And then she quoted Bible verses in Psalm 37:1–2, which says, "Do not worry about the wicked or envy those we do wrong. For like grass, they soon fade away. Like spring flowers, they soon wither."

Ms. Comfort left Accra to be with her family for a while, and Jack told her to tell the head pastor to extend their periods of staying because it wasn't easy winning souls at Ada like they thought, and so Michael also expected his share of tithes and offerings because that was his church branch of Ada, and so Jack was the one sent to the headquarters to give a small amount of money they called monthly returns to Michael at Nugua. And so because he wasn't having his own living place, he was tinier because he wasn't working, so he barely ate. He had no good clothes on before they came to Ada Junction, and so he saved some of his shared money to buy new clothes and shoes. He also bought a medium-sized briefcase like a businessman, so this way, he gained weight, and he was in new clothes and shoes, with a briefcase, to his hometown. At Accra, everyone was amazed, and they asked him if he traveled to the States because they didn't see him like that before, especially how he gained weight, because when you gained weight in Ghana, that means you are rich and have nothing to worry about. And one more thing was, Bondee's relative came to the church, who was in her forties, had fibroid, and she looked like she was five months pregnant, so she came over to be healed, so just like those days, I had guinea worm disease, which my parents thought was spiritual attack, and so she also spent all her money on herbalists and fetish priests, instead of going to the hospital to be removed.

She gave up hope, and she was waiting to die because she was so tiny and unhealthy, and so her last hope was to be healed by those fake men of God, and so Jack had been acting as a prophet among them, so as soon as he saw her in the church service, immediately, he was in motion like a fetish priest, and he pretended the Holy Spirit was using him, and he said, "Woman, forces of darkness had placed a big pot inside your belly, and they filled it with your own blood, and that was the reason it looked fat, and you looked so tinier, like that." And so she should fast and bring water, with Florida water perfume, olive oil so that he blesses water for her to drink, at all times, and she should rub the olive oil after bathing and much more. She should come to church services at all times, and he would continue praying for her, and soon, in the mighty name of Jesus, she would be healed. And to be honest with you, it was my first time seeing a woman with fat a belly, though she wasn't pregnant, so I was sad and felt sorry for her for not going to the hospital all those years. Though God is a miracle worker and she did the right thing to come to the house of the Lord, but met wrong acting man of God. And so though she did all she was told to do and she also gave those money they asked her, she eventually died in a couple of months later, and then the same Jack, who was supposed to heal her, accompanied us to the cemetery, and he stood as a pastor to bury.

Largea told me that he loved me and he wanted to marry me and buy me a sewing machine for me to learn how to sew in Accra, and so it was like he read my mind about how badly I wanted to become a seamstress, that it didn't happen, but I told him point-blank I had a husband, so I didn't want another one. And so I didn't know what his reasons were, but one time, in the middle of the night, I was fast asleep, outside on the hallway, next to the chief's daughters, and I heard someone calling my name: "Atswei, Atswei, Atswei!" And so I suddenly opened my eyes, and then I saw Largea on his knees behind the mosque net, and he told me that Jack was calling me. And so I was mad at him, and I told him to tell Jack. I had no business with him until tomorrow, daytime, and the next morning, when I asked Jack why he sent for me at late night, he denied it, and he said he didn't send Largea, but I didn't believe him. And so since then, though I wore a pantie, I added pants to it, and I covered myself also with cloths, and I kept on wondering about the kind of people I was dealing with, who were claiming to be men of God but were rather wolves in sheepskin. And I even told myself that if I didn't have a boyfriend, I wouldn't be with any of those scammers, because being in a relationship with them is like being with the devil himself. And so months later, a fight broke between those faked pastors, because, according to Jack's confession later, they stopped talking to themselves, because Solomon was in love with Tsotsoo, and he was shy to tell her, so he told Jack to tell Tsotsoo his feelings toward her, and rather, Jack had sex with her in the same room in the middle of the night. And Solomon got mad at him for being a bad friend.

Days later, Largea thought he was Jack's best friend because he brought him to the church in Nugua, and he told him that he loved Kai and she didn't want to be with him, and so he should convince her to become his girlfriend, and rather Jack had sex with her in the same dark room in the middle of the night. And so Largea was so mad and disappointed in him, and so Solomon, Largea, and Akronkron teamed up against Jack, and they stopped talking to him or stepping out with him, and so he was on his own, and he was crafty, selfish, and greedy among them, and he rather went to tell Ms. Allotey that his friend hated him without him doing anything wrong to them. And so because such issues between them are so delicate to tell Ms Comfort when she asked them, and so she thought Jack was telling the truth about his friends hating him. And so she went to Nugua and reported them to Michael, and for that reason, he ordered all of them to return back to Nugua, except Jack, to be with Ms. Allotey. And so after his friends left for Nugua, he made that confession to me, in which he wasn't honest with Ms. Comfort about his friends, and so I asked him why he did such bad things to his best friends, and because of his lies, they sadly left and he was enjoying everything now. And one more thing about Jack was that, naturally, he is a good liar who can put his hands in fire for him to be believed than the rest of them and is so controlling, and he also seems like he is always the victim. And so now that he was alone, he continued with his crafty ways in getting more money from the offertory, because he one time passed comments unaware that whenever he gets Grandma's tithes and offerings, he left for Accra to shop for new clothes and shoes.

I was surprised to hear that because the church tithes and offerings were supposed to be saved by Ms. Comfort, so that at the end of the month, it was divided into two, and half of it was sent to the headquarters before Ms. Comfort, and Jack shares the rest. Besides, food was available, and even before dinner was cooked, they asked Ms. Comfort what she would like to eat, and it was prepared. And so for Jack to make that statement, it means, he steals Grandma's tithes, from the offertory on Sundays after service before the money was counted, and so aside from all those bad behaviors, he is also a thief who is stealing from God. And though I didn't ask him why he does that, I realized more how fake he is, and he would be rewarded for his own actions toward God and the way he treats people. And after his friends left, he wanted a bed and mattress in the room and to furnish it for himself because they slept on mats on the floor for months till they left, and so Grandma had Mom's bed from Lolonyah, and she bought tsatsa on the bed for him to sleep on and the chair inside, and he bought a plastic wardrobe, and he placed his stuff inside. And a couple of months later, another church branch was opened, at Old Ningo, which wasn't far from Ada Junction for Solomon to head, and we, as a church, were told by Michael, to visit them, on one weekend, to have services with them.

During the due date, for us to leave, just about an hour's time, I was busy dressing up in the room, and Amos was outside playing with his little car made out of milk cans with wheels on it and a rope tied to it for pulling it, and so as he was moving backward, his slippers hit the charcoal pot, then the boiling soup that was being prepared by a tenant, in the compound poured all over the ground, so close to where Amos fell, after he hit the charcoal pot filled with fire, which could have poured all over himself, and he might die right away or be disfigured out of severed burns for the rest of his life. But God miraculously pushed him aside from the boiling soup, and thankfully, just a small amount of soup poured on his left upper hand through his armpit. When we heard him screaming, I rushed outside together with the neighbors to pick him up, and because it was the weekend in the evening, I couldn't send him to the health center, but I went to the drugstore to buy him pain relief, syrup, and also a

217

spray for burns. And so it was a great miracle and surprise to me and everyone in the house for how God saved Amos's life, and I had tears of joy, and I was grateful to God for not giving up on Amos since the day I got pregnant with him. And so I had no choice but to leave with them. I really loved my job as an interpreter because I learned from Ms. Comfort. The Bible in John 9:1 says, "While it is daytime, we must do the works of Him who sent Me." Night is coming when no one can work. I was the only person who understood and spoke both Ga and Ada languages well and also Ningo language, which is a combination of both Ga and Ada languages.

When we arrived at Ningo in the crusade, grounds, there was no electricity, so we used lamps throughout the service till the end, and we couldn't win new souls to few souls Solomon had, because their beliefs were the same as the Ada, so they weren't easily convincing to leave their churches or leave their voodoos to join the new church, especially when they saw that Jack's faked miracle for healing the blind didn't work. His fake prophecies mean nothing to them. And one more thing I noticed between the Ningo people and the Adas was that we are more generous givers than them, because though the members knew that we were coming, they didn't prepare food for us to eat after the the church service, so I was smart enough to carry with provisions for breakfast and agblemaku and okro soup for dinner, and I even shared with a couple of people. And so in the next Sunday too, we were served with small kenkey and fried fish with pepper after the end of the service, but Amos and I had good breakfast, and then we returned back to Ada Junction. Also in terms of giving offerings, they didn't really give, though Jack tried the appeals for funds, tricks with more quotes from the Bible, but it didn't work. And so when I thought of how my son was saved by God, the more I show my gratitude by volunteering in his work, and so thankfully, a few weeks later, his wounds were healed and left with his scars. That keeps on reminding me of the accident that day.

When he was eighteen months, he had severed measles, and he cried at all times in a whispering voice, and he was so weak he couldn't eat, and he couldn't suck my breast too because he had sores all over his mouth and his whole body, and I thought he wouldn't make it, and that was the first time I sent him to the health center since his birth, and I didn't even send him to have immunizations. And so he was treated by a doctor with a few injections, medicines to drink, calamine, lotion to apply his body, and gentian violet to use cotton and applied it in his mouth sore. And he had the contagious disease from neighbors, kids in the house, and so I continuously prayed for him apart from the medicines he had, and by the grace of God, he was healed in no time.

I was still living with Grandma, and I ignored her cheating, and so she continued to buy me smoked fish. She added her own interest for me to sell. I did my best by respecting her and taking her orders, knowing that it was a temporary job, and soon God will open new doors for me. But Ofliboyo never worked, and Grandma provides her cloths and blouses, all her needs, including her two kids, and I didn't complain about that. And since I moved in with her, she bought me only four yards, cloths, sold cheaper, because they were rejected from the cloth factories in Ghana, and they named them "fence cloths" and with different blouse. And so I wore it sometimes to church service, and so later, she deliberately bought me another two different types of fence cloths, which was six yards each, to sew and wear to church, then a new blanket, also surprisingly from Ada Foah market, without me asking her to buy anything. And so I thanked her, and I thought she felt guilty about what she was doing to me, and so I felt calm inside, then I stuffed them in my big basket, which was the only thing I had to put my outfits inside, but one time, Ofliboyo came for a visit, also to get money and things from Grandma, like he normally does. And so I was busy outside for dinner and also for Jack and his girlfriend, Georgina, since he didn't sometimes like the food prepared from Bondee's house. And all the while, Grandma and Ofliboyo were having some conversations in the room, and I went to the room to drink water, then I saw Ofliboyo put my cloths in the basket she brought along with her, and she was ready to leave, and so first I got confused, and I thought maybe that might be Grandma's because she bought things she bought me, and so just for me to be sure, I poured my cloths on Grandma's bed, and I went through them. And to be honest with you, all those new things she bought me weren't in my basket, and so I asked Grandma, "Where are my cloths and blanket?" And she said, "Oh, I just gave them to Ofliboyo!"

And so out of shock, I was like, "What? But why mine and not yours?"

And so, you know I was expecting her to say, "Oh, don't you worry at all, Atswei. I will replace them soon!" Even if it was a lie, but she started yelling at me that she gave them for me, and now she had changed her mind and she gave it to someone else.

And so I stepped outside with loud crying and saying, "This is not fair at all. After all I did for you, is that how to pay me back? Why did you give them to me in the first place?" Grandma didn't feel a little bit guilty for that, and to calm me, rather she followed me outside, and she started cursing me in proverbs in the Ada language, "Keep walking, but I'm right behind you." And to me, it means that since I have the nerve to talk back at her for demanding my rights, it shall never be well with me, and so on the other hand, I should continue enduring all the injustices she did to me without complaining. And another proverb also she said, "As for me, I'm carrying a pot of water, but soon you will meet someone carrying a pot of palm wine." And my understanding of that means, if I think she is treating me badly, rather I will be treated so terribly by someone soon. And so I was depressed and terribly hurting about how my own grandma had been greedy, selfish, and heartless to me, and on top of that, when I complained just once, she started casting spells on me for worse things to happen to me in life rather than best things, and meanwhile, she forced me to be with her against me. And so I was so overwhelmed, and I told her that God is the only judge between the two of us and, someday, we see who is the guilty one.

I really missed Ashaiman more, because aside from Amartey, who raped me during my pregnancy, Maa and her family treated Amos and me so well, so kind, and with respect, and I never worked, but both of our needs were provided, and I had a brighter future there to become rich and independent until Grandma forced me to be with her through the elders of my family in Lolonyah. And I knew that she wasn't a good grandma to me since my childhood, Lolonyah, when I was little, and she took care of Ofliboyo, who had mental illness, but she always came first, and she didn't really care about my well-being, and so I depended on my great-grandma and Korleteynye, who lived in the next house to keep on surviving, and I also moved around to old folks in their houses. And so because I was so smart and eloquent and curious, they gave me a nickname: "Atsweiodjadjeotso." This, in the Ada language, means "Atswei a talkative," and then they said, "Who is this little girl?" And then I told them in such an enthusiastic, funny way, "Ami Atsweiooo, ami Atswei!" In the Ada language, it means "It's me, Atswei. Oh, it's me, Atswei." And then all questions they asked me about my family. I had answers to those, and they fed me because of that, and all the while, Mom and Adzoa were staying with Dad in Labadi. And amazingly, she likes Adzoa also more than me in those times, which made me feel rejected way back in those days, when I was just five years old, before I had that guinea worm disease, but what I didn't see coming and I never thought of was that in my eighteenth year, Mom would die, and I would be living with her, and she would curse me if I complained about her wrongdoings toward me. And so after those curses, I was comforted by the neighbors, and Ms. Comfort also encouraged me with Bible quotes in Psalm 109:28, which says, "Then let them curse if they like, but you will bless me! When they attack me, they will be disgraced! But I, your servant, will go right on rejoicing! And someday God will pay me back, big time, for all cruelty done to me."

And so though I heard her and after giving it some more thoughts, I decided to go back to Ashaiman and now that Amos was walking, he will be at daycare center, and I will go back to lotto ticket sales I planned for before Grandma forced me to stay with her, and so the next day I told her I was visiting my family for few days at Ashaiman, and I packed clothes for Amos and me and clothes in the same basket I had to Ashaiman, and so after I told them what happened, they all felt sorry for me, and I blame Maa, somehow, for letting me go, because even if that was traditionally done, I told her how hard Grandma was so hard to deal with, and even when Mom was around, they argued, especially when she was in sick bed, so she should have explained that to the family members to allow me to continue living with them. But she told me that she couldn't go against the tradition because she would be blamed if anything happened to us under her care, and so now I went there, and Grandma rather didn't treated me well. He would have no one to blame but herself. And so I was calm and at peace to be back again with an honest and caring family, who never frowned at me, yelled at me, or insulted me in any way, but I felt loved, and then I gave Adzoa a message from Grandma to come over and visit her. And so she went the next day to Ada Junction, and then I resumed my normal chores excitedly, and I saw how much they also missed me because Adzoa couldn't replace me since she was a lazy type, and she was a spoiled brat when Mom was alive, and so two weeks later, when she returned back from Grandma's, I was shocked to see that she bought her two different kinds of colorful cloths, which was six yards each, and she also sewed them.

It hurts me more, and it confirmed that Grandma didn't really like me, no matter what I do to please her, and that also reminded me of how I was rejected and badly treated by my own close family when I was little. And what I didn't understand was, why didn't she choose Adzoa to stay permanently with her since she loved her that much? And what I learned from some people is, if they love someone, they don't let them do anything at all for them, but they are treated with care and respect, and all their needs are provided with, which is quite opposite from Mom's. And so I was still at Ashaiman, and my mind was made up to carry on with my plans toward the future for both Amos and me to send him to a daycare center, after I hired a kiosk, and I had it registered to start selling lottery tickets, but I also felt so bored. I missed church and my interpretation, and I felt guilty for leaving God's unfinished and thinking about myself and my child alone and also because I lived with pagans who talked about nothing else but voodoos, and I hate the fact that I couldn't convince them to be Christians. And so I decided to go back to Ada Junction not because of my grandma but to continue doing the work of the Lord rather and gain a better reward someday, which lottery sales can't give me already. Ms. Comfort told Adzoa to ask me to return back to continue God's work to receive blessings from it. And Maa and her family didn't like the idea that I was going back to Grandma's after all she did to me, but I left anyway back to Ada Junction, and I continued with all chores, and she also continued cheating me in terms of smoked fish sales, but I pretended like nothing happened, and I didn't complain, but I was still hurting inside because seeing her reminds me of what she did to me, especially those curses, and she didn't regret, apologize, or replace me with those things.

I continued going to church as an interpreter, and more than ever, I focused on God, and I keep my faith, trust, and hope for abundant blessings someday in order to shame Grandma and all those who hurt me in the past. And I wasn't expecting any apology because Ghanaians, as far as I know, don't apologize to their children whenever they hurt their feelings, because to them, they own them, like part of their properties, like forever, and rather most of them control their grown-up children and their wives or husbands like puppets, and in the least mistakes their children make in terms of talking to them or something else, they freak out, with insults and curses until they go to their knees to beg for their forgiveness, especially pagans. And the Gas even has a saying that "tse kpaa bi fai" means "Father, never apologize to the child." And so they took advantage of that saying and continue hurting their children, and it doesn't matter how old they are. And so a couple of months later, after Georgina moved in with Jack, Bondee sponsored Georgina's engagement, and she became Jack's wife because Bondee didn't want him to have a relationship of any kind to the rest of the youth in the church, and so I was their cook, and at the same time, I fetched water from the well for them to drink and bathe, and I took it as part of my volunteer work for God. And Adzoa also returned to Grandma's for a few weeks after I came back, and she told me that she was dating Amartey, and she got pregnant, and they had the baby, aborted at a clinic, and right now, she was a couple of weeks pregnant again, so this time, they wanted to keep the child, and so they already told Maa and the family.

In fact, hearing the bad news broke my heart, because at least one of us should have completed form 4 education successfully and much more. Why does it have to be Amartey who raped me? And also Maa wasn't only Grandma's half sister, whose daughter was Amarkuo.

223

Amartey's father was one of Grandma's siblings, called Lomo, and so both sides are close families. And I was even wondering if he raped her the same way he did to me, and Adzoa felt embarrassed to tell me because it's difficult to talk about rapes those days since they wouldn't believe you, and instead you're the victim, who rather turned out to be a bad girl and tempted the man to rape her. And I wanted to blame her, but I kept quiet, because who am I to judge her for not completing her education and getting pregnant? Since I was a bad example to her, I couldn't also tell her that I was raped by Amartey because I hadn't gotten over what he did, so I just didn't feel like talking about it. And so one thing I observed was that Adzoa and Jack became close friends and they spent more time in the prayer room in the afternoon and after dinner, and so I went on with my chores, and she told me that they were studying the Bible, so because of the hot temperature in the room, she joined Amos and me to sleep outside in the same tsatsa and mosquito net, and so Amos slept in between the two of us. And I didn't have much experience when it comes to the way someone breathes after sex, and so each late night, she joined us inside the mosque net. She breathes heavily and faster than normal, but I thought she went to pee, and she got scared of the darkness, and she runs as a result of that. And so not knowing the secret behind all was that she and Jack had an affair on her first visit before she left, and all the while, Georgina was still Jack's wife, and he was cheating on her. And so they continued to have sex in a place called prayed room, and later on, Georgina found out about their relationship, and one time when Jack, Georgina, and Adzoa went for dawn preaching at a village called Korlekope, which is a mile away, for some reason, Georgina and Adzoa started fighting each other, and so when they came back home, she couldn't tell me until someone from the village told me after the evening service before I took my time to see a little scratch on her face, and she lied that Georgina was jealous with the relationship between Jack and her, and so for that reason, she started the fight, and so I couldn't figure out what the fight was about because I thought, since she was pregnant with Amartey's child, there wasn't any way to be sleeping with another man. And so I told her to be careful, because, since I arrived at Ada Junction, I didn't have fights or arguments with anyone, except Grandma, and so their secret affair grew up to the point that they decided to have an abortion in Accra and then get rid of Georgina, so they get married. Only God knows the one responsible for the pregnancy because it doesn't make sense to me to abort someone's child so easily without his permission and get married right away.

The night before their due date, we were having evening church service, and then a surprise guest, a guy preacher, with his Bible in his armpit, came out of nowhere and visited. And so Jack told him to preach since he was the messenger, so the preacher based his sermon on the child abortion, that a child is a gift from God, and so no one has the right to get rid of it no matter what, and so those of us who have that intention should better watch out as they would be punished by God, and he also said that with God, all hidden things are visible to him. Also, he talked about those who were cheating on spouses, committing adultery, and that is in the Ten Commandments in the Bible. God speaks against it too. And all the while, I had no idea what was going on between those two, and their evil decision, God was against it, and so he sent his messenger, who came from the Volta Region, to warn them, and though I liked the sermon, only those two were the guilty ones. And surprisingly too, Amartey came from Ashaiman the next morning. They were supposed to be at Accra for the abortion, and he said he got worried because Adzoa said she was spending a few days over, and it had been weeks, and she didn't return back, and so she asked Adzoa to pack her things to leave, and so they left in an hour for Ashaiman. And so months later, Adzoa sent a message that she had a baby girl, and so we were all happy for her, and then Jack made an announcement at church that everyone had to buy baby's clothes, pomade, or things that the child might need and those who wanted to donate money to the child and to dedicate the child also, then he set a date for us to leave to Ashaiman with Bondee's truck. And so he behaves like he was the child's father, and meanwhile, Amartey was a Muslim, whose child didn't need dedication, but she was given a Muslim name right away in a week's time. And so for real, we went on a trip to Ashaiman and to surprise Adzoa on a Saturday when she and her baby were lying on the floor in the same small room with the door widely opened because of the heat, and Amartey and all the family weren't at home, except a couple of tenants, and so we sat on one of the benches in the compound, and we prayed for the child, and we presented her our gifts to the child, and since Grandma couldn't come with us, she gave me things for the child and money, too, and we bought food on the way, which was kenkey and fried fish and boiled lobsters, with hot peppers, and all Adzoa provided was water to wash our hands with and some to drink, and we all ate together with lively conversations. And so we returned to Ada Junction after spending some time with her, so thereafter, Jack confesses everything in detail to me, about their relationship and the abortion plans. Because he is a good liar, he told me that was Grandma's idea. He and Adzoa should be in a relationship and get married. And so his story didn't make sense to me at all because Grandma was among those who sent Georgina's traditional rights to her family, and they were living together in the same house, and why would she encourage you to marry her pregnant granddaughter?

I knew Jack also as a cheater and a he-goat type of person who sniffed every teenager or woman that crosses his path by having sex with her, and so when I thought over all that was said and done, Adzoa also had to be blamed, because how could she have an affair with him when she was pregnant with someone else's child, and she agreed to abortion? And since she never told me about her affair with Jack, I was so disappointed and ashamed even to ask her about this disgraceful act, and one good thing I did, too, was that I kept her secret well and I didn't tell anyone, because if Maa and her family, including Amartey, heard about it, I don't think that child would be accepted in the family, especially since there was no DNA test in the system in those days to prove if he was the father and even the child, and Amartey had nothing in common, like a little resemblance, though she looked somehow like Adzoa. And so Jack had no shame at all or regret for this shameful act, which is a sin before God, but he told me later that the two loved each other, and so after she had that child, they planned to continue their relationship, secret and get married eventually. She would stay at Ada Junction for good.

I told him I am quite opposite of Adzoa in everything, and Grandma even knew me. Well, if I set my mind on something, that's it, so because she knew that I had a serious boyfriend, she couldn't force me into any relationship; else, she couldn't even convince me to marry the rich chief, who might have promised her things, like free accommodations or a brand-new house, if he married. And one more thing to growing up among fetish priests, I studied them so well to know how great and mightier God is, and I also knew how every knee bows before him and every tongue confesses that he is the Lord, like in the Bible in Romans 14:11, and they also know that they can't do anything without God with all powers they think they have, because I've never seen any of them pouring libations with either alcoholic drinks or a calabash of water and not calling God's name first and then lifting the drink toward heaven, and they address God with honor and respect, and they lift his name so high, like in the Ashanti language: "Otswediapong, Nyame" means "supreme God"; "Okatamansu," like a top security man who guards the whole nations; "Oyeadueyie" means "a handyman who fixes anything before they asked him to have a drink, to help them in all things that they do, and their voodoos rather comes last." And so because of all years of my observations, I am one, in a million, who knows God better, and with my own life experiences, I know that God is capable of doing anything, and that lifts my so spirit high it increases my faith and my trust in God, and I put him in the first place before anything else, and for that reason, too, I blindly respected and served any one that claimed to be the messenger of God in order to receive more blessings directly from him. And so one time, when Ebennezer came around, I asked him to go to for prayers, and so it was Jack who prayed for us, instead of Ms. Comfort, so after the prayers, he said he saw a brighter future for both of us, and so we should continue being together, and we would be successful someday, which wasn't a prophecy to me, but he was using his wisdom to fool Ebennezer, like he fooled anyone else, and after the prayers, I introduced Ebennezer to him as my boyfriend, my future husband, and the father is Amos, and he said, "Oh, that is great," and he encouraged him to focus on his education, achieve his goals in life. And then we started outside.

He held Amos's hands, and we walked on the pathway, and we continued to talk about our future, and we confirmed the rule number one: no sex until after marriage, no matter how much we desired. And something else which was special about our relationship was that we didn't doubt the love we had for each other, though he likes girls and he continued to have sex, but in my case, though I was around matured young men in the house and in the neighborhood, he believed in me that I wouldn't cheat on him or break his heart, which belongs to me.

I also knew that regardless of his cheating, he wouldn't break my heart by leaving me for someone else because I was a fishmonger, and since his main subject was agriculture, he might get a real job and forget about Amos, like his father did to her mom and him. And so you know, when I was in school, the friends I mostly played and joked with were boys, and Eva was my only best girl friend, and I saw all those boys like brothers I never had, but with Ebennezer, I had different feelings toward him since the day I met him, so after everything that happened, he came looking for me, wherever I was, and so I didn't have any doubts that we would spend our lives together, especially how gentle, sweet, caring, and humbled he was to me, and even one of her girlfriends told me that girls fall for him because of his nature, since they barely receive such treatments from other boys. And also one more unforgettable experience I had in forms 4 was that my classmate Grace took me, one time, to Ada Foah, where the sea and the River Volta crash, and it sounds like bombs burst each time they crashed. Because they lived in a village close to that area, they have experienced that, and when she told me about it, I curiously wanted to see for myself.

That morning, I lied to Kakinye that we forms 4 students were supposed to be in school for a program, and so I left right away, and I walked about a mile to Azizanya village, and then I continued to walk to a couple of villages close to the beach before I arrived at Grace's village, and so we left right away after I greeted her parents. And she had some snacks and water for us, and though I was tired, I couldn't wait for the site scene, and so we didn't see any village but bare sandy path, and so we kept on walking, and we heard loud sounds, like a bomb blast, and so I was scared, and she said, "I haven't seen nothing yet." And then as we continue to walk, the pathway turns small, and then I saw the Volta River on my left side and then the sea on my right side and to be honest, I was very afraid, and the worse part was that as we kept walking, the sandy paths turned smaller, and the sea waves run into the Volta River, and as we went so close, then I saw the sea and the Volta River crash to each other in intervals, and they blasted like a bombshell, and the two acted like they hated each other, so they were fighting, as if they were on the battlefield. But Grace was so relaxed, and she told me that many dead bodies were found on that pathway because some get drowned in the sea or in the Volta River, and the bodies eventually dropped off there before they came to pick them up for burial, and in fact, that story rather scared me to death, and then my thoughts told me, *What if a big wave of the sea carried both of us inside the river? Who will save us?*

And so it means we would also die just like that, and then I started feeling uncomfortable, but one thing I had the courage to do and am grateful for was when she asked me to fetch water in between the sea and the river with my hands repeatedly to wash my face and to wish for anything, and I did exactly that, and I wished for long life, good health, and prosperity, and during those times, I was already pregnant. And so I told her that we had to leave right away, and so we returned back to their village to have the snacks and water, and she walked me halfway home, so I thought of that scary experience for a while. First, I blamed myself, but later, I was thankful to God for seeing that site scene. And so one time at Ada Junction, Jack and I were discussing the Bible in Isaiah 40:31, which says "They that wait on the Lord, she renew their strength; They shall mount up wings as eagles; They shall run, and not be weary, they shall walk, and not faint." And so I will patiently wait on the Lord for you, sweetheart, to complete his education, get a job, and save money to marry me and instead of him, to encourage me, to stick to my words, as he claimed to be a man of God. Rather he said he didn't think that handsome young guy would marry me after he settles down since he had eyes on ladies who haven't had a child before and with their firm breasts, because mine now are flat, out of breastfeeding.

I laughed at him, and I told him that he didn't know my Ebennezer well like I did and the kind of love we two shared, and my hopes is in the Lord, and so even if he disappointed me, though it will hurt me, there is still hope for me as long as God lives, and so I will get a better person than him. And because he couldn't persuade me to leave Ebennezer, he changed the subject, and we talked about something else, and so later, I knew he would do exactly what he said to me, if he were to be Ebennezer, and even how he cheated on Georgina with Adzoa, and he forced his way to abort her child and marry her instead and then dumped Georgina, proof of the type of man he really was. And so apart from all those bad behaviors of Jack, he is verbally, emotionally, and physically abusive, because several times, we heard him yelling, insulting, and beating Georgina with his door locked, and so when she started crying out loud for help, we couldn't open the door to save her, and later on Jack would step outside sweating and tell lies that she was cheating on him when she told him that he was going to her dad's place. But meanwhile, Georgina would be inside the room all day long, and he warned her not to share what was actually going on with them. And so I asked myself, if he was a real man of God, would he abuse her, even if she was cheating? And so because of his nasty behaviors, aside from Grandma and me, none of those tenants joined the church, and he didn't even listen to Ms. Allotey whenever she tried to correct him to stop that, since it's a disgrace to pastors especially, since one time he left for Nugua church for ordination service for the young pastors, and he said he was among them, but he came back without certificate of ordinations.

What blew my mind away was that pagans in the house rather treated their wives and girlfriends with respect, and though they argued in their rooms, they didn't hit them or insult them. And so I felt sorry for such a beautiful, classic young lady who completed her secondary education and should be working and find a real man, who would treat her nicely, instead of Jack, with a fat mouth full of lies, who couldn't offered her anything but pain and suffering. And also one of our middle-aged neighbors traveled to Togo to buy clothes, cloths from Holland, perfumes, watches, slippers for sales, because things shipped to their harbor are duty-free, and so for that reason, things are cheaper to buy and sell, and so do many Ghanaians. And so I gave her money, and she bought me cloths, designer perfumes, pomades, and a wristwatch, because God, amazingly, touched customers' hearts, and no matter what prices I came out with on the fish, they bought right away, and so I gained many profits to save for those things.

In early 1975, Jack's mom came over to look for him, and she was short, four feet and eight inches tall. She was fat, had a round face, smaller eyes, pointed nose, and regular-sized mouth, but she dressed like a pauper because of the way she dressed in worn-out cloths, slippers, and scarf, and so that was strange to me, because no matter how the Adas dress anyhow, at home or in farms, whenever they step out for any occasion, like funerals, outdoorings, or traveling, out of villages or towns, they dress decently in their best cloths, pure-gold jewelries, slippers, scarfs and watches. I mean the bottom line is that they dressed appropriately and were presentable to prove that they are really hardworking. And so for Jack's mom, Selina, to travel from Accra, the city, where people are more civilized, to be in those worn-out cloths made me realize the type of family he came from, and instead of him being humble and being a good person, rather aside from his bad behavior, he pretended like he came from a royal family, and he also looked down to those Adas, who were kind to him. And so later on, I also thought that maybe her mom was the pauper, because way back in Labadi at the family house I lived in, the Gas dresses well to funerals, outdoorings, and especially Homowo festivals.

After she introduced herself, we offered her a seat and water to drink, food to eat. She was so outspoken, and at that time, Jack wasn't home, and she had the chance to tell us about Jack's two wives he currently have in Accra, and he also had three kids with those women, and two of the kids were dumped by his wife for her to care for, but she wasn't working, and she also had couple more teenagers she was caring for, and so she went to the church at Nugua, and she was directed to come over. And so she came for Jack to give her money, to provide for them, and then I knew that was the Lord's doing, to unmask him to be known as the kind of man he was, because how possible could it be that he had multiple wives in Accra and then fooled the members that he wasn't in any relationship in Accra and he married Georgina and at same time he wanted Adzoa also? And so he when he arrived home, he let her mom leave in no time after they talked in the room, but what he didn't know was that we heard all we needed to know about him. And so when he left for Accra days later, he brought a five-year-old son called Sammy, who was smaller than his age. He had kwashiorkor because of malnutrition, and he was skinny, and his eyes turned red, and everyone stared at him like he was an alien, so different from the neighborhood kids, so people kept asking, "Who is this kid? And where did he come from?" And then he lied that was his son from his divorced wife, and he brought him over to his mom's place because she was jealous, then he even told me one time that he told his mom to stop talking about his childhood's behaviors and also her private matter, but she didn't listen. And so I noticed that though no one said anything to him, he knew her mom well, so he figured out she might have told us things about him. And so my point was that if he had nothing to hide, why would he shut him mom up, not to discuss anthing about him? And that proves how worse he was since his childhood and in his own hometown. And so later on, he was embarrassed because of his own son, and for that reason, she begged a middle-aged member called Soyonye in the church to care for him at Korlekope, where she lives, a village where there wasn't a school to go to in his fifth year, and so it proved that he, being a assistant teacher at Nugua, was also part of his lies, because he should have known better than anyone else to let his son be with him and go to the school around, and also if he was an assistant teacher, why didn't he look for a teaching job since the church wasn't growing and rather decreasing after all his tricks?

He continued to steal Grandma's awesome tithes from the offertory without nobody noticing, except God, and he saved enough money to buy old-fashioned small couches, a dresser, and a center table from Accra, and he hired a truck over to furnish his room. And so suddenly, Pastor Michael came from Nugua on a surprise visit, with lots of envelopes, with the church's name boldly printed out and also fundraising service in aid of a church building and the exact date of the event on them, and so I was wondering why Jack built a medium-sized palm branch, shed, and we worshiped there, and during rainy season, we returned back to the hallway to worship, but we hadn't acquired any land yet for church building, and so what were those envelopes for? And there I figured it out myself that, just like Jack said, stealing from God is kind of wisdom to keep on surviving, and so Micheal was also using the same common sense to steal from God to live. And so Jack told me to accompany him to Big Ada to distribute the envelopes to the rich people over there in order for them to put huge money inside since I was the interpreter, and so when we arrived at Big Ada, the first house we went inside was the "Gabon house," which was boldly written on the front walls of his one-story building. And so we met an elderly man in his sixties who spent half of his life in Gabon, in the West Coast of Africa, and with his breakthrough, because of being hardworking, he bought plots of land, and he built the story building after he returned home. He also had single rooms across the the story building and a large compound where people hired for engagements, and they were fenced and gated.

I was impressed with his success, story, and so we gave him an envelope after he asked a little bit of the church, and he promised to send someone to return the envelope to us on that Sunday because he wouldn't be able to come. And so from there, we went to invite a chief from a particular tribe called Nana Pediator, who was in his late forties. He was handsome and humble because of how he invited us right away to his living room, and he was a Christian, and he said he was chosen to be a chief in his young age as soon as he completed his secondary education, and he also said pouring libations and traditional duties as a chief meant nothing to him, because he is a committed Christian who goes to church, and whenever he was invited to such occasions, he honored that and he prayed to God and even some of the traditional rights someone had do for him, and so he promised to come to the function because he was available. And then we also went to self-contained houses and invited individuals, then we returned back home, and we also invited rich elderly people also at Ada Junction and nearby villages for days. The rest of the envelopes were given to the members of the church to distribute to their family and friends. And then at the set date, Sunday, in the late morning, Nene Pediator arrived, so well-dressed in an Ashanti Kentey cloths and in pure gold necklace, bracelets, and rings, and with his Oheneba slippers, and he was escorted by one of his elders carrying his stylish umbrella as soon as he got out of his car, and he was given a seat in a couch. And so we started to service with opening prayer, and then we continued with worship and praise songs by us the girls, and then Jack said the main intentions of the service was to raise funds in aid of the church building in order for us to worship in a real church rather than the palm branches, shed. And then Micheal and four of his three young pastors arrived, and a few invitees also came, though we expected more than that, then Michael made the appeal for funds, and he started calling big donations and kept on reducing it because people couldn't give, and I also gave what I couldn't afford.

And thereafter, a funny way for people to give money in such programs is called "Kofi," which means "Friday male born," and "Ama" means "Friday female born." And what happens is that Michael started calling days of the week from Monday borns, and then a song was chosen by one of them, then all Monday borns danced to the center of the church, where a basin was placed on the table, and they put their money inside. After that, the money was counted separately, and then he continued by calling Tuesday borns. Same procedure was done, and so he went on and on until Sunday borns were called, and so after counting all those money separately, the winners of those days were called according to how much they gave, and the loser was also called, which was interesting to watch how people gave generously, because they didn't want their day of birth to lose. And then Jack asked for general offerings, and then all envelopes were collected from the individuals, and after that, Nene Pediator was asked to say a few words of encouragement, and after he finished, he gave his generous donation, which was in his envelope, before he left, then closing prayer was said, and benediction was given, and the program came to an end. But something unbelievable happened, and that was as soon as the program was over, instead of Pastor Micheal allowing the money to be counted, for everyone to know how much they had from the program, rather, he ordered the money in a medium-sized bucket with lid to be put in the trunk of his car, and then he told Ms. Comfort and Jack to come over to the Nugua to get the share of the money, which was supposed to be used to build a temple for the Lord.

One more interesting thing about Ghanaians when it comes to addressing their chiefs, each region has honoring terms of saying "Your Highness": in the Ga language, "Nii"; Ada language, "Nene"; Ewe language, "Togbe"; and Ashanti language, "Nana," etc. And so the actual stool name of the big Ada Chief is "Pediator" and "Nene" is "Your Highness." So the day Michael took the fundraising money away was a shock to the members because no pastor did such a thing in the church, and especially Jack was so disappointed more than anyone else because his intentions was that the money would be counted and, as usual, in front of everyone, but in the room, Micheal will take his share, and he gives them theirs, too, because he definitely knew that Micheal is also crafty just like himself, and there wouldn't be any church temple for worship. And also when it comes to money and a human being drowning in the river where Jack is supposed to save one, he will choose money over the human being, and so you know how much he loves money more than anything else, he wouldn't be stealing tithes and offerings for his selfish reasons without thinking that money is the Lord's. And so Jack was hurting so badly because he said it was him who worked so hard for organizing the fundraising service, and what made him more depressed was that he did went to Nugua to collect the share for both him and Ms. Allotey, but unfortunately, Michael refused to give them any of the money, and he kept on tossing him for three days, and so he returned back with nothing but anger. And though the members still gave Michael benefits of the doubt, he would bring the money back to build the temple, since Bondee offered him a free land, but as a smart nineteen-year-old, I knew he was fake, like Jack, but he sounded like a nice person, and so I respected him for that, but what he did by stealing money which was supposed to be used to build God's temple was a worse thing that a real man of God wouldn't do. And so afterward, one evening, at church service, Michael came unannounced, and he took the pulpit to preach during his sermon. One lie he came out with was, he went to a church conference in the US, and then he performed a miracle by praying for people with bald heads, and their hair grew instantly, and that showed how God uses him for his miracles, and then he said, as a result of that, he would be performing more miracles at Accra Chorkor, where he had his first church temple.

He gave the chief money to let his gongon play gongon to the whole town and surrounding villages to bring people with all disabilities to Chorkor for miracle healing, and so the villagers believed in him, though they haven't seen him before, but all they wanted was to get their health back, and so they contributed money for more trucks, because Bondee offered one truck, and so actually, three more trucks were hired with disableds and their families. And on the set day, Ms. Allotey, Jack, Georgina, Amos, and I joined them because I was the interpreter and more so I wanted to witnes those miracles myself, though I knew it was all made up to get more money from the naive Adas, and so we had tambourines, and we sang songs of praises on the way to Nugua, the headquarters. And I was shocked to see Michael having church service in a rented self-contained house he lived in, with canopies fixed in the compound and benches arranged as seats, with just about twenty members, instead of a cathedral with comfortable seats, and so we were asked to sit down. And then they started with worship and praises, and then Michael gave a short sermon, concerning giving, and then "here we go again," he started calling an amount of money for people to get up and give, expecting the Adas to give, but they were surprisingly looking at him because that wasn't why they came, and so he ended the service, and we weren't even given water to drink, and we were all smart to carry food and water with us. And then he told us to get back to the trucks to Chorkor, and there the real miracles were going to happen in the pool, and so we went inside in haste, and we drove to Chorkor, then I saw a worn-out wooden building, like it was rejected, for years, in the midst of fishermen and fishmongers and their families close to the beachside.

We were told to change our clothes before entering the pool called Chemu, so close to the sea, and as we all went inside that nasty, stinky water, then he and a few of his young pastors, including Jack, were in with us, helping out the disabled from drowning alongside their families, and then Michael told us to hold each other's hands, then he quoted the Bible in John 5:1–13, which was a miracle that happened at a poolside by Jesus. And he talked about the cripple Jesus met in Jerusalem at the sheep gate pool, called in Aramaic Bethesda, and he was there for thirty-eight years, and he said, whenever an angel came around, to stir the water, someone gets ahead of him inside the pool and gets their healings, and so Jesus asked him if he wanted to be healed. And he said "yes," and he told him to fold his mat and leave, and instantly, he walked on his own back home. And so he told us to bathe in that pool for the miracles to happen, and all those while I observed what was going on, I knew he was just fooling the Adas, and so he prayed, as we bathed, and then he said all those we received that their miracle should raise hands, but no one did that, and so he told us to step outside the pool, and then out of shame, he said no miracle happened, because they didn't have faith. And so the Adas, who spent money and wasted time, hoping to return back home with great joy, were really disappointed, and they were whining about that throughout, until we got home, and that confirmed that the type of people those two were all scammers, but I continued in my volunteer service, knowing that at the end of time, in the Bible in Romans 14:12, which says, "So then, each of us, will account for ourselves to God."

And so those poor cripples return back and crawl on the floors, with their Afro Moses, slippers, made out of tyre, to protect their knees and hands, so it had that name, because Mose wore that kind of slippers, and so it turned to fashion those days, and people wore them to functions, and the farmers also wore them to their farms, because normally, they walked barefoot to the farms. And so because of Grandma's hard work, without resting, she didn't notice he wasn't young anymore, because aside from those four days of sales of smoked fish, she also went to the Volta River at Ada Foah to buy big sharks home, and with her butcher knife, she cut them into medium sizes, and she kept awake to smoke them, then in the morning, she carried them in baskets to the market to sell, and she nearly crippled out of that, so she was in bed for weeks, though she went to the health center, and she was given medications to take and rest, but that didn't work. And so she was in pains, and she got weaker each time, then I figured out something I didn't know, that was God using me, so I heated water in the bucket a little warmer, then I put a towel inside, and I squeezed it, and then I massaged her whole body, especially her joints in her back, repeatedly, until the water was cold, and then I rubbed with pain-relieving ointment, and at the same time, twice a day, I prayed to God for a miracle. Grandma didn't believe it will happen through me. And she was scared she might either die or turn crippled, so she sent a message to Lolonyah and to inform her family, so her sister Korletenye came over to visit her, and miraculously, she got better a few days later. She got on her feet and started walking again. I was grateful to God for her true miracle, about Michael and Jack, who claimed to be men of God, and yet they couldn't perform. And so later on, just like what Sarah overheard, those three angels told Abraham that a year by this time, they would have a son after he treated him nicely in the Bible in Genesis 18:10, and exactly, I overheard Korletenye tell Grandma, "Atswei is gifted with blessed hands," and "That is the reason why you are walking again," and then I smiled like Sarah did, and I am grateful to God for knowing I had a gift I'm not aware of, then I entered the room, and I served them with dinner, but none of them told me in my face.

And so a couple of months later, the church wasn't the same, but aside from their monthly share of the offerings, they weren't in need of food or anything else, but Jack was still mad because of that fundraising money Michael took all for himself and because he saw how generously they gave during the fundraising service, and so he decided to start his own church at Big Ada in order for him to have everything for himself without sharing with anyone, and also because he is a lazy type of person who wants the easiest way to become rich without working so hard for it, from the way he talks. But meanwhile, there is a saying: "Working so hard, that's what successful people do." And so he had a meeting with us teenage girls and boys, who were the only ones committed to the church, and that was Lehuyo, Patience, Elizabeth, and me, then the three Emmanuels, the drummers, also Georgina, and Bondee's youngest, a pregnant wife, called Akuyo. And so he had sweet talks with us, and he said God revealed this big dreams to him and have his own big ministry, and he would acquire plots of lands and build a mission home, a temple, and a big school attached to them, and if that happened, he would give us good salaries each month, and we would need anything. But as soon as we get there, foods will be cooked for us anytime.

And so we were impressed with his dreams, because we wanted to get out of poverty, especially me, who wanted to leave Grandma and move on with my life, rather than being a fishmonger for rest of my life, and so we said we were in with his plans. And so that means if we follow Jack to Big Ada, then Michael had no more members in Ada Junction, except Grandma, because he also convinced Soyonye to be his cook, and Jack didn't care because of his selfishness and greediness. And so because he still steals Grandma's tithes, offerings, which are more than the whole month, church tithes, and offerings, he saved enough money, and he went to Accra for a few days, and he printed posters with his full picture inside, and under it was a real man of God, "seven days, miracle, crusade, so all people, with disabilities, like blind, cripples, and death, should come over for healing, from 7:00 p.m. to 10:00 p.m. at Gabon House," and all those words were boldly printed inside the posters. And then he bought a new set of drums like base drum, side drum, and conga drum, and he also bought a local build amplifier and speakers too. And after he returned back with all church equipments and I told him that I was a little concerned about breaking out with Michael's members, he told me not to worry about it, because he told him he quit his church, and that still didn't make sense to me, because if he quit his church, it doesn't mean he had to take his members away from him. And I stopped talking because that's his problem, and so the next day, Jack, the boys, and I went to Big Ada with those posters and cooked starch, too, but we went to talk to Gabon about our plans, and we also wanted to hire his compound for seven-days crusades and also to hire an old abandoned, self-contained building in an old cemetery by the roadside, across the street, which belonged to his family. And so he told us he would give us his compound for free, since were using it for God's work, and his son-in-law, called Ebentse, who is a photographer in the town, had a big generator, machine, for hiring too and much more. He would let us know the price of the building later. And then we thanked him with much joy, because things started working for us, and then the boys went to the south side of the town, with posters and starch, and Jack and I also went to the north side, and we started pasting the posters on all walls and polls, with no restrictions. In two days' time, we posted one hundred posters, except ten of them, which he handed over to some people, and among them was a black-beauty student called Ama, and he told her to be there. And the self-contained building was rented for us, so cheap, and Ebentse also didn't charge for the generator because he belongs to Presbyterian Church and because we were using it for God's work, and then we cleaned the four beds and doubled living rooms, without a kitchen, self-contained house, somehow, because time wasn't in our side.

Our first night at Big Ada, that self-contained house, Jack and Georgina had a room, and next room was for prayers and consultations, then the other two rooms, one belonged to the girls, and the next one was for boys, so Jack and Georgina moved in with all their belongings, but we brought few of our things, with mats, and in the girls' room was a old twin-size bed and mattress, and so I took it as mine, and I covered it with a sheet, and Amos and I started sleeping in that bed with second thoughts. What if someone with any disease ever slept on it or someone died on it? But rather I was thankful for sleeping on a bed for the second time at the age of nineteen. The first crusade was in the evening, around 6:00 p.m., when all of us were supposed to be there, to start with prayers, worship and praise songs, to draw the attention of the crowd, and we girls had our heads scarfed with pieces of white material, and then Jack called me, and he told the rest to leave, then he gave me like white power mixed with incense, in a metal plate, to burn them with charcoal fire, and when I asked him what that was, he told me that he went to see a Muslim, imam for consultation, toward the crusade, so he gave him that to burn, as soon the crusade started, in order for the smoke to draw more crowds for far places to the crusade grounds. And also he was given some concoction, called "rukutu," which was Islamic words written on the slate, and then it is washed inside a bowl, with a little amount of water, and then mixed with honey to have two tablespoons, before he stepped in the crusade grounds, and whatever he told the crowd, they would listen, and also he would perform miracles too.

He also told me he was told that, without powers of voodoos and Malams, his church will never grow, and that was his reason for consulting, a malam, in order for him to have breakthrough. And so in fact, I was shocked, because it was my first time hearing such words from a self-claimed man of God, without a tiny, little faith in him, and rather asking help from malam to grow a church and win more souls and then perform miracles too. And also because I saw hundreds of fetish priests, rather than asking help from God first before anything else, but I said nothing else to him because he knows what he is up to, and God won't hold me responsible for that, so I did what he told me to do and placed the burning incense outside the door entrance, and I left him by himself, and then I went to the crusade grounds, to help my teammates. And so at the crusade grounds, we had a crowd who came over, not because of that incense power, but because there wasn't electricity in the town, so there wasn't any source of entertainment, except during Asafotufiam festivities, and so they saw the crusade entertaining and much more. They curiously wanted to see those miracles performed, like it was boldly written on the posters, by self-called Evangelist Jack. And so I walked through the crowd, to join my team on the stage, who were singing praise songs, in both Ga and Ada languages, and the three boys too were busy playing drums, then both young and old folks in the crowd were also happily singing and dancing alongside, and then I called for testimonies, for those whom God has done something, and to pick a song and dance in circles and put money in the offertory, which was in the center of the grounds, and whoever wanted God to do the same things or more should follow them to give offerings to the living God. And that was something Jack told me to say, in order to get more money from the people, and so they formed a long line, and they started to give a longer testimonies and then pick a song, and then we helped them to sing, and so then they were followed by friends, and they danced around, and then they put money in offertory, and afterward, I blessed them, and so I asked for thanksgiving offerings too, and they danced around to give in the offertory.

Since Jack heard all that goes on, because the house is just across the street, and so he came through the crowd as soon as the last offerings were given, then he climbed the stage, and he dressed in white shirt and pants and in high-heeled shoes, then the crowd cheered him, and with hands clapping, he started to preach the sermon, which he said, "Say me amen," in every sentence he made, so he was named "Say me amen osofo." "Osofo" means "pastor" in Ga and Ada languages, and all the while, I was the interpreter, and at same time, I read each Bible quotation he based on givings and miracles in the Bible in John 9:2–3, 6–7, and Jack talks about when Jesus, the disciple, asked if his parents sinned and he was born blind because of that? And he told them that neither of them sinned. But this happened so that God's words should flourish. And after he finished talking, he spat on the ground and he mashed till it turned to clay, and then he rubbed the blind's eyes with the clay, then he gained his back after Jesus instructed him to wash in the pool of Silaom. And I keep on interpreting them, until the sermon was over, and the three blind elderly men paddle a canoe from the other side of the river in the night to the crusade grounds, who desperately wanted to be healed, like they heard for five good days, and each night he had a story to tell him, after he prayed for them, and he encouraged them to keep on coming, and he placed the microphones in their mouths, and he asked them what they see.

Each of them told him, point-blank, that they saw nothing, and then he pointed his five figures to them, and he asked again, "How many figures are these?" And they told him they have no idea. And honestly, I was ashamed of standing by his side, and he was speaking through me in performing a fake miracle. And he also told the crowd to place their hands on hurting parts of their bodies, and he prayed and prayed, and he asked if someone had received a miracle and to raise the hands, and nobody did, and though they entertained themselves, they left so disappointed, especially those three blind men, and also a young, beautiful, crippled teenager, who also came to be healed, to still crawl home, through the darkness, because no miracles happened. But he had enough money for those five days because of the wisdom he told me to use, in terms of those testimonies and offerings, and he also made an appeal to fundraising, and he said because of expenses, he opened a bank account at Ada Foah in his own name and not in the church's name, so every day, he and his wife checked those lots of coins, and food expenses were taken from it, then I sent the rest of the bank. And on the sixth day, early evening, Jack's head pastor, Micheal, reported him to the Ada Junction Police, to be arrested for stealing his members, to form his church, and so Jack was informed by Soyonye, who spotted Michael's young pastors in the house, when we, the team, were busy singing songs of praises without even a crowd but some of the youth in the town, and so Jack sent us a message through Soyonye to stop the church, and then he was so afraid he would be arrested in the house and so walked through the darkness to Ebentse's house to spend the night over there, so after Michael's, those two young pastors and the police officers waited for some time, and there wasn't a crusade going on, and Jack, the accused, wasn't there, like those complaints said; they returned back to Ada Junction, with the hiring car and not their own car, because in Ghana, there are no cars for individual police officers to drive, so if a complainant wants someone to be arrested, then he has to hire a taxi for them to make the arrest, and so if you can't afford taxi fare, then it means they can't help you.

We were worried about him, but on the other hand, he brought it for himself, out of greed and selfishness, and I'm okay to be honest with him about my concern for the wrong thing he was about to do, and he told me not to worry. And so since that night, he told us started holding church services in those double empty living rooms in the house instead and also because he announced to the people in crusade grounds be coming for prayers and consultations in his prayer room, from 9:00 a.m. to 4:00 p.m., to pray for them and also to give them his gifted prophecy and to solve problems, so some people who weren't living in Big Ada but from other surroundings later heard about Jack, so they started came to consultations, and he continued his faked prophecies. He told them items they should buy like Florida, devil, incense, money, draw oil to be mixed in holy oil, etc. to use after bathing, in order for their businesses to prosper and to be very rich and also for them to be healed and good thanksgiving money in envelopes, then he said, instead of them, buying those items themselves, he told them to bring a fixed amount money, in order to buy everything himself, and have them blessed for pickups, and so Jack went on with his new tricks to turn rich the easy way like he planned.

Seriously, I hate that, as his interpreter, sometimes, I felt like he used me to fool those naive people, and then I reminded myself that I was just a messenger used to deliver messages or his spokesperson, and so I would be held responsible, and much more, since we came over, I didn't eat lunch and dinner cooked for them, because in Tuesdays and Fridays, I still go to the market to sell smoked fish and, on my way back to Big Ada, bought all things I needed, and I also had my own cooking pots, plates, cups, spoons, and I prepared my own food, and I shared with Amos and Akuyo, who was like Amos's babysitter, and she cared for him at all times, and rather I gave tithes and offerings, and so I didn't have anything to do with those filthy money. And also Jack acted like the fetish priests, because one time, a woman came to prayers for bodily nerves, pains, and Jack told her she was afflicted with "dadikojo" spiritually, because of Mom's past experiences concerning "dadikojo" I told him about. And so he told the woman to provide money for other items, but she should buy a dozen eggs and bring it over to him. He would pray for her, and everything the enemy put in her body will be removed by God and placed them in eggs rather, just like how Jesus transfered those demons from the man inside those pigs, in the Bible, Matthew 8:28–34. And so in the prayer room, Jack gently and carefully pushed needles attached to back threads as much as he can inside each eggs, until the dozen eggs were filled with small needles and thread, and so because she told that woman it would take a week for that miracle to happen, so though he tried his best, there were small cracks, and the eggs got rotten, and it stinks in the prayer room, no matter how much Florida water perfume he sprayed. And so he announced to the little youths he connected to the church, as his members, to tell people in the town about the unbelievable, real miracle of casting "dadikojo" inside eggs, so that evening, we brought more lamps outside, and we arranged benches in a circle too for people to sit on, and Jack ordered for fire on charcoal pot, and he placed the eggs in a cooking pot, well covered with lid on it in the center, where the service was going on. He asked someone to continue to fan the fire for the eggs to cook in no time. And so Jack continued to encourage those around about how powerful God was, and in twenty minutes' time, I took the eggs off the fire, and I poured the hot water, and I added cold water to the eggs in the cooking pot and brought it over to Jack, and so as we kept on singing, then he peeled off the eggs gently in front of the audience, and then when he finished, he called that woman to come over, then he broke the cook eggs one after another, and then he asked the audience, "What do you see in those eggs?" And they all shouted, "Needles, and black threads!"

Then he told them to clap for Jesus, because from "today, she is untied, and saved, from the forces of darkness, that afflicted, her, with dadikojo, and she won't be poked by needles anymore." And there you know the kind of man Jack is, and aside from all those bad, unfair behaviors, he is heartless, like a vampire, who doesn't care what type of blood he sucks, because Jack doesn't care how poor you are, but he tricks people to get more money, and he doesn't care where you get them from, even if you have to borrow it, so thereafter, the woman was still in pain, because nothing changed, and so she quit coming to the church. And so I curiously continued being his interpreter and watching everything about him; else, I won't be writing a story about him. And so since Ada Foah and Big Ada is just a walking distance, Ebennezer came around to visit us, and sometimes, he came with a girlfriend, and I shared my leftovers with them, and one good thing about him was that he joined the service and he played drums whenever it was evening church service until the service was over before we talked. And so he told me he was on school vacation; he was staying in his uncle's self-contained house, which wasn't far from us, and he told me to pass by anytime, and so one time, Georgina and Amos stepped outside for a while, and they haven't returned, and so

I went looking around for them, then to the exact house Ebennezer told me he was, and then I knocked the door, and so when he opened the door, I entered. "Oh, my god!"

That was divine intervention, which saved me from having another sex with him for the third time, because of how handsome he looks. He was half naked, with only a towel on his waist, and his bare hairy chest. And then my aroused feelings I had for him alone were unstoppable, and the way he looked at me in the eyes confirmed he felt the same way too, so I couldn't sit in the couch. He offered me to, so I stood up, and every part of me was so ready for sex, which I missed, since 1973, after he got me pregnant. And so when he said, "Atswei, mo yee." In Ada language, it means, "Atswei, you are welcome," and he asked how Amos was doing.

And thank God he reminded me of the promise we made not to have any sex until we married, then I told him that I had to leave now, because we have a prayer meeting in an hour's time, and then I stepped outside, breathing faster, then he changed into his clothes to meet me, and he walked me halfway home, and he asked the reasons for my reactions, which he also knew, but I told him. It was nothing, and he smiled at me. And one thing Jack said repeatedly to me after consultations, hours, as I was about to leave the prayer room that I disliked and I didn't know his intentions behind was, whenever Ebennezer comes around especially with his girlfriend, I was wasting my time with Ebennezer, and as soon as he finished his education and he gets a job, he won't notice Amos and I exist. Can't I see for myself? He brings his girlfriend with him, and I also fed them with my leftovers.

I smiled at him, and I told him, "My God, won't let that happen, and if Ebennezer doesn't love me, why would he waste his time coming around with a girlfriend he loved, instead of spending more time with her?" And I didn't mind sharing leftovers with them, because in the Bible in Proverbs 25:21, it says, "If your enemy is hungry, give him food to eat; If he is thirsty, give him water to drink." And so how much more my boyfriend, the love of my life, and the father of my son? And so one more thing Jack did was that he raped all my teammates, girls, one after another, in the house, and he gives them fake promises to keep quiet, then a woman, in her early twenties, called Hogbayo (meaning "Sunday born girl," in the Ada language), who had three-month-old child, and she staye, in Accra for a few years, and so she understood the Ga language, and she joined the church, and so for that reason, Jack told me to take a break from interpreting. And later on, he raped her too in the prayer room, and she went back home, hurting, and she told her pagan parents about what Jack did to her, and Hogbayo's father went straight to the powerful shrine, called "piemi" in the Ada language, and he summoned Jack over to curse him and his entire family to death, if he denies raping her.

When I asked him, he lied to me; they had sex, but he didn't rape her, and my question was, why do you have to have sex with someone, as a man of God, when you already have a wife in the same house? And it is a disgrace to me, as his interpreter, seeing him doing that, and people might think I am one of his victims, and he told me that was a temptation, and I advised him to go see Ebentse, who is respected and in town, and tell him the truth, then he and Soyonye went to see him because he was ashamed of himself. And so that due day, Ebentse, Jack, and Soyonye went to Ada piemi, to meet with the fetish priests, their elders, and also Hogbayo with her parents, and so Jack confesses he actually raped her, and it's unbelievable. Jack, man of God, was on his knees, in front of voodoos, and begged for forgiveness, and the fetish priests said he was lucky to confess; else, he would be cursed, and his entire family would die, one after another, and he will be the last to die, so he was warned against raping the Adas, and he was charged with a lot of things, including a fixed amount of money, and so he paid everything, in cash, out of God's money to those fetish priests before he was free to go. And so Soyonye and Jack, he turned back home, and he was so ashamed, and he couldn't tell me in details, like Soyonye, so Hogbayo stopped coming to the church, including most of the youths, whose parents heard about what Jack did, so the the membership totally reduced, so most times, it was just us, the team, worship, and people stopped coming to prayers, too, and Soyonye also left back to Korlekope to continue her farming, and Jack couldn't even feed the team twice a day like he used to, so Patience and his year-old son also left back to Ada Junction.

When I remembered, since Jack and his friends arrived, he was the bad nuts among them, and all worse things he continued doing; it is a disgrace to God and real men and women of God. Though no one is perfect, but for him to use God's name for his selfish interests... But he believes in Malams, powers and also to turn into a rapist to worse was the last thing a man of God, with his Holy Spirit in him, was supposed to be doing. And what even hurts me was that Georgina thought I was his lover, because of how he stepped out with me, if he wanted an interpreter, and so one, she tried to fight me, as a result of that, and I put in her place, and I told her that I wasn't interested in him, but I had a serious boyfriend, and also because I'm not so cheap like she thought. Besides, I was the only person Jack hadn't raped. And so I went to the room, and I packed my things, and Amos and I left for Ada Junction to focus in selling, and if Ms. Comfort had new members, I would be her interpreter and patiently wait on the Lord. And then Jack came over to Ada Junction the next day to apologize for his wife's behavior toward me in front of Grandma, but still, my mind was made up, and then Grandma's convicting made me change my mind, because she told me to see that as my temptations, but "you never know" what God's blessings had for me there, and so he waited for me to repack again, and we returned back to Big Ada. And so I thought that what Jack went through from raping would make him stop raping other girls for good, and he would focus on his wife, who was twenty-four hours a day in the house. But I was wrong, because he raped very brilliant Ama. We first met when posting the posters, then he was able to convince her that really, he was in love with her, so as soon as she finished her education, both of them would move to Accra and start a new life, so he continued having sex with her, because she was born and raised in Ada, and she never traveled to Accra before, so she thought she had fine chances.

One time, his brother, Kwabena, came from Chorkor for a weekend visit, because he completed his form 4 education, and he learned electrical, and he worked at Accra Electricity Company, so he liked Ama when he saw her, and out of respect, he asked Jack.'s permission to date her, but he was shocked to hear him and said, "Ama is untouchable. Because he is mine." And then Kwabena asked him, "So what about your wife, Georgina?" And then he smiled and said, "Don't pay attention to her, because she is living with me, for some reason, but I will dump her in no time, when I'm ready." And he also said, "Even King David had wives, but he still had lovers." And so I was sitting with them, on a bench, in front of them, in the living room, and then, Kwabena, and I looked at each other's faces, and we shook our heads, then we laughed, because I just couldn't believe what I just heard from Jack, and Kwabena went to Chorkor, and he didn't return back. And so months later, he eventually impregnated Ama, and when she told Jack about that, he told her to give the pregnancy to her boyfriend, and Ama told him that his boyfriend was out of town for a while to work somewhere else, and so he can't tell him she was pregnant. And unfortunately, Ama's parents were out of town, also working, so Ama was living with her fetish priest grandma, who could easily summon Jack to her shrine for refusing to take his responsibility, but one thing about the Adamgbes is that when someone is pregnant, she shouldn't be stressed out with such cases until after delivery, so for that reason, the grandma was patiently waiting for the child to be born and to see the resemblance, though she wasn't okay her brilliant black-beauty granddaughter was pregnant and had to go through that and also put her education on hold. And so months later, Ama had a cute light-skinned baby girl, and Jack and his mother have black skin color, but his brother Kwabena had light skin, and the secret Jack hid from everyone is that his father's mom had a lighter skin color, but his father's dad had black skin color, and so his family is mixed with black and light skin colors and brown and black hairs. And so that type of kids or grown-ups with light skin color and brown hair is called "ofili" in Ada language, which means "albino." And so Jack, a self-claimed man of God, denied his own fresh blood, born in 1976, at Big Ada, and he hid it from Ama and her family, so since her Grandma didn't see resemblance for the fact that Jack is black, they let Jack walk away free, but my question is, "Though he fooled the innocent Ama, but can he fool God too?" In the Bible in Romans 12:19, it says, "Dear friends, never take revenge.

Leave that to the righteous, anger of God." For the Scriptures say, "I will take revenge; I will pay back, says the Lord."

Eventually, the entire town realized who Jack really was, and so his crafty tricks came to an end, and nobody stepped a foot in his house for anything, so for that reason, we, as a team, from Ada Junction, were his only membership he preaches to, and even the three Emmanuel returned back to their hometown to struggle to survive, since all those promises were fake, and when he started earning money from the crusade and his dubious ways, he didn't share with anyone, and much more, he couldn't feed them again. And so Jack is persistent and didn't give up easily, when we were about to return back to Ada Junction, but he told us that his auntie and part of his family are in powder business, so they buy bags of raw powder, and they mixed them with perfume oils, and they had them in plastic containers, for sales, and some of them also put measured an amount in smaller white plastic bags, for sales, and also they mixed some with mints oil to cure heat rashes, and they make good money from that. And so he was going to Accra to buy raw powder in bags, and he would buy small envelopes, with the printed words *miracle, healing, powder, for all purposes, like malaria fever, tuberculosis, disease, measles, injuries, and also as fertilizer, for farmers crops to grow well.* He would also have tiny bronze crosses made from the black smith and placed them in each of those powder, in the envelopes, to be used as protections, lockets, and he would make good money from that, and this time, he would pay us good money from that new business. And so we decided to give him the benefit of the doubt, since we didn't have any future plans yet. And so Jack went to Accra for days, and I was wondering where he was going to get money for all he was going to do.

And then I knew he still had money saved in the bank, and he pretended like he didn't have any money, and that confirmed the type of person he is, and I knew that even if he had a breakthrough with the fake miracle, powder business, we wouldn't enjoy part of his success. And so when Jack returned from Accra, he brought everything like he said, and he also brought large quantities of white polyester materials, with dresses magazines attached to them, for the four of us

(Georgina, Elizabeth, Lehuyo, and me) to have it sewn by Gabon's baby daughter, who is a seamstress, with a bow tie and long gowns to wear, for sales, in marketplaces, and to scarf our head with pieces of the material, in such hot, sunny weather. And so she took our measurements, and then Jack turns to our instructor, and he had smaller measuring cups for them, and so after we poured a big bag of raw powder in the basin, then we mixed it with Florida water perfume, and we stirred with our hands to separate and had it well mixed, then we started measuring the powder inside those envelopes, and someone had to put those tiny crosses inside; someone also sealed them with cooked starch, and so it took us days to finish a good amount of powder. And so he went to convince those boy, back, because they will play the drums, and we will be singing worship and praise songs to draw people's attention, before Jack introduces his powder, and I will interpret to them to understand before they buy them, so our dresses were ready, and we collected them and fitted in before we brought them home. And so Jack was able to convince three Emmanuels back with his lies to help with his powder business, and he had a tailor to sew them white shorts, sleeveshirts, shorts, pants, and we the girls also were so ready and happy for wearing American-style dresses, without thinking about the weather, from the beginning, but my main concern was that Jack isn't gifted with any type of miracle healing powers, but God gave him smartness to convince someone to believe him instantly, so blindly, so he should have used his talent, wisely, to earn his own money, rather than playing tricks on people to rob them, and also he used the same talent for trying to be nice to girls and young women, from the start, and then he rapes them unaware. And honestly speaking, I told Jack multiple times that he should be an actor instead for a living, to make more money for himself, because of how people fall for his lies, but not a pretending man of God, because his behaviors don't seem like a man of God. And so I knew this powder business wouldn't succeed, because though the Adamgbes are kind, humble, generous, and so naive, that doesn't make them so stupid, for Jack to continue playing tricks on them all the time; else, the crowd he had at the crusade grounds would still follow.

I also wondered how is it possible that just a powder could heal those diseases and fertilize farmers' crops? Though I knew that with God, nothing is impossible, God doesn't work through hypocrites, like Jack. And so on our first day, we left home at 10:00 a.m, all dressed up in white clothes, including Jack and his big Bible. We wore any type of slippers, with the powder in baskets, drums, local tambourines, and two yards of white material, to be laid on the floor, for people to throw offerings on it, then we picked a truck to Ada Foah market on Wednesday. And so we settled at the center of the market, where there was a space, in the morning sunny day, and Jack laid the material on the ground, and he displayed some packs of powder on it, so he prayed, and then we started singing worship and praise songs, with drumming and dancing, with big smiles, like Jack told us to do, and little by little, people started gathering around us to see what was going on, and then Jack started talking about his miracle powder and what it does, and he picked one, and he mentioned it one by one, and he told them to mix some with shea butter, to rub themselves and their kids, in case they had any of those diseases, and the crosses inside was for protections against forces of darkness, then he told farmers whose crops don't grow well, because of no rain, they should buy a good amount to sprinkle in their farms, and God will give them dew from heaven, and their crops will flourish, and he quoted Genesis 27:28.

He told them the price, and so those people bought the fake miracle powder, desperately, because of their situations, so we all started selling and putting the one in the basket until all were sold before we girls realized how warm we felt and sweated and looked so tired and hungry too, because he told us to fast in order for the products to sold out. But Jack had a big smile, and he kept talking about how great the sales went, and so he returned back home, and he had Georgina cook for him and the rest of the team, but he didn't give us anything, he said, after we finished selling those bags of powder, then we would have our share of the money. And so on Friday, we went to Ada Junction market, and we had some sales, but not as much as Ada Foah, because he was noticed by some of the villagers, and we returned back on Saturday to Ada Foah market, and the sales reduced, because there wasn't any miracle, and then in the second week, the sales kept on reducing instead of selling more. And so Jack and we went to visit a pastor he met at Ada Foah market, at Ocanseykope, on one weekend, and his church, he was able to convince his members, who were mostly farmers, and he made good money from there, and so he told that pastor to introduce him to other pastors around, and so we went to Pute, the next village from Ocanseykope, to visit another pastor and his church members, who were mostly fishmongers, and Jack convinced them, and he made good sales from there. And one more selfish thing Jack did also was that he took pictures with us and some visiting members, with a banner on the background, with the words boldly printed out "St. Adorkor African Universal Church," just a couple of weeks, on our arrival to Big Ada by Ebentse, then later we, as a team, in white clothes, were ready for his miracle, powder, sales too. He let us took pictures, and he added copies in an envelope and with attached letter, and he sent it to the US, in Florida, to the Africa Universal Church Inc., and he told them we were all his church members, and he also claimed that Laura Adorkor Kofi, who died on March 8, 1928, was his real auntie, and so for that reason, he needed an invitation to visit the church, in the States.

Because of his same selfishness and greediness, he didn't give us anything of those money he made from the powder sales since, but he continued to encourage us with fake promises. One more thing he did, after he found out that the powder business didn't go well, because "seeing is believing," and so the Adas stopped buying the powder, because there wasn't a single miracle that happened in the powder. And so Jack joined pastors association in some of the surrounding villages, including Ocanseykope and Pute, and so the pastors agreed on dates for individual pastors' fundraising services, in order of them to come together with their members, to help financially, to raise money, for the aids of church buildings. And so Jack was so crafty, and luckily, he was the only literate person among them, and so he convinced them to push his date ahead of others, because of how he was able to make more money for some pastors, on their fundraising services, which happened each month per pastors. But what they didn't see coming was that he wanted to use them to get more money and then run away from Big Ada, because everybody knew about Jack, with his nickname, which says, "Me amen osofo, abonuatualo," which, in the Ada language, means "rapist pastor." And so on Jack's set date for the service, he already told Gabon to give him his big space for the fundraising service, and he hired canopies and benches and everything was well fixed and arranged, and meanwhile, his printed envelopes were already distributed, and so we, the team, were the only members of his church, but because those naive pastors believed in him, they also saw him like a godsend, who encouraged them with sweet talks, Bible quotes, so for that reason, they all came alongside their members, and they really gave generously toward the church building he claimed he was going to build, and so honestly, at the end of the service, he had more money than any other pastor's fundraising service. And so he was so happy, for his breakthrough, and we also thought he was going to give us some of the money, because of all those sacrifices we made, no matter what terrible things people say about him and how he kept on lying about helping us to have a great life. And so Jack went to Accra the next morning, for days, and on his return back, we surprisingly saw him riding on a big Tomos motorcycle he bought from Accra, out of the fundraising service, so we were shocked, including the people of Big Ada, then he said, since there was nothing, to do over there, so we had moved back to Ada Junction, a little far from Michael's church, to start another church all over again.

And so Jack really fooled the Adas, including us, to get what he wanted, and so he rented a single room, far away from the Kasseh Chief's place, in the farms owned by an elderly woman farmer, who had four single rooms, and she lived in the other side of those rooms, and he built a shed with palm branches, and he started a church, in which only Soyonye and a kenkey seller and his sister, who lived close by, were his membership. He told Soyonye convinced me to return back and help with the interpreting. After we returned back, we decided to go our separate ways, and so the girls went back to their houses, and they stopped going to his church; rather they followed their parents to the church of Pentecost, and so

Akuyo, Amos, and I also went back to stay with Grandma, and she, being so kind, aside from provisions, for breakfast, she bought him. She also told me to prepare dinner for Jack and sent it over for him to eat and return the dishes back home to wash. He had a fight with her wife, after the fundraising service, and so she also went to his father's place, and she sometimes visited him. And one more thing Grandma always told me was, "Sharing food is not a big deal to her at all because if you feed someone, then you have sent that person to the toilet to have feces," so that was her reason for still feeding Jack. And so Jack's escaping from Big Ada became top news and spread over Adamgbe District, and some people made jokes about him. The youths composed a song that says, "Me amen, osofo, juwo, yahe, motor le, emafo ke je," which means "Jack robbed us to buy a motorcycle and then ran away."

And he was lucky that those frauds and raped cases happened in Adamgbe District, because if it were to be any other developed country, he would have been jailed for a long time. And so Jack couldn't talk to me directly, because he knew how disappointed I was with all those disgraceful acts, and so he used Soyonye if he wanted to talk to me about something, concerning church, because he knew how I respected her, like a mom, so afterward, I went to the church and help with worship, praise, and interpreting, and Jack himself turned to a drummer, and he played his base drums, when worship and praise were going on, and then he preached during sermon periods, because the three Emmanuels also quit the church. And so one time, Soyonye told me Jack wanted to have a meeting with us, so we all went to his place, and he told us that he, Soyonye, and I should have seven-day vigil in his room and prayed to God to increase the church, and he would have preferred the church, but it wasn't safe, because it was a shed, also because of the mosquito bites. And so Soyonye's encouragements made me decide to help, because she told me not to worry, but on her way to Jack's place, she would call me, so for both us to go to sleep over and keep wake and pray, then we would take a break to sleep, and at 3:00 a.m., Jack said he would call us, again, to continue praying, until 5:00 a.m, and then we would return back to our homes. And end of December 1976 and early days in January

1977, Soyonye and I started sleeping over Jack's place, in a mat on the floor, in between his couch and his bed, and after hours of singing and praying, we break to sleep a little, then Jack woke us up at the time he said, to continue the prayers, then we returned home like she told me, around 5:00 a.m, for six days straight, and so I thought I was safe, and Jack won't get a chance to rape, and I knew all about him and his capabilities, but he didn't give me any doubts. He could possibly rape me, because we sat in a prayer room for hours, reading the Bible, debating, but I didn't see that coming in a millions; else, I wouldn't last around him, because I'm so smart to know if someone is trying to play games on me. And much more I made it clear many times to him that I had no feelings for any other man than Ebennezer, and so on the seventh day, which was supposed to be the last day of the vigil, surprisingly, Soyonye didn't come over to call me like she used to, and so I got worried about her, because she was always punctual in everything.

After thinking about her, I decided to go to Jack's place and asked him if he had any news of Soyonye, so he told me he hadn't heard anything about her, but I shouldn't worry, because she might be doing something else and she was running a little late, since she was a woman of her word. He played Jim Reeves's song on his little type recorder machine that uses batteries and the song "This World Is Not My Home, I'm Just Passing Through." And so it was getting late, and Soyonye still hadn't come, so I decided to return back home, but he told me that because it was the last night, so I should sleep over, for just the two of us to pray, and so I agreed right away without having any second thoughts. Also because it's like you know someone, for years, as a terrible person who does bad things to other people, and so you think he won't harm because of all sacrifices you made for him to get all those money without giving you a penny, and also your family is being so nice to him. But what I didn't know about him was that, aside from all horrible behaviors, he is also a beast. And so I didn't hesitate to lay the mat on the floor, in the dark room, with freed mind, to lie down, with my clothes on, and then I slept right away, without noticing it, and then I heard my name mentioned, "Atswei!" And I said, "Hmm! What is it?" "Is it time for prayers already?" And he was like, "Oh no!" "I just wanted to talk to you about something." And so I said, "Can't it wait till tomorrow?" And he said, "Oh, it won't take much time at all."

I reluctantly sat on the mat, and I asked him what that was all about. And then I heard a shocking news from him, telling me about how much he loved me all those years since he set his eyes on me, and so after long times of his prayers, he asked God to confirm it to him, and before he ended his prayer with "Amen," I just said "yes" in my dreams. And so I started boiling up from the start till he finished, because I imagine his evil intentions, I told him, "With all due respect, you are like a brother I never had. And as long as I live here, I will continue serving you and your wife. And he was insisting it was God who said so, and I was like 'Well, God hadn't told me so.' And so give me some time to think and pray over it." And so I just told him something, just for him to leave me alone for just that night, and he will never see me close to him again, and that was my plan, in the middle of the night. And then he told me, "Okay, let's go back to sleep," and honestly, I couldn't sleep again, out of shock and anxiety, because I thought I was exempted, so I was just waiting for the first cockcrow to leave right away, because he lived in the thick bush farms with trees and noises of bats, other birds, and animals sounding more scary, and moreover, it was about half a mile from Grandma's. And all of a sudden, he jumped on me like a hungry lion, and he started pulling off my clothes, and I started crying out loud and was like, "Why are you on me? Please, please don't do this to me," and though I tried pushing him away from me, he acted like a real beast, and so he heartlessly raped me without pitying me, and because there weren't any houses around and the elderly house owner lived at the far end of the house, nobody was able to save me, no matter how loud I screamed.

So I cried the whole night, and with his great satisfaction, he snored louder, so as soon as I heard the first cock crow, I got up and dressed up and felt body pains and filthy. Especially my underpart hurt and was like a raped virgin, and I was almost like one, because I had sex twice, in 1973, and I was raped at Ashaiman, in the middle of that same year, and since then, I never had sex again, until he raped me in 1977, and that was three years later. But I forced myself and left, and on my way to Grandma's, I asked God multiple times, "Why does he have to allow this to happen to me, after all I'd gone through to have a son, and how dedicated am I to him?" Serving him well and giving my tithes and offerings? Why does he have to allow some people to use his name his name in devilish ways? And so I was confused, emotional at home, and a whole lot of thoughts went through my mind, like, *What if he didn't use a condom and I got pregnant again without being married? And what would happen if my boyfriend found out? And how about my sister he had affair with? Now do I break this news to her?*

She wouldn't believe me that I was one of his victims. And I knew that Jack actually wanted to rape me for a long time, but words in our conversations discourage him, and since he doesn't give up easily, the way he thought of as fine chance to rape him was to use Soyonye, which perfectly worked for him, after one year, ten months. And so that early morning, he came after to the house, and in fact I put my frustrations on him, and I told him that God knows and he also knew who I really loved, by telling him multiple times, and he still tricked me, then he raped me, so he had reasons he's bad for discouraging me, many times, to stay away from Ebennezer, because he would disappoint me. And then he begged me when I told him I was going to tell Grandma that I shouldn't tell anybody; else, his life is over here, but he loved me for real, and he wanted to marry me, to spend the rest of his life with me. And so I asked him, "How about Georgina?" And moreover, I loved only one person and not him, and even if he really loved me, like he claimed God told him to tell me, I told him to give me some time to think it over and to ask God by praying over it, and also is rape the best solution for expressing his love for me?

And then he returned home, with no regrets, or apology, for me. And I was so overwhelmed, and I couldn't stop myself from crying outside. Meanwhile, everybody was sleeping, and there I knew all he told me right now was just for me to shut up my mouth. I was so confused, and I couldn't think straight if I should tell Grandma or not because in those days, if someone had come to my rescue, in an act of rape, then you get a witness, in case the rapist denied, but since nobody witnessed that they might think that I deliberately went to tempt his place him, unless I sermoned him at a fetish shrine, like Hogbayo's parents did, after he raped her, which was the last thing I would do, since I have nothing to do with fetish priests. And so no matter how much I was hurting, even when I was pregnant and raped by Amartey, because later, I told myself I was already pregnant, and much more his family's goodness toward me eased my pains, but Jack's case is a horrible experience for me, but I kept it a secret and told nobody, and I had emotional pains. I cried myself out when I was alone, and I asked God questions like, why do I have to continue to suffer whenever I thought things are working for me for good? Like in the Bible in Romans 8:28, it says, "And we know those who love God all things work together for good, for those who are called according to his purpose." But it is quite opposite of what is in the Bible.

And still God didn't answer me back, and the worse part also was that Jack didn't use a condom when I asked him, and that worsened my depression, because grown-ups say, if you stop having sex for years, and then you have sex, one time you can easily get pregnant, so a couple of days later, I had bad feelings. I could get pregnant out of this rape, and so I mixed a lot of Nestle coffee, with plenty of sugar, inside a cup of hot water, and I drank with an empty stomach, so in case, any tiny sign of pregnant should melt, completely, in order for me to move on with my life and deal with those rape situations emotionally for the rest of my life. And then unfortunately, I missed my period weeks later, and I cried on God's shoulder and I prayed that history shouldn't repeat itself. Because I didn't know where to go from here to a hiding place, and I didn't know how to take it this time. Then I waited for two weeks for a miracle to have my menstrual cycle, but still nothing happened, so I went to tell Jack, and he told me to wait for another week, and that made me more frustrated, because I never missed my period that long, and much more, I had a whole can of Nestle coffee, with plenty of sugar, so that no matter how tiny a clot may try to stick inside me, it had to melt. But I still didn't menstruate, and that scares me to death. And so

Jack took advantage of my frustrations, and he deceived me with his sweet talks to calm me down that I shouldn't worry about anything, but he would tell Grandma about his feelings toward me, that he would marry me and spend the rest of his life with me and I would be the luckiest and happiest woman on earth, because he would do all it takes to make me happy before my pregnancy started showing so nobody would suspect that he raped me, and he even swore with God's name to impress me. But I didn't believe any of those.

Mom, Odoi, and me, in Elmina at Bakatue Festival in 1966.

CPSIA information can be obtained
at www.ICGtesting.com
Printed in the USA
BVHW030118270221
601199BV00001B/35